THE FATHER OF JEWISH MYSTICISM

NEW JEWISH PHILOSOPHY AND THOUGHT
Zachary J. Braiterman

THE FATHER OF JEWISH MYSTICISM

The Writing of Gershom Scholem

DANIEL WEIDNER

TRANSLATED BY
SAGE ANDERSON

INDIANA UNIVERSITY PRESS

Originally published in German as *Gershom Scholem* by Wilhelm Fink Verlag

© Wilhelm Fink GmbH & Co. KG, Paderbom 2003
All rights reserved by and controlled through Wilhelm Fink GmbH & Co. KG, Paderborn

This book is a publication of

Indiana University Press
Office of Scholarly Publishing
Herman B Wells Library 350
1320 East 10th Street
Bloomington, Indiana 47405 USA

iupress.org

© 2022 by Daniel Weidner

All rights reserved
No part of this book may be reproduced or utilized in any form or by any means, electronic or mechanical, including photocopying and recording, or by any information storage and retrieval system, without permission in writing from the publisher. The paper used in this publication meets the minimum requirements of the American National Standard for Information Sciences—Permanence of Paper for Printed Library Materials, ANSI Z39.48–1992.

Manufactured in the United States of America

First printing 2022

The translation of this work was funded by Geisteswissenschaften International – Translation Funding for Work in the Humanities and Social Sciences from Germany, a joint initiative of the Fritz Thyssen Foundation, the German Federal Foreign Office, the collecting society VG WORT and the Börsenverein des Deutschen Buchhandels (German Publishers & Booksellers Association).

Cataloging information is available from the Library of Congress.

ISBN 978-0-253-06207-9 (hardback)
ISBN 978-0-253-06208-6 (paperback)
ISBN 978-0-253-06209-3 (ebook)

CONTENTS

*Abbreviations of Frequently Cited Works
by Gershom Scholem   vii*

Acknowledgments   ix

Introduction: Intellectual History and Writing:
What It Means to Read Gershom Scholem   *1*

PART 1. POSITIONING SPEECH:
Scholem's Political Education

1. Revolt and Romanticism: A First Language   *16*
2. Confusion and Polemics: Taking a Position   *22*
3. Asceticism and Silence: Gaining Authority   *28*
4. Esoteric Zionism: Politics and Language   *36*
5. Victory's Despair: Reality and Crisis   *44*
6. Looking Back: Rewriting the Past   *56*

PART 2. PRACTICING THEORY:
Scholem's Early Reading

7. Language and Truth: First Steps   *72*
8. Lamentations: Thinking Language   *80*
9. Tradition, Teaching, Doctrine: A Jewish Form of Truth   *87*
10. Paradox: Fragments of a System   *98*
11. Prophecy and Messianism: Rethinking History   *111*
12. Revelation: Problematic Foundations   *126*
13. Philology: Poetically Spoken   *144*

PART 3. PRODUCING HISTORY: *Scholem's Scholarship*

14. History of Religion: A Paradigm *163*
15. Myth and Mysticism: Fundamental Concepts *169*
16. Gnosticism, Misunderstanding, and Symbolism: More Operative Terms? *178*
17. History of Messianism: Continuity and Rupture? *186*
18. Explosion and Historical Test: The Essential Plot *192*
19. Jewish Modernity: A Test of the Present *201*

Conclusion: Authority and Silence *209*

Bibliography *215*

Index *233*

ABBREVIATIONS OF FREQUENTLY CITED WORKS BY GERSHOM SCHOLEM

GERMAN[1]

Br I, Br II, Br III	*Briefe.* Edited by Itta Shedletzky and Thomas Sparr. 3 vols. Munich: C. H. Beck, 1994–1999.
T I, T II	*Tagebücher nebst Äufsätzen und Entwürfen bis 1923.* Edited by Herbert Kopp-Oberstebrink, Karlfried Gründer, and Friedrich Niewöhner. 2 vols. Frankfurt: Suhrkamp, 1995–2000.

ENGLISH

FBJ	*From Berlin to Jerusalem: Memories of My Youth.* Translated by Harry Zohn. New York: Schocken Books, 1980.
JJC	*On Jews and Judaism in Crisis: Selected Essays.* Edited by Werner J. Dannhauser. New York: Schocken Books, 1976.
KS	*On the Kabbalah and Its Symbolism.* Translated by Ralph Manheim. New York: Schocken Books, 1969.
LL	*A Life in Letters, 1914–1982.* Edited and translated by Anthony David Skinner. Cambridge, MA: Harvard University Press, 2002.

---

1. Passages from Scholem's letters and diaries that are not included in the English collections *A Life in Letters* and *Lamentations of Youth* have been translated from the German by Sage Anderson.

LY	*Lamentations of Youth: The Diaries of Gershom Scholem, 1913–1919.* Edited and translated by Anthony David Skinner. Cambridge, MA: Harvard University Press, 2007.
MI	*The Messianic Idea in Judaism and Other Essays on Jewish Spirituality.* New York: Schocken Books, 1971.
MS	*On the Mystical Shape of the Godhead: Basic Concepts in the Kabbalah.* Translated by Joachim Neugroschel. Edited and revised by Jonathan Chipman. New York: Schocken Books, 1991.
MT	*Major Trends in Jewish Mysticism.* New York: Schocken Books, 1961.
PM	*On the Possibility of Jewish Mysticism in Our Time and Other Essays.* Translated by Jonathan Chipman. Edited and selected with an introduction by Avraham Shapira. Philadelphia: The Jewish Publication Society, 1997.
SS	*Sabbatai Sevi: The Mystical Messiah, 1626–1676.* Translated by R. J. Zwi Werblowsky. Princeton, NJ: Princeton University Press, 1973.

ACKNOWLEDGMENTS

DECADES AGO, WHEN I PREPARED my master's thesis on Sigmund Freud and Walter Benjamin, friends suggested that I have a look at Benjamin's intimate friend Gershom Scholem. So I went to get a book on the symbols of Kabbalah, a topic that was for me then probably the most obscure I could imagine. I was surprised to read its lucid and brilliant description of kabbalistic symbolism, a description that came along with striking insights into the nature of language, history, religion, and tradition. I continued to read Scholem and was taken by the richness, depth, and elegance of his thought and writing as well as by the trajectory of his life and his different friendships, mirrored by a rich correspondence that allows the reader to witness rigorous and dramatic intellectual dialogues.

Some years later, when preparing my dissertation, rumors of more material had already reached me. Ambitious texts from the young Scholem, which had circulated only in fragments, were just about to be published as part of Scholem's early diaries. After some inquiries and conversation, there was a scene I still remember, when Herbert Kopp-Oberstebrink handed me a couple of thick folders containing the manuscript of the second volume of these diaries that he, as well as Friedrich Niewöhner and Karlfried Gründer, kindly allowed me to consult. I began to conceive a doctoral thesis that should deal with the relationship of Benjamin and Scholem, encouraged by my supervisor, Gerd Mattenklott. I marked excerpts, making notes upon notes on what seemed to be a vast dialogue between Benjamin's and Scholem's early esoteric writings. I traveled to Jerusalem to find even more materials in the Hebrew National Library with the kind support of Margot Cohnn and later Stephan Litt, and I had countless conversations in the cafeteria of that library where you always find someone working in this field. I felt that something large was emerging and that I simply lacked the key to unlock this huge mystery, the one perspective from which everything would fall in place.

In the end, I did not find the key. Friends and colleagues made skeptical remarks about my ideas, and I realized that I could not put them together in a coherent way. Sketches and notes generated further sketches and notes, but nothing like a dissertation. I remember many helpful conversations in these days, with Carsten Allefeld, Stefan Beier, Iris Hölling, Thomas Meyer, Christoph Schulte, and others. At some point, I took a step back and decided to limit my thesis to Scholem and to change my approach: it seemed to me that I first had to describe what was happening in Scholem's texts before I could try to unlock their deeper, systematic meaning. And that is what this book mostly does, resisting the temptation of finding the esoteric key but trying to understand how Scholem writes and what effect this has for his intellectual project. In this way, with more modest claims, I finished my dissertation, which was defended in 2000 and came out as a book in German in 2003 with the patient help of Susanne Hetzer.

The story does not end here. I did not immediately continue to work on Scholem, but he remained a good guide into the field of religion and literature, modes of secularization, and German-Jewish culture in a broader sense—the major topics of my work in the decades after my dissertation. This work was possible only with the kind support and close collaboration of a number of colleagues and friends, beginning with Sigrid Weigel and Eva Geulen, the directors of the Berlin Center for Literary and Cultural Studies, my academic home for a long time, along with Center colleagues Ernst Müller, Martin Treml, Stefan Willer Kai Bremer, Claude Haas, Caroline Sauter, Yael Almog, and other friends in Germany and Switzerland, including Stephan Braese, Robert Buch, Birgit Erdle, Joachim Jacob, Andreas Kilcher, Andreas Mauz, and Andrea Polaschegg. No less important were international colleagues and friends David Biale, Brian Britt, Carolin Duttlinger, Amir Eshel, Peter Gordon, Mike Jennings, Nitzan Lebovic, Vivian Liska, David Myers, Gerhard Richter, and Liliane Weissberg, who allowed me to take part in discussions that interestingly came back to Scholem again and again over the years. Friends and colleagues from Israel—Amir Engel, Ilit Ferber, Paul Mendes-Flohr, Menachem Lorbeerbaum, Rivka Feldhay, Galili Shahar, and Yfaat Weis—gave me glimpses of the complex, forceful, and, at times, tragic aspects of Israeli existence that was so central for Scholem. I gratefully remember so many discussions from Berlin to Jerusalem that helped me understand, at least for a moment, what was at stake in the texts I had read and reread over the years; or, more modestly and more often: moments in which I understood that I had misunderstood these texts.

I thank all those mentioned and many others, among them my students, for such moments that I hope will also continue in the future.

During these years, some friends finally convinced me that it might be worthwhile to translate the German book, since the more exciting discussion was taking place outside Germany. So I sat down and shortened the old dissertation significantly, omitting some typically German academic arabesques and trying to integrate new insights without undoing the structure of the entire book. This process would not have worked without the help of my patient, critical, and supportive translator, Sage Anderson. I would also thank Zachary J. Braiterman for including this book in the New Jewish Philosophy and Thought series and Vinodhini Kumarasamy for the careful editing of the text.

THE FATHER OF JEWISH MYSTICISM

INTRODUCTION

Intellectual History and Writing:
What It Means to Read Gershom Scholem

IN THE LAST PAGES OF *Major Trends in Jewish Mysticism*, Gershom Scholem quotes a now well-known Hasidic story:

> When the Baal Shem had a difficult task before him, he would go to a certain place in the woods, light a fire and meditate in prayer—and what he had set out to perform was done. When a generation later the "Maggid" of Meseritz was faced with the same task he would go to the same place in the woods and say: We can no longer light the fire, but we can still speak the prayers—and what he wanted done became reality. Again a generation later Rabbi Moshe Leib of Sassov had to perform this task. And he too went into the woods and said: We can no longer light a fire, nor do we know the secret meditations belonging to the prayer, but we do know the place in the woods to which it all belongs—and that must be sufficient; and sufficient it was. But when another generation had passed and Rabbi Israel of Rishin was called upon to perform the task, he sat down on his golden chair in his castle and said: We cannot light the fire, we cannot speak the prayers, we do not know the place, but we can tell the story of how it was done. And, the story-teller adds, the story which he told had the same effect as the actions of the other three. (*MT*, 349–350)

According to Scholem, this story epitomizes the history of Jewish mysticism that has fallen into oblivion in modern times. It also describes "the position in which we find ourselves today, or in which Jewish mysticism finds itself" (*MT*, 350). As Scholem indicates, we do not know the secret, but we still have the story, and we have it thanks to the meticulous historical reconstruction that fills the nearly four hundred pages of his magisterial book. "The story is not ended, it has not yet become history, and the secret life it holds can break out tomorrow in you or in me" (*MT*, 350). Thus, with this final anecdote, what had seemed to be solely a scholarly work by Scholem seems to turn into something more—namely, the continuation of a story, the handing down of a mystery that might become visible again even at the very end of this chain of generations—albeit in the weak form of a philologist who does not even leave his castle.

However, it remains uncertain whether the miracle will indeed occur and whether the secret will actually resurface. In the story that Scholem cites, the final miracle is already different from the preceding miracles. Whereas these simply happen, the last one is added by the "story-teller," an anonymous figure not previously mentioned, who by nature has an interest in the force of narration. Scholem's commentary leaves no doubt but that the story in question is "not ended," yet he shifts to the mode of possibility as to whether it will return to life. In fact, Scholem closes this section—and the entire book—with a different gesture: "But I have come here to speak to you of the main tendencies of Jewish mysticism as we know them. To speak of the mystical course which, in the great cataclysm now stirring the Jewish people more deeply than in the entire history of Exile, destiny may still have in store for us—and I for one believe that there is such a course—is the task of prophets, not of professors" (*MT*, 350). Scholem's account is similar to the past but also different. It contains life, but that life remains concealed. Scholem believes in a "mystical course," but he does not speak of it. What emerges here is a polysemous field that is decisive for the suggestive power and attraction of Scholem's text, awakening curiosity even among readers who have little historical interest in the Kabbalah, who sense in the text something alive, something that cannot be pinned down precisely. Is it something that holds his account together, endowing the abundance of information, citations, and reflections with consistency and cohesion? Is it a particular kind of reading that makes it possible to discern "major trends" in this overabundant field, or a particular kind of access? Or is it some surplus that goes beyond this, transforming the historical narrative into something more and ultimately performing the miracle? Scholem's source for the story remains open: Is it a Hasidic narrator, or is it Shmuel Yosef Agnon, as Scholem once suggested? If the "story-teller" of the Hasidic story is as central as he is indeterminate, how much more important is the narrator of this account, the one who cites the story—that is, Scholem himself? Is he actually a kabbalist or just a good historian? Neither? Both?

It makes little sense to try to resolve these questions, for it is clear that Scholem's conclusion, along with his book as a whole, depends on the impossibility of such an answer. This impossibility is linked to the historical span of the book as well as its historical place. *Major Trends* takes an expansive approach, encompassing all of Jewish history from late antiquity to the present, and it appears unlikely per se that this history would simply come to an end. At the same time, the book was written in the 1940s, in the face of what is referred to as a "great cataclysm," which constitutes such a radical break in Jewish history that its end may be a possibility after all. With an understanding of who narrated this account—and how, and why, and when—the life evoked in Scholem's conclusion takes on a different meaning. We can situate Scholem's gesture in entirely different contexts—for example, that of newly emerging Kabbalah scholarship, Jewish historiography, history of religion, or reactions to the catastrophe for European Jewry. *Major Trends* can also be situated in different ways in Scholem's life: as the fulfillment of a youthful dream, as a goal finally reached after long exertion, or, in light of the book's dedication to his recently deceased friend Walter Benjamin, as a gesture of resignation or mourning. To speculate further, if Benjamin—for a time, at least, for Scholem—was precisely that prophet who could tell not only the past but also the future of Jewish mysticism, what does his death mean for the project as a whole?

Just as we can hardly say what is actually happening here, so too is it difficult to determine the context. Contexts are always manifold, and strong texts also prove resistant to contextualization: they want to say more than can be said "about" them; they link different and often contradictory meanings in a way that cannot easily be grasped or recounted. In any serious engagement with Gershom Scholem, it is important to keep these difficulties in mind and develop one's own path. What can intellectual history contribute to understanding Scholem, and what does it mean to place Scholem's writing at the center of this inquiry?

Today, Scholem is considered one of the most important Jewish intellectuals of the twentieth century and an eminent representative of Jewish thought in times of crisis. In addition to his pioneering studies on the Kabbalah, this recognition is based on his influential essays on tradition, messianism, and Jewish history; his friendship and correspondence with Walter Benjamin and a host of other prominent contemporary thinkers, such as Martin Buber and Hannah Arendt; and his exceptional life story and memoirs. However, Scholem is also more than just an intellectual. Otherwise than the literary or essayistic style of the final pages of *Major Trends* might suggest, much of his writing is highly academic. Scholem's work follows the constraints of different academic disciplines—critical philology, history of religion, and Jewish history—and to a large extent, it is determined by the inner logic of these disciplines. In fact, the effect of the closing gesture we have just read relies on this difference between different forms of writing; the sober report of historical detail has its own life in relation to the life of prophetic proclamation. It would be too simple to reduce this difference to an opposition between history and philosophy, or between a "mere" historian of the Kabbalah and a "secret" kabbalist. As we will see, the blurring and undoing of such distinctions is essential to Scholem's writing. Instead, it is necessary to keep in mind that Scholem writes in different registers: philological, personal, philosophical, and political. None of these registers is totally coherent in itself, and each of them follows a different logic that has to be modeled differently.

It is not easy to position Scholem historically. His work is closely tied to Jewish history, with the pivotal moment of his research—the 1941 publication of *Major Trends*—coinciding with the deepest period of crisis. However, Scholem cannot be situated within any single history, as his life was constituted by passage between different milieus and very different historical contexts. Born into assimilated German Jewry, he became a German Zionist who also maintained contact with intellectuals far less sympathetic to Zionism, among them Arendt and Benjamin. He immigrated to Palestine and found a Zionist reality very different from the German intellectual landscape, and he went on to establish himself in Israel as a university professor and internationally as an important—if not the most important—interpreter of Judaism, at least for postwar Germany. The question of how to strike a balance between these very different contexts, and how to conceive the trajectory from one to the other, remains a major problem for any work on Scholem, but it also constitutes a primary source of fascination.

Scholem's fame and the difficulties already mentioned are reflected in the remarkable research devoted to his work, to which this study is indebted. In 1979 David Biale provided a first introduction with *Gershom Scholem: Kabbalah and Counter-History*. Based primarily on Scholem's memoir *From Berlin to Jerusalem*, Biale's book presents an impressively coherent image, at the center of which stands the antagonistic and anarchistic impulse that shaped Scholem's youthful Zionist rebellion as well as his later attempt to counter the bourgeois histories of liberal Judaism by writing the history of mysticism. Forty years later, three more books appeared almost simultaneously, offering different forms of intellectual biography. With the successive publication of Scholem's correspondence and early diaries since 1994, these books are based on a different body of source material that allows for an entirely different and much more detailed description of his life.[1] All three books are also post-Zionist, questioning Scholem's clear trajectory "from Berlin to Jerusalem" and thus in a sense presenting counter-counter-histories, to borrow Biale's terminology.

---

1. See also Aschheim, *Scholem, Arendt, Klemperer*.

Biale himself published *Gershom Scholem: Master of the Kabbalah* in 2018, emphasizing that it is precisely Scholem's contradictoriness that makes him so interesting today. With recourse to Scholem's diaries and letters, Biale tries "to enter his inner life and view him not only as a thinker and a writer but also as a human being," presenting him as "not an ethereal intellectual but a fully embodied person, filled with passion and paradoxes, much as he described Judaism itself."[2] Indeed, in several respects, Scholem's early writings demonstrate that his life's path was far less linear than his retrospective accounts would suggest.

The two other books likewise rely on new material, albeit with very different emphasis. In *Gershom Scholem: An Intellectual Biography* (2017), Amir Engel endeavors to consider Scholem's work and life as a unit determined by "two transitions—from Berlin to Jerusalem and from fringe to mainstream."[3] Engel argues that immigration induced a profound crisis in Scholem's self-understanding, expressed in his engagement with Sabbatianism, and that it was only after the Holocaust that Scholem identified more and more strongly with Israel. The dramaturgy of Noam Zadoff's *Gershom Scholem: From Berlin to Jerusalem and Back* (2017) is practically the reverse. Zadoff concentrates on Scholem's life after immigration, interpreting the postwar period in particular as a crisis for Scholem, after which he oriented himself increasingly toward Europe and Germany, culminating in an "effort to tie together the ends of his life and create a biographical continuity in gestures toward his childhood, whose scenery had been lost."[4] Both of these biographies show the fundamental difficulty of linking life and work, and of weaving the different phases of Scholem's life into a narrative without distortions. Their dramaturgy also makes it clear that, as counterimages, they still depend on Scholem's self-image "from Berlin to Jerusalem," supplemented with "but only later" (Engel) or "and back" (Zadoff). It is questionable whether any such formula can express the entirety of a life, and even more questionable whether this formula could be conceived in terms of spatial movement "from . . . to"—if anything, the matter at hand plays out "between" Berlin and Jerusalem.[5] In the following study, I will be less invested in establishing a clear plot than in tracing ambiguities, and less interested in mapping changes in location than in charting transfers and displacements.

---

2. Biale, *Master of the Kabbalah*, XI.
3. Engel, *An Intellectual Biography*, 203.
4. Zadoff, *From Berlin to Jerusalem and Back*, 231.
5. See Weidner, "Berlin und Jerusalem."

This book grew out of a dissertation written between 1997 and 2000 in Berlin, initiated primarily by my engagement with Scholem's early diaries. It appeared as a book in German in 2003, and it has now been revised for English translation with attention to literature published in the interim. In particular, sections dealing with Scholem's later development have been shortened, as this has been more widely and effectively addressed in subsequently published research. The book concentrates on the young Scholem, specifically his intellectual and scholarly development leading up to immigration. At times I expand my focus to discuss Scholem's academic publications, especially in the third chapter; these texts are fundamentally shaped by his academic socialization in Germany, through the methods of historical and critical philology and the paradigm of the history of religion. One thesis of this book is that the history of religion as developed in German biblical and religious studies around 1900 is of decisive significance for Scholem. As Biale has once again emphasized in his recent book, this early period is of particular interest due to vital and contradictory aspects of Scholem's development. His situation as a young thinker outside of institutions and without a defined intellectual project allows us to observe his thinking as it unfolds. The nature of the sources—diaries, letters, many drafts and notes—reveals even more about *how* Scholem thinks than *what* he thinks, making it possible to explore his development through his writing.

Scholem was a manic writer. In his youth, he kept notebooks and diaries, generated excerpts and working drafts, and wrote a multitude of letters, poems, aphorisms, political essays, manifestos, and translations. Later, he wrote historical essays and biographical essays on contemporaries, a memoir of his friendship with Benjamin, and his own memoir. At the same time, his extensive work on the Kabbalah grew and grew through a constant process of revision: Scholem liked to have a copy of his own books bound with blank pages inserted for further observations. His existence revolved around "script," and he is often associated with the image of a modern scribe, studying, handling, interpreting, and commenting on texts.

Considering Scholem's writing, one is faced with the question of how to avoid what Quentin Skinner has called the "mythology" of intellectual history, which all too often simply attributes systems of coherent ideas on certain themes to great thinkers, whereas thought is actually a situational response that responds to specific, usually very concrete contexts.[6] As apt as this critique is, it sets up major methodological issues. If different statements are no longer

---

6. See Skinner, "Meaning and Understanding in the History of Ideas"; see also Palonen, *Quentin Skinner*.

necessarily coherent but rather potentially contradictory or unclear, how can we understand them at all? What can take the place of the apparent coherence imposed onto a life or system? It seems to me that this can only be an act of construction that articulates the problem to which the text responds. This involves conceiving of thinking as a process of question and answer to be traced by interpretation. In turn, interpretation can shed light on how particular solutions evolve in this process—for instance, figures of thought, terminological decisions, or formulations that become increasingly stable without necessarily leading to a "system." It is only by taking this literary or rhetorical dimension seriously that one can take the texts seriously as texts and not only as receptacles for ideas.[7]

Speaking in totalizing terms of Scholem's work or thought suggests a consistency and autonomy that he neither claimed nor achieved, in my view. Instead, I take his *writing* as my object of study, not in the sense of a free expression of subjectivity but rather in the sense of *work* as a theoretical *praxis* that unfolds in an already structured space.[8] Rather than reading Scholem's writings as a (canonized) corpus, I read them as attempts to deal with historically concrete tasks and as dynamic acts of writing that produce and establish meaning. This is not a question of aesthetic taste, and I will be less focused on Scholem's "style" than on the literary practices—broadly conceived—that constitute his texts, such as citation, allusion, self-commentary, or metaphor. Concentrating on these techniques casts the polysemy of Scholem's texts in a different light: no longer an indicator of "depth," it appears as the result of conscious work devoted to expression. Scholem's esotericism does not consist in hidden theological and metaphysical ideas behind his statements. It is rather a form of concealed—or, more precisely, indirect—communication, a form of allusion and suggestion that should be read with respect to its effects rather than decoded. These effects are not always consistently planned, and they do not merge into a hidden author standing behind everything. It is precisely the contradictions and complexity of Scholem's writing that make it so interesting and so nimble.

Beginning with "writing" as a broad formal category, it is necessary to differentiate between different ways of writing. Scholem never writes *one* text that is at once Zionist, Jewish, true, and individual. Instead, as he establishes himself

---

7. See Weidner, "Reading Gershom Scholem." On the criticism of documentaristic prejudice in intellectual history, see also La Capra, *Rethinking Intellectual History*.

8. On the concept of a theoretical way of writing in the sense of *écriture*, see de Certeau, *The Writing of History*, esp. chapters 1 and 9.

more and more, his texts spread across different genres, themes, and forms. While his various ways of writing are always interrelated, and the themes interconnected, a reading that follows these links quickly runs into a dangerous circle. This is what happens, for example, when one attempts to read Scholem's early notes directly alongside his later essays, deducing from similar formulations that Scholem already represented a kabbalistic theory of language in his youth. Thwarting a more precise reading, this approach overlooks the fact that such "similar" formulations have very different functions in the context of a historical essay or a speculative aphorism; the appearance of evidence shores itself up in coils, while in many cases it is no longer possible to state the question to which the formulations at hand actually respond. Typically, as is also common in research on Benjamin, this leads to a stringing together of suggestive quotes that all "have something to do with one another."

A more precise reading must at least attempt to differentiate, identifying different problems and working out distinct answers, which may be similar but are not necessarily identical. Such an approach is *constructive* in that problems must be isolated and explicitly named. Indeed, such selection is necessary in order to understand what Scholem is saying; by establishing a sufficiently saturated horizon through specific problematics, it is possible to read his texts in context—not the other way around. The widespread practice of narrating a life while occasionally dipping into details regarding the surrounding environment in order to explain certain turns will not suffice here. Scholem's expressions are too open, suggestive, and idiosyncratic for a method like this.

Reading Scholem calls for discernment. What is nested together in life must be disentangled in research, a possibility demonstrated by broad research on Scholem published in recent decades. Jay Howard Geller has reconstructed the story of the Scholem family, and Ralf Hofrogge and Mirjam Zadoff have described the life of his brother, Werner, as a Communist.[9] Eric Jacobson has underscored the importance of anarchism for the young Scholem, Christoph Schmidt has analyzed his relation to political theology, and both his personal and intellectual relationships to Martin Buber have been explored by Klaus Davidowicz and Shaul Magid.[10] Scholem's theoretical reflections are discussed by Robert Alter in connection with Jewish modernism, by Stéphane Moses with the Jewish theological tradition, by Andreas Kilcher with German Romanticism, and more specifically in relation to Walter Benjamin by

---

9. See Geller, *The Scholems*; Hoffrogge, *Werner Scholem*; Zadoff, *Der rote Hiob*.

10. Jacobson, *Metaphysics of the Profane*; Schmidt, *Der häretische Imperativ*; Davidowicz, *Gershom Scholem und Martin Buber*; Magid, "For the Sake of a Jewish Revival."

Irving Wohlfahrt, Werner Hamacher, Ilit Ferber, and others.[11] With respect to Scholem's historical research, there are so many valuable resources and discussions that it is difficult to list even the most important, such as Joseph Dan's summary of Scholem's findings, Eliezer Schweid's critique of Scholem's image of biblical and rabbinic Judaism, Elisabeth Hamacher's analysis of his relation to the phenomenology of religion, David Myers's study of the context of twentieth-century Jewish historiography, and Boaz Huss's analysis of Scholem's reluctance to engage with living kabbalists in the Yishuv.[12] Particularly elucidating is Moshe Idel's general and radical critique, arguing that Scholem's picture of the Kabbalah is limited and one-sided, excluding the more practical and magical streams.[13] Furthermore, all these studies refer to much broader backgrounds, both in intellectual history, as in the history of Zionism or historiography, and in theory, as in discourse analysis and philosophy.

Such research allows us to consider Scholem in perspective—or rather, in different perspectives. The present book offers readings of three different aspects of Scholem's writing; entangled in his life, these aspects have to be untangled analytically. Each reading has its own methodology and also its own theoretical background—namely, the sociology of intellectual discourse, epistemology of question and answer, and history of science—to be spelled out in the introduction to each of the three parts. The first part analyzes the political dimension of Scholem's early writings, exploring how he became a Zionist, how he defined and claimed his position, and how he figured both the Zionist movement and his own position in a way that fully legitimizes his Zionism and his manner of belonging to Judaism. The second part discusses the theory of Judaism and its philosophical and theological implication as developed by the young Scholem in his diaries, highlighting how some of these ideas can still be discerned in Scholem's later writings. On the basis of these analyses, the third part seeks to elaborate how Scholem's scholarly conception of the Kabbalah emerged and what implications it has for his object of study.

---

11. Alter, *Necessary Angels*; Mosès, *The Angel of History*; Kilcher, *Die Sprachtheorie der Kabbala*; Hamacher, "Bemerkungen zur Klage"; Ferber, "A Language of the Border."

12. Dan, *Gershom Scholem and the Mystical Dimension*; Schweid, *Judaism and Mysticism*; Hamacher, *Gershom Scholem und die allgemeine Religionsgeschichte*; Myers, *Re-inventing the Jewish Past*; Huss, "Ask No Questions."

13. Idel, *Kabbalah: New Perspectives*.

PART 1

POSITIONING SPEECH: SCHOLEM'S POLITICAL EDUCATION

The title of Scholem's memoir *From Berlin to Jerusalem* places emphasis on the most distinctive trajectory of his biography. Turning away from a fully assimilated parental home and toward Judaism, he went on to become one of Judaism's most significant interpreters—or even its embodiment, for many. He subjected German Judaism to an extremely sharp critique, distancing himself from his origin in a manner that intensifies the tension inherent in any biography, between the story of a life as it is lived and as it is narrated in retrospect. Yet this tension hardly surfaces in Scholem's text. With the calm hand of a memoirist, he details the experiences and encounters along the path laid out by his title: "This path appeared to me to be singularly direct and illuminated by clear signposts" (*FBJ*, 1). The text foregrounds clarity, set up in contrast to the milieu of Scholem's origin. He casts assimilated Judaism as "self-deception," noting that "its discovery was one of the most decisive experiences of my youth" (*FBJ*, 26). Thus, it was "no miracle" that he became a Zionist (*FBJ*, 40). Drama, crisis, and the problem of memory, typical themes for the genre of the autobiography, play only a secondary role in the text.[1]

Published much later than his memoir, Scholem's early letters, diaries, and essays present a very different picture of his development. These texts demonstrate that his path was not smooth and direct but marked by intense crises and conflicts, and that these crises and conflicts remained far less resolved than the memoir suggests. Scholem began his diaries in 1913, at the age of fifteen, and he wrote with relative consistency until the early 1920s. In these diaries, reflections generally outweigh mere observation. They are full of judgments, indictments, and justifications aimed at himself and others as well as attempts to say something significant regarding Judaism and Zionism. Elements that come to light only in the margins of the memoir dominate pages of the diaries.

Schematically, we can divide the diaries into three phases. In the first period, from 1913 to around the summer of 1916, entries are primarily composed of short notes on everyday experiences and thoughts. The bulk of diary entries date from a second phase, between the summer of 1916 and the summer of 1919. Alongside daily reports and more and more self-reflection, there are stand-alone texts and collections of fragments in which Scholem reflects on Judaism, Zionism, and related topics, striving to sketch something like a theory of Judaism. I will explore this theory at length in part 2. In the third phase, from 1919 to 1923, there is a sharp drop-off in regular notes and an increase in stylized compositions. Independent texts, often extremely esoteric in nature, supersede the openness typical of the diary genre. The still-unpublished diaries from after 1923 also resemble those from this third phase: with some exceptions, such as the account of Scholem's trip to Europe in 1946, there are hardly any continuous passages chronicling events.[2] Scattered throughout, there are also private texts and poems written with an eye to self-understanding, to which we will return below. Scholem's letters reveal a similar development toward increased

---

1. Scholem seldom explicitly distinguishes between the remembering I and the remembered I, but he does do so in some significant passages, for instance, when discussing the character of tradition (*FBJ*, 47–50), anarchy (ibid., 53–54), or Zionism (ibid., 54–55, 151, 166–167). The same is true of the strongly autobiographical text *Walter Benjamin: The Story of a Friendship*; this generates extraordinary tension, precisely because Scholem does not endeavor to balance out differences and difficulties; see esp. *Story of a Friendship*, 83–91. At times, however, he does distinguish between the remembering and remembered I; see, for example, *Story of a Friendship*, 65ff. On the form of the autobiography, see also Mosès, "Gershom Scholems Autobiographie," 3–15.

2. Zadoff quotes from the 1946 diaries in *From Berlin to Jerusalem and Back*.

stylization, becoming more and more erratic and often difficult to understand, even for their original recipients.[3]

While Scholem's letters and diaries were not written or intended for publication, he carefully saved them and drew on them extensively, not only as material for his autobiographical texts but also as a source of formulations to be further developed in his later writing. This double function informs my reading here, allowing me to trace the young Scholem's development within a network of relationships, readings, and ideas. These are also Scholem's first attempts at writing, in which he experiments with different formulations, styles, genres, and figures of thought in order to find a way to express himself. The development of his intellectual position and the acquisition of a language of his own—the formation of lifestyle and style of utterance—thus go hand in hand.

Scholem's memoir and his diaries are not simply private texts. He wrote as a Jew, and his texts appeared in the context of the "Jewish question" and the "cultural revolution" of Judaism in the early twentieth century, which led to a proliferation of discourses on Jewish belonging that still hold fascination for us today. For lack of political institutions, the "Jewish question" was negotiated in Jewish literature, in the broadest sense. Conversely, this means that such literature has a particular relation to the question of belonging; Jewish discourse of the period is metapolitical, as it envisions a community that does not yet exist. This is especially clear with respect to cultural Zionism, serving the specifically German semantics of *Kultur*, a culture that helps to simultaneously articulate national particularity outward and a societal claim to leadership inward.[4] Cultural politics as well as metapolitics are the domain of intellectuals, those who occupy neither a fixed position in society's institutions nor a stand-alone position of unquestioned "artistic" subjectivity.[5] Such intellectuals do not avail themselves of special scholarly or aesthetic discourses, instead employing continually contested everyday language. Claiming to be the legitimate speaker of a group, the intellectual actually generates this group through an "alchemy of representation": "Group made man, he personifies a fictitious person, which he lifts out of the state of a simple aggregate of separate individuals, enabling them to act and speak, through him, 'like a single person'. Conversely, he receives

---

3. See discussion in Goetschel, "Scholem's Diaries, Letters"; Aschheim, "The Metaphysical Psychologist: On the Life and Letters of Gershom Scholem." On the diary in general, see esp. Lejeune, *On Diary*.

4. See Bollenbeck, *Bildung und Kultur*. On the symbolic dimension of Zionism, see also Berkowitz, *Zionist Culture and West European Jewry*.

5. On the problematics of the individual, particularly in the German Jewish context, see Mendes-Flohr, *Divided Passions*, chapter 1, as well as Löwy, *Redemption and Utopia*, chapter 3.

the right to speak and act in the name of the group, to 'take himself for' the group he incarnates."[6] With respect to Judaism in the early twentieth century, this alchemy took place in a particular field of power: Jewish discourse was not only the discourse of a minority but also part of a complex mass movement—namely, Zionism—and thus its politics of representation differed from the lonely incantations of invisible communities that some German intellectuals developed during this period.

Within this framework, the political dimension of Scholem's writing does not consist primarily in his opinions and judgments, which—unsurprisingly for a young Jew of the day—are numerous, radical, and idiosyncratic. Instead, it is the relationship of his discourse to the community that he represents that is political. Seeking a place for himself, he struggles for legitimacy as a Jew and as an intellectual, constantly distinguishing between "true" and "false" representatives of Judaism and developing an ever more complex account of his own position.

Inquiring into the political dimension of Scholem's writing allows for a meaningful analysis of his use of language, from tentative borrowings from other languages, to rhetorical mechanisms of self-legitimation, polemics, and explicit reflection, to various forms of indirect communication, as well as reflection on political linguistic phenomena. Rather than being a simple precondition that "naturally" sets the course of his life, Scholem's Jewishness becomes recognizable in writing aimed at the acquisition of a language of his own. Through a complex process, the direct, appellative gesture of his earliest writings disappears as his texts become more and more "objective" and his judgments more stable. Invoking silence again and again, his formulations become deliberately opaque, and his language becomes highly evocative, suggesting something while saying nothing fixed. Over time, this language spreads across different stages and genres, with Scholem writing as a historian, as a political essayist, as a contemporary, and as an autobiographer, gaining the pronounced authority with which he ultimately interprets the story of his own life.

The chapters of part 1 will trace the different phases of Scholem's shifting political ethos, analyzing the correlation between his imagined position and

---

6. Bourdieu, *Language and Symbolic Power*, 106. See also Bourdieu, "Intellectual Field and Creative Project," 89–119; Ringer, "The Intellectual Field, Intellectual History," 269–294, and the subsequent discussion. Otherwise than Bourdieu's field theory suggests, however, we are not dealing with an economy of complete, reciprocal recognition but rather with unilaterally raised *claims* to legitimacy, often associated with the term "charisma." On Scholem, see Bollack and Bourdieu, "L'identité juive," 3–19.

his mode of writing. His philosophical reflections and central relationship to Jewish tradition will be addressed in part 2. We will first consider how Scholem adopted language from the youth movement while at the same time striving to find his own radical position and language. This attempt, described here in terms of a revolutionary and Romantic ethos, reached a crisis with Scholem's break from the youth movement and with Buber; he subsequently developed a new ascetic ethos, essentially consisting in the withdrawal of direct expression. This position also allowed Scholem to process his disappointment in light of the actual Zionism that he experienced upon immigration to Palestine in 1923. After World War II, he was circumspect in speaking out on these questions, while he found a form that allowed him to interpret his own origin in his essays on German Jewry and contemporaries.

ONE

REVOLT AND ROMANTICISM
A First Language

IN HIS MEMOIR, SCHOLEM TELLS of a "terrible scene... at the dinner table" that took place in January 1917: his older brother, Werner, had been arrested at a Socialist demonstration against World War I. When Gerhard cautiously tried to defend Werner, their father "flew into a rage and said he had now had enough of the two of us, that Social Democracy and Zionism were all the same, anti-German activities which he would no longer tolerate in his house, and that he never wanted to see me again" (*FBJ*, 84).

In a nutshell, this scene contains Scholem's youth: fathers, sons, Germans, Socialists, Zionists. The father's reaction is more than just patriarchal violence in a traditional generational conflict, since one can safely assume that it was by no means only the father who attacked the son. For the son, the father is the embodiment of self-deception, with a value system he radically rejects. Inversely, for the father, the son's projected identity is not merely questionable but totally incomprehensible, as another memory shows: "My father had said to me, 'Why don't you become a rabbi? If you want *Yiddishkeit* so much, then become a rabbi and you'll be able to keep busy with *Yiddishkeit* all your life.' I told him, 'I don't want to be a rabbi.' Papa didn't understand what I wanted: *Yiddishkeit* without anything? I called it Zionism" (*JJC*, 10). Scholem wants to turn away from self-deception, but he does not yet know where to turn or what it would actually mean to be Jewish. Thus, his Zionism—pure "*Yiddishkeit*"—is still anything but clear. More than anything, it has the negative force of repulsion. "It seemed very rational to me," Scholem writes, looking back on his Jewish awakening. "Today I ask myself whether it was really all that rational" (*JJC*, 7). In fact, not only did Scholem have to find his way to this pure *Yiddishkeit*, but he also had to find modes of self-description and self-fashioning that would allow him to make this passage. Self-fashioning is not accomplished all at once by decision but rather step by step through practice, and Scholem's vehement revolt against his parental home was only the first step. To move on, he initially participated in the discourse of Martin Buber but soon tried to surpass it through radicalization, which finally led to disappointment.

Looking back, Scholem once said that his Jewish consciousness was "a revolt against the life-style of the run-of-the-mill bourgeoisie to which my family belonged" (*JJC*, 2). This revolt, and generational conflict, is far from unique. With the stagnating process of Jewish integration, Scholem's generation was in a position of particular tension: forced by Jewish parents into German culture yet rejected by that culture, they had to search for new options to define their way of being Jewish.[1] As in the surrounding German culture, "youth" thus became a central problem, leading to renewed interest in the past: "Like every generation of revolting sons, this generation of young Jews skips over the line of their assimilated fathers to look for a tradition in the deeply staggered background of generations that have already become historical, against which venerable backdrop their fathers must appear as pale specters."[2] The dialectics of tradition unfold here as generational conflict.

The intense conflict with his father played a decisive role in Scholem's development, as demonstrated by his early writings. Although we do not see much evidence of ambivalence on the son's part, the vehemence of the conflict indicates that this is more than just a normal adolescent crisis. The mode of breaking with his origins, manifest for the first time in confrontation with his father, persists most remarkably in the formula with which Scholem bids farewell to Europe and distances himself from world war in his privately published pamphlet *Blau-Weisse Brille* (Blue-White Spectacles) in the autumn of 1915: "We wanted to draw the dividing line [*Scheidelinie*] between Europe and Judah: 'My thoughts are not your thoughts, and your ways are not my ways'" (*T I*, 297–298). Scholem repeatedly asserts that the particular problems of German Jewish identity never played a role for him—for example, in a letter to Werner Kraft from the summer of 1918: "The confrontation with German culture which presents so many Jews with such painful dilemmas has never been

---

1. See Schatzker, *Jüdische Jugend im zweiten Kaiserreich*; Hellige, "Generationskonflikt, Selbsthaß."
2. Mattenklott, "'Nicht durch Kampfesmacht und nicht durch Körperkraft...' Alternativen jüdischer Jugendbewegung," 346. On Scholem's rebellion, see also Mosse, "Gershom Scholem as a German Jew," 119, as well as a psychoanalytic interpretation in Mosès, *The Angel of History*, chapter 8.

a problem for me.... I have never found or sought out values whose legitimacy was rooted in the German essence" (*LL*, 58).

This distancing becomes more and more apodictic. At first Scholem speaks in a cultural-critical idiom of the "decadence" of Europe that he wants to leave behind. In 1916 he no longer criticizes Europe but excludes it: "What is a *Western Jew* [*Westjude*]? He in whom the spiritual orders of Judaism have collapsed in contact with 'Europe,' spiritual disorder, from the Jewish point of view. This Europe does not appear visibly as an *element* of the Western Jew, at most it manifests itself *immanently* in the *condition* of the orders, in the *manner* in which they are situated" (*T I*, 457). Western Jewry does not really exist; not a mixture and much less a synthesis of Judaism and Europe, it is merely a ruin of Judaism without its own rationale, as shown by its "confusion" (*T I*, 457). Judgment on Europe is bracketed, so to speak, and at this point Scholem does not know what more to say about it.

Retrospectively, Scholem notes that in his youth, "confusion" was his favorite word (*JJC*, 11). "Confusion" applies less to the Germans than to the Jews here, and it is less of an argument than a gesture that forecloses certain problems: the entire question of German Jewish identity is categorized as a pseudoproblem on which one must simply turn one's back, erecting a *Scheidelinie*.[3] With this original division comes great determination: "I relate everything in my field of vision to Judaism. Someone could perhaps call me one-sided, but that's just the way I am" (*LY*, 25). As we will see further on, strict separation and criticism of confusion also shape Scholem's influential description of the self-deception of assimilated German Jewry written after World War II.

In a diary entry from 1916, Scholem connects the "*decisive* change" in his attitude with "the declaration of total revolution" (*LY*, 132–133). Revolution is an issue that he discusses with his left-wing Socialist brother—for example, in a letter from 1914: "You, that is, you Social Democrats from the Marxist side, are firmly convinced that 1. one can prove Socialism, and 2. the prerequisite for S. is materialism—historical and philosophical.... Dear Werner, I do not believe in the philosophy of history, whether it comes from Hegel (id est Marx), Ranke, or Treitschke, or for all I care not even in the negative of Nietzsche.... I mean, if there is anything one could prove with history it is at most—anarchism, nothing more" (*Br I*, 11). Anarchism, which entails the claim that

---

3. Goetschel highlights the "curious tension in Scholem between a profound engagement with historical understanding and its very opposite, a passionate, if not fanatic rejection of certain options for historical action" as the "blind spot in the epistemological grounding of his project" ("Scholem's Diaries, Letters," 80–81).

the revolutionary act is *always* possible and that there is actually no historical "situation," is indeed opposed to a philosophy of history that would dismiss moral claims in the name of "historical necessity." This is precisely what the anarchist revolts against when he employs skepticism and morality at the same time: the anarchistic free act is radical, moral, and unanalyzable, beyond tactical or psychological considerations.[4] The anarchistic emphasis on outrage as *conditio humana* offers a possible interpretation for generational conflict, implying not only critique of the ruling order but also skepticism toward the more established institutions of critique, such as the Social Democratic Party, the kind of "organization" that Scholem sees as a "murky sea that collects the lovely flowing streams of thoughts" (*LY*, 22); despite all this, anarchism is not sufficient for him: "I, Gerhard Scholem, do not stand on the ground of anarchism. . . . For it does not know unity" (*Br I*, 6).

Scholem's demand for something beyond anarchism became entirely clear in June 1915 after hearing a lecture by the Nietzschean Kurt Hiller, who called for radical renewal and for youthful, unburdened turning toward new shores. In his diaries, Scholem rejects this point of view, as it knows no "problems, polarities, and tragedies. . . . Things are in fact very different from this. The path of youth is full of abysses, and difficult contradictions cannot simply be passed over silently, but in one way or another they must be actualized. . . . Leaping over the chasm is no solution to the problem. We can't leap" (*LY*, 58–59). To "actualize" these abysses while never being able to leap will forever be the task of Scholem's identity; he never becomes a "pure" anarchist, and even in his youthful writings, anarchism is less of a worldview than an instrument that allows him to take a stance against his older brother. Other discourses follow, amalgamating with anarchistic conceptions.

The confrontation with his father demonstrates that the young Scholem did not merely want to become Jewish; he wanted to become a Zionist. Zionism is a central and continuous element in his biography, the significance of which is a matter of debate.[5] As is the case with his later treatment of German Jewry, Scholem superimposes a retrospective interpretation onto this aspect of his youth in his memoir, emphasizing that his decision for Zionism was above all a decision against self-deception and for himself: "Those aspects of Zionism

---

4. On Scholem's anarchism, see Löwy, *Redemption and Utopia*, chapter 4, and Jacobson, *Metaphysics of the Profane*, chapter 2.

5. For Arthur Hertzberg ("Gershom Scholem as a Zionist"), Zionism is key to Scholem's character and has a religious component, while David Biale ("Scholem und der moderne Nationalismus") emphasizes its secular nature.

that dealt with politics and international law were not of prime importance to many of those who joined the movement. Of great influence, however, were tendencies that promoted the rediscovery by the Jews of their own selves and their history as well as a possible spiritual, cultural, and, above all, social rebirth" (*FBJ*, 54). Looking back from an autobiographical perspective, however, Scholem also highlights that the Zionists' relationship to history was not an easy one: "For from the outset the struggle between a striving for continuation and revivification of the traditional form of Judaism and a conscious rebellion against this very tradition, though within the Jewish people and not through alienation from it and abandonment of it, created an ineluctable dialectics that was central to Zionism" (*FBJ*, 54). While Scholem does not find it necessary to go into political details here, the expanded Hebrew edition of *From Berlin to Jerusalem* hints at the fact that he was not aware of Zionism's "dialectics of continuity and revolt" in his youth, "for we did not yet see the abyss that would open up between the different interpretations of such sweeping slogans in the attempt to realize them."[6] The "renewal" of Judaism can only appear as a simple (undialectical) undertaking as long as it is not (politically) realized, and the different interpretations—continuity or revolt—can only coexist as abstract slogans, not in concrete, public action, as demonstrated by the Sabbatian past as well as the Zionist present, as we will see below. The fact that this realization entails potential danger is acknowledged by contemporary Zionist discourse, especially in the writings of Ahad Ha'am, which Scholem highly valued. For Ha'am, political Zionism is more than insufficient, actually hindering necessary Jewish renewal, which requires cultural work and the cultivation of an "awareness of ethical chosenness."[7] The main danger of Zionism lies in its great gestures of symbolic policies, "in that premature 'victory' . . . granted to thought *through the fault of its proponents. For by wanting to accomplish something great ahead of time*, they left the

---

6. Scholem, *Von Berlin nach Jerusalem*, 187, 188. Translator's note: The 1994 expanded German edition of *Von Berlin nach Jerusalem* contains a translation of Scholem's additions and revisions from the 1982 Hebrew edition (*Mi-Berlin l-Irushalayim*). When the author quotes sections from this expanded edition that are not contained in the 1980 English edition, I am translating from the 1994 German edition, in which these disparities are signaled by italics.

7. Ha'am, *Am Scheidewege*, vol. 1, 262. See also Klatzkin's critique: "How can one simultaneously deny God and affirm chosenness?" Quoted in Rosenberg, *Das verlorene Land*, 138. "Cultural Zionism believed it had found a safe middle ground between politics (power politics) and divine revelation, between the subcultural and the supra-cultural, but it lacked the sternness of these two extremes" (Strauss, preface to *Spinoza's Critique of Religion*, 6).

tedious track of natural development and transplanted a new, tender thought into reality before it was ripe."[8]

Scholem shares in Ahad Ha'am's criticism of a purely pragmatic politics: "In this respect I am an Ahad Ha-amist and religious, but more religious than Ahad Ha-am. I don't believe in a world of total secularism in which the religious factor will not manifest itself with redoubled strength" (*JJC*, 34). Toward the end of his memoir, portraying his arrival in Jerusalem, Scholem once again invokes the "historical consciousness" that was immanent in his Zionist youth: "With our return to our own history we, or at least most of us, wanted to change it, but we did not want to deny it. Without this *religio*, this 'tie to the past,' the enterprise was and is hopeless, doomed to failure from the start" (*FBJ*, 166–167). Here, Scholem seems to share the standard Zionist view that Jewish history is an essentially autochthonous process as well as the doctrine of the negation of Galut.[9] However, this perspective conceals the fact that modern Zionism was a mass movement precisely because it remained European and bourgeois in many respects, skillfully reaching compromises. German Zionism in particular took on the function of a "supplemental nationality" or the "fabrication of a national culture with which Jews could identify without setting foot in Palestine."[10] Yet Scholem fervently rejects precisely this kind of symbolic Zionism. For him, Zionism is a purely intra-Jewish movement, not a European national movement and certainly not a movement of colonial expansion. As a result, nationalism and colonialism—the "Arab question"—come into his focus only indirectly, as misinterpretations of the genuinely Jewish nature of the issues.

---

8. Ha'am, *Am Scheidewege*, vol. 1, 35.
9. See Volkov, *Jüdisches Leben und Antisemitismus*, 102ff.; Schweid, "The Rejection of the Diaspora."
10. Berkowitz, *Zionist Culture and West European Jewry*, 6. See also Mintz, "Work for the Land of Israel"; Feisel, "Criteria and Conception in the Historiography."

TWO

CONFUSION AND POLEMICS
Taking a Position

IN SCHOLEM'S YOUTH, SUCH FALSE Zionists played a role above all in his confrontations with the Jewish youth movement, where he first experienced the tension between political aims and metapolitical slogans. He also encountered the link between political and philosophical discourse in Martin Buber's teaching of *Erlebnis*, which had a strong impact on young Jews of the day. In this context, the young Scholem first developed his own language and distinctive political ethos, in which revolt slowly transformed into rigor and critique.

Generational conflict as well as the tension between Jewish and German cultural belonging culminated in the Jewish youth movement, which adopted the cult of the natural and healthy from its German model. The assumption here is that Jewish awakening should take place "via detour at first.... As the individual gains a natural relationship to his surroundings, ... and as the senses, corporality, this-worldliness, and personal courage gain greater significance for his existence, his position on Judaism must shift."[1] This ideology of authenticity finds expression in Martin Buber's religious and cultural criticism, which has strong anarchistic overtones.[2] Buber links the refusal of compulsory education with a "religious" condemnation of bourgeois profanity.

---

1. Calvary, quoted in Schatzker, *Jüdische Jugend*, 272. See also: "Engagement with Nietzsche or with Hölderlin can make us into Jews more strongly than forced return to a ritual whose meaning we do not believe in" (quoted in Reinharz, *Dokumente zur Geschichte des deutschen Zionismus*, 68–69). See Schatzker, "Martin Buber's Influence on the Jewish Youth Movement in Germany." On the political implications, see also Linse, "Die Jugendkulturbewegung"; Hermann, "Die Jugendkulturbewegung."

2. On Buber's thought, see Mendes-Flohr, *From Mysticism to Dialogue*, as well as Löwy, *Redemption and Utopia*. Distance from the state and authority also differentiates these

In a highly effective manner, he transfers the discourse on youth onto the problem of the Jewish cultural revolution. Emphasizing the personal element, for Buber the Jewish question is actually a question of personal authenticity fused with cultural-critical topoi: Western man rationalizes, his gaze dismantles reality, and for him, "the world appears objectified, as a multiplicity of things," whereas to "Oriental" man—with the Jew as paradigm—"the world appears as limitless motion, flowing through him."[3] Buber's success within Zionism and the youth movement is based primarily on the way he uses decidedly modern, European figures while projecting a primal Judaism (*Urjudentum*) in contrast to modern decadence. Especially with his writings on Hasidism, he meets the needs of his audience through a well-considered balance between exoticism and adaptation to contemporary taste that includes philosophical consecration of the emphasis on authenticity in his doctrine of lived experience (*Erlebnislehre*).

The vocabulary of "youth," "movement," "renewal," and "experience" also becomes part of Scholem's language, and he employs this vocabulary with the vagueness that is essential to it: "youth" is the substance of "movement" or vice versa; "movement" is "creative," the overcoming of differences, but it is also associated with "depth," "mysticism," and above all, "sacrifice."[4] Scholem thus argues within the discourse of the youth movement and *Erlebnislehre*, but this does not prevent him from also criticizing the youth movement. He firmly opposes World War I from early on, going so far as to publish the illegal pamphlet *Blau-Weisse Brille*, full of the most intense polemics against the enthusiasm for war among Jewish youth. Yet these polemics also draw on the rhetoric of the youth movement, surpassing it: "We do not have a Jewish youth movement but rather immobility. Three words, and at least one was always missing: Jewish movement without youth—Jewish youth without movement—youth movement without Judaism" (*T I*, 291). Jewish youth is not a movement because it is not radical. The Jewish movement—Zionism—is devoid of youthfulness and creativeness, while the youth movement is devoid of Jewishness. Scholem has

---

intellectuals from Ringer's "Mandarins," yet by no means does this lead to a realistic attitude toward politics, as shown by the example of the Forte circle or later "Secret Germany."

3. Buber, *On Judaism*, 59.

4. For example, Zionists are described as "people of longing," and they attempt "to restore youth to their people, and to evoke the curse that lies upon them" (*T I*, 47). "But only the movement that demands great and true sacrifice carries continuous life within itself" (ibid., 308–309). "Three things seem to me to be essential for assessment of the existence or state of the movement: 'form,' 'content,' and the spark of the decisive event that connects them and welds them into a 'movement'" (ibid., 314–315).

a radical position but as yet no language of his own aside from the language he adopts from the youth movement.[5]

We can observe how this adoption functions in a fanciful sketch from the summer of 1914 entitled "Travel Thoughts." Nietzschean topoi of escape into the mountains, praise of loneliness, and ecstasy are linked with a sense of mission, since Scholem is not in the mountains to be lonely but to draw strength in order to accomplish the "work of redemption down below" in the world of the ghetto: "I want to fetch the fire from the mountains, the fire of myth, the fire of the soul of humanity. This fire is threatening to go out in you, and then you would die. I am making this journey not for myself alone, I am making it for ten million" (*T I*, 34–35, 36). He is not just a person in the community but rather its mandatary, with messianic undertones. Not so uncommon for a pubescent youth, for Scholem this thought is intimately connected with the possibility of his own language. As the bringer of myth, he is at once a poet: "I'll have to compose the myth of the coming reality" (*LY*, 64).

This self-imagination is even more clearly visible in another poetic entry from May 1915, which Scholem characterizes as a "new myth, an unconscious product of poetic compulsion" (*T I*, 115). He recapitulates the story of Zionism in Buber's language and then proceeds to introduce a figure who surpasses Buber: "This young man went alone through the world and looked around to find where the soul of his nation awaited him. . . . Deep down inside he knew that he was the Chosen One who was to search for his people's soul, and to find it; that he must equip himself to pave the way. . . . To do so he needed knowledge of the nations" (*LY*, 57). Scholem thus figures himself as the hero who will consummate what Buber only pointed to.

Alongside such flights of fancy stand articulations of doubt and skepticism. Scholem had read Fritz Mauthner and Ernst Mach very early, and he was familiar with both linguistic and epistemological skepticism. Differently than he suggests in retrospect, however, this skepticism is accompanied in his early writings by a range of firmly atheistic avowals that lead to a deep existential crisis, as we will see shortly. These avowals also modify his ethos, rendering his own "mission" and his entire position questionable, as demonstrated by a

---

5. Scholem's critique published later in *Der Jude* follows a similar scheme. The Jewish youth movement lacks that which decisively constitutes movements in the first place: "they are not continually reborn out of the flow of movement" (*JJC*, 49). This is its failure, and the fact "that in the decisive moment our youth succumbed to the war" appears secondary, the "final and greatest triumph of confusion and the deepest fall we have experienced" (ibid., 50). See Mosse, "Scholem as a German Jew," 120–121.

passage from the autumn of 1915: "Occasionally I have a deeply sad feeling of being a tired and burned-out Jew (though I still can't say what's behind this feeling).... At this moment I no longer believe as I once did that I'm the Messiah. Which is sad, because the minute I recognize my inability to bring about renewal—my own renewal—I cease being a Zionist, or at least a Zionist in the sense I consider necessary" (*LY*, 68). The very possibility of being a Zionist seems to depend on the messianic claim. Consequently, Scholem now has entirely different visions of his own role and of the "myth" he has to compose: "What must and will be written is a novel about a young man who travels to the Land of Israel and is shattered" (*LY*, 82). It is failure that is paradigmatic now, not the heroic overcoming of all contradictions. Elsewhere Scholem is even more direct, having devised the "novella of my suicide"—namely, "I would shoot myself after concluding that there was no solving the gaping paradox in the life of a committed Zionist" (*LY*, 90–91). As we can see from such passages, Scholem's development did not unfold as smoothly as he suggests in retrospect. Instead, it was accompanied by intense crises, most extremely the weeks in a military hospital where he had himself admitted as a schizophrenic in order to get out of military service. Only allusions from his letters indicate that his nerves were indeed affected, he had lost his balance, and his mental condition seemed questionable to him at the time.[6]

More than just instability, Scholem's vacillation between different positions and idioms in his texts is also what enables him to be radical and polemical. In May 1915, he writes that it is becoming increasingly clear to him "that I have ample ideas of my own, but these cannot arise out of my treasure trove without some external catalyst. I always have to be *against* someone, I present my own viewpoint in response to his.... It is in this sense correct, but *only* in this sense, when people claim that being in opposition is for me an integral part of life" (*LY*, 53–54). Scholem goes into opposition in order to *say* something: his tone is radical so as to express the need to take a position. His desire to use language radically is visible in many statements that must have been barely comprehensible to his contemporaries, as his argumentative effort is often incommensurate with the pragmatic question being discussed. Thus, Werner Kraft writes, "We

---

6. See *Br I*, 69, 77, 88; *LL*, 43, 53. Looking back on his youth, Scholem refers to this as "the six most intense weeks of my life" (*JJC*, 16), which he deliberately kept silent about throughout his life (see also *T II*, 28). However, soon after he was exempted from military service, Scholem stressed that his illness had been feigned and his dismissal from the military a triumph of his intellectual efforts (*T II*, 99, 93). See also the discussion in Biale, *Master of the Kabbala*, chapter 2.

seem to be speaking to each other across an abyss" (*LL*, 56), and Erich Heller confesses, "I had understood *nothing* of what you said" (*Br I*, 190). Scholem subsequently attempts to demonstrate to Heller at length that comprehension was not possible for fundamental reasons, so he had not even tried.

With no language of his own, Scholem also hesitates to go public. In 1919 he writes to Buber, "I do not yet have the courage to let anything be printed before I can come up with a terminology that cannot be misunderstood" (*Br I*, 204). For a time, especially in 1916, he experiments with an "ideology" of "Zion" that would constitute such a language: "Ideology should speak to those who at some time and place found Zionism as a demand within themselves, as something finished and unmediated, who ask about the structure and the law of their cause" (*T I*, 299). With this language, Scholem also begins to distance himself from Buber's position: "Youth has no ideology that can give voice to what youth has *recognized*. Buber has written about what youth has experienced, not about this. Ideology is about knowing. No Zionist ideology can be based on Experience. I had once thought otherwise but have changed my mind. There must be knowledge" (*LY*, 84). Above all, ideology legitimizes Zionist *speech*—including his own: "Screaming is a necessary stage before a person throws himself into work" (*LY*, 130).

The objects of this ideology, which is never actually formulated, are the central problems of cultural Zionism: the relation to tradition, social responsibility to fellow Jews, and the cultural-critical position toward Europe (*T I*, 199). The central term of "ideology"—and its ultimate solution—is "Zion," yet many different things fall within this scope. "Zion" is not only the "meaning of Jewish history" (*T I*, 341) but also the "idea of mysticism" (*LY*, 126) and a "religious symbol" for "the *Jewish* concept of redemption, a concept not corroded away by Christianity" (*LY*, 122). "Zion" absorbs all concepts; in Scholem's expositions it appears as a place more than as an answer to a particular question. It is the "*standpoint* from which one can gain the decisive insight" (*T I*, 341). Indeed, Zion here is less a concept than a marking of his own location: Zion is where Scholem speaks. Later, as his doubts regarding Zionist politics increase, Scholem considers the possibility of being forced to leave Palestine again, in which case one would need "to be a Zionist in 'Zion'" (*Br I*, 137).

In this language, all problems are already solved. Unrestrained engagement with tradition will emerge in Zion, social problems will give way to a "synthesis" between deep socialism and aristocracy or a "penetration of the most revolutionary spirit with deepest awe and the strongest feeling for dignity" (*T I*, 344). What is more, "all else will find its creative outlet in the Land of Israel, where everything that is beautiful and is at all available to us will be created anew, and where new symbols will emerge" (*LY*, 122). Yet "Zion" is not only the site of coincident opposites but a political term as well: "Berlin [that is, political Zionism] is the ideology of the politician, the tactician, and the phony; Heppenheim [that is, Buber's cultural Zionism] is the ideology of confusion; while Zion, our Teaching, is the ideology of dogmatism, truth, and *one necessary* standpoint. Berlin requires Zion for logical reasons; Heppenheim out of experience and desires; Zion demands itself" (*LY*, 121). Scholem himself is working through doubt as to whether this is merely a rhetoric of self-affirmation: "So where do the demands of Zion come from? From itself! Is this verging on nonsense? Not in the least, for it's the only adequate expression for our way of thinking" (*LY*, 121). It is precisely this polemic that stabilizes his own position. The more Scholem sets himself as a Zionist against the other semi-Zionists, the more plausible he finds this position that seems like a tautology at first. His position thus begins to gain immunity against critique, as demonstrated by Scholem's response to Buber's critical remark that his polemic is only negative: "One cannot articulate his incomprehension any more clearly, for *what* should it mean that my essay is 'purely negative'? First of all, it is not, because to criticize from Zion is the most positive critique conceivable, and second, it is not the fault of the author but of youth, in which there is nothing of Zion" (*T I*, 456). Thus, speaking of "Zion" is also an immunization strategy. Having taken up the right position in Zion, one can no longer be affected by critical responses. On the contrary, Scholem proceeds to criticize Buber in turn.

THREE

ASCETICISM AND SILENCE
Gaining Authority

SCHOLEM'S GESTURE OF REVOLT TURNED him into a radical, while the cultural Zionism influenced by Buber outfitted him with a vocabulary that he could use to express his position: that of a Zionist able to criticize everyone from within Zion, even Buber himself. Yet the full development of his own position required a second step, expanding his criticism beyond Buber to include the radicalism and enthusiasm from which he himself started. This move placed Scholem precariously as an outsider in a no man's land, and it is from here that he took decisive steps into the intellectual ethos that shaped the rest of his life. We can observe this above all in texts written from 1916 up to Scholem's relocation to Palestine in 1923, which reveal both a deep crisis and a new strategy—namely, that of self-limitation and silence. In these texts, Scholem no longer expresses himself directly and simply. The proclaimed Zionism of "ideology" becomes an esoteric Zionism, and the ethos of revolt and messianism becomes a more indirect and allusive doctrine of the interrelation between religion, politics, and language. The Romantic ethos gives way to a more complex mode of expression determined by ascetism.

Scholem's distancing from Buber was initially prompted by the latter's positive stance on World War I. In the summer of 1916, for example, Scholem describes Buber as an "apostate," who "lost himself, and who thinks he is fighting for the Jews when he is planting German oaks. Buber is lacking *mathematics!*" (*T I*, 362). Around this time, Scholem is also becoming more and more wary of *Erlebnislehre* and Buber's interpretation of Hasidism, and this distance leads him into a deep crisis. At the end of 1914, he writes about his "doubts on mysticism and on Martin Buber's conception of Judaism. . . . I'm in a severe crisis and everything is vanishing from under my feet" (*LY*,

45–46).[1] Buber still embodies authentic Judaism, but there is also something false in this that Scholem cannot yet grasp: "the more Buber is valued, the more ruthlessly he must be challenged when he betrays Zion, the more we would be glad to see him on our side, the more severely he must be condemned when he makes leaps of unpermitted mysticism" (*T I*, 362). Scholem continues to work through this ambivalence during the period that follows.[2]

Rather than the authenticity of the *Erlebnislehre*, Scholem now seeks order and clarity. The previously welcomed merging character of *Erlebnis*, its overcoming of all contradictions, now appears suspect to him: "*Erlebnis* is no *spiritual* order. . . . In the concept of *Erlebnis* as it is now applied like a mystically conclusive magic formula, antinomic layers lie interwoven on top of one another" (*T I*, 507). Scholem's critique is directed not at the epistemology of *Erlebnis* but at its morals: "*Erlebnis* and magic are ultimately identical. Who does not think of a magician when thinking of Buber?" (*T II*, 201). He does not want to—and cannot—completely reject Buber, because at this point he does not have another standpoint available to him. But he can figuratively condemn him, for the "monstrous thing about Buber is that he somehow has the truth, but he conceives of it falsely. In no way can you disprove Buber, but you have to overcome him—just as I have overcome him" (*LY*, 137). Overcoming *Erlebnislehre* does not mean critically destroying it but rather reinterpreting it as part of a demonic counterworld, the "world of Tohu" (*T I*, 507–508).

Buber the "magician" still holds value for Scholem, but this significance is skewed and inverted: "I must say it again and again: Buber is somehow ultimately concealed, but he *is* in the ultimate place. This is naturally twice as terrible but also twice as great as the platitudes and non-errors (not truths!) of many others. Buber is a heretic teacher [*Irrlehrer*], but a teacher, one who has something of the teaching" (*T I*, 388). The formulation "*Irrlehrer*" appears again and again, precisely characterizing the relationship to Buber, who embodies something central that Scholem cannot exactly describe—thus prompting ever fiercer critique. In the summer of 1917, Scholem finally writes to Werner Kraft that "Buber is inherently anti-Jewish" (*LL*, 57) and that he bears the traits of

---

1. See also *T I*, 91–92.
2. "This year I did not think of Buber much," he writes three years later, "in the earlier years the confrontation with him was an ongoing act that occupied me. Now it is finally done. Now Buber is only a paradigm for me (invaluable, certainly)" (*T II*, 430). Escha Bergmann, Scholem's first wife, recalled in 1959 that Scholem got the "'fright of his life' from Buber, and because he did not want to fall into the way that Buber spoke, he kept silent." See Schmuel Hugo Bergmann, *Tagebücher und Briefe*, vol. 2, 308. On the ambivalences in Scholem's later critique of Buber, see also Davidowicz, *Gershom Scholem und Martin Buber*.

the "diabolical" (*Br I*, 94). While others do not know about the truth, Buber keeps it silent. Literally demonized, Buber thus becomes the embodiment of a superior yet negative principle.

For Scholem, overcoming Buber entails overcoming his own origin, which encompasses the biographical phase of Buber enthusiasm as well as a condition of possibility for his own Jewish identity. Is there any way to renew Judaism other than Jewish Romanticism? The danger of Buber is therefore also an internal danger. His "influence" cannot be overcome and cast off in one step but only via an indirect and complex path, to be traced in the remaining course of part 1. The fact that this ambivalence is never completely resolved is revealed by later controversies in the years after World War II. Even though Scholem repeatedly emphasizes the groundbreaking accomplishments of his elder in revealing the mystical and mythical dimensions of Judaism—"in one sense or another we are all his disciples" (*MI*, 229)—he also completely revises Buber's view of history and calls his authority into question. For Scholem, Hasidism actually belongs in the line of development of the Kabbalah and cannot be viewed separately, and thus it is by no means antignostic as Buber asserts. Closing his critique of Buber's view of Hasidism with the remark that "we shall have to start again from the beginning" (*MI*, 248), Scholem once more claims to consummate what Buber only initiated; his "deliberate misunderstanding of Buber's work" thereby concludes a process that began in his youth.[3]

Turning away from Buber also forces Scholem to give up his own language of "youth" and "Zion." This leads to a crisis in the spring of 1917 that finds expression in a special book of his diaries with the title *Exemplum non datum: The Example Not Given*. This book is full of self-reproaches, contrition, and self-accusations that he is neither really a Zionist nor a proper Jew: "Am I a Jew? No. A human being? No. An upstanding youth? No. What am I then? A nihilist who, spurned by God, goes behind God's back because He's rejected him" (*LY*, 173). The central theme of these crises is loneliness, and Scholem often portrays himself as the lonely, heroic radical. However—and this is what is new in these reflections—he also starts to question the heroism and depth of this loneliness. He refers to himself as a "holy swindler" and "spiritual hypocrite" (*LY*, 173), mendacious precisely in his radicality: "Once upon a time there was a fellow whose life was a failure but who didn't find the courage to put an end

---

3. Davidowicz, *Gershom Scholem und Martin Buber*, 105–106. Buber felt himself intentionally misunderstood in this controversy. See Freedman, *Martin Buber's Life and Work*, vol. 3, 230–299. On deliberate misunderstanding and its modes, see Bloom, *Anxiety of Influence*.

to it; the coward couldn't bring himself to do it. He therefore played a game. . . . He was extremely radical, so radical that no one could impress him with any demand. Far surpassing all demands, he didn't need to fulfill any. He discovered a science that allowed him to hide the emptiness of his heart behind the fullness of his spirit, and—desecrating something very respectable—he called his science Zionism" (*LY*, 172). Scholem often mentions suicide during this time: "I am such a liar that I may have to make believe I live a heroic life because I'm too dishonest to kill myself. Suicide requires completeness" (*LY*, 180). He notes the "sneaking arrogance of thinking what would happen if I were dead in a month" (*LY*, 207). His own radicality and the surpassing strategy of Zion are becoming dubious to him, and he can no longer decide if he is a radical or merely a hypocrite. After having rejected all other Zionists, critique now backfires on him, and he loses the language he had gained: "To me, the words people use have something ghostly about them. I exist *before* language" (*LY*, 222). He also loses his sense of a special vocation: "I see my thoughts but I have no visions. That was a hoax on my part. I only have a very lively fantasy in my thoughts" (*LY*, 176).

To escape his own mendacity and spiritual hypocrisy, Scholem initially subjects himself to silence: silence is "renunciation of the periphery and of hubris" (*T II*, 158). His skepticism regarding enthusiasm and grand rhetoric now turns against him in ascesis, which enhances itself through limitation. We can even see a kind of self-demonization at work here: "I now know unimaginable things since death has become my bedfellow. I am restful, but dead. Just a nudge and *I'll also* become a ghost" (*LY*, 260). Stabilization through silence is highly precarious, and Scholem must find a way to speak in spite of this precarity.

In addition to skepticism, it is the influence of another figure that enables Scholem to free himself from Buber's "magic" and find his way through this crisis to a new position. Scholem met Walter Benjamin in 1915, and Benjamin rejected Buber from the outset. Without question, Benjamin became the most significant among Scholem's friends, not only in the years that followed but for life. The "influence" in question lies far deeper than what is normally described in literary and cultural history. Especially between 1917 and 1919, the two philosophized together so intensively that their respective considerations can hardly be understood in isolation from one another, as we will see in part 2. Moreover, during these years, Benjamin also represents a position that enables Scholem to position himself differently. In 1916, after the intense conversations of one visit, Scholem writes: "to truly follow Benjamin would require making some extraordinary revisions"; above all, in light of Benjamin's position, "I'd have to repudiate the sort of Zionism other people proclaim" (*LY*, 139). As we have seen, this initially leads to a profound crisis, with Scholem calling into question his own Zionism and Jewishness. The crisis only ends when Scholem receives a short letter from Benjamin for his twentieth birthday in December 1917, in which Benjamin thanks Scholem for his commentary on Benjamin's text on Dostoevsky. Scholem enthusiastically notes: "These ten lines bring healing to my life.... What kind of affliction can affect my heart now that *this* has occurred: now that God himself, speaking through the mouth of his truest servant, has awakened my *courage*. Yes, if I could only have him near me—and I want to have him very close—my healing would be complete" (*LY*, 202). The burgeoning friendship is described here as a religious experience with erotic undertones. As is typical for a prophetic speech, it is not clear who is actually speaking, whether the "he" in the last sentence is God or his prophet. Scholem sees all the precarities and contradictions of his own existence legitimized by Benjamin. Several months later, he writes to Escha Burchhardt: "I know no one else besides my friend who has become such a teacher to me, owing not only to the ingeniousness of his mind, but also to the sterling purity of his existence" (*LL*, 78). Although he is hardly knowledgeable about things Jewish, Benjamin is stylized as a teacher, and the mimesis goes so far that (in the original German) Scholem even forgoes commas just like his friend.

Scholem retrospectively reflected on why his expectations had been so "excessive," remarking that due "among other things, to his complete seclusion and the tenor of his utterances, Benjamin's figure had assumed a prophetic proportion in my eyes."[4] In any case, Scholem's vast expectations were not met by studying with Benjamin in Bern beginning in May 1918. On the contrary, Scholem found himself disappointed. Only a month after arrival, he notes in his diary that his "life converges on suicide" and that Walter and Dora "are literally driving me to my grave" (*LY*, 240). Scholem refers to Walter's "mendacity," which clearly disappoints him: "Walter may be whoever he is, but he has boundaries over which he won't step, which I experience daily. Metaphysics turns him into a lunatic" (*LY*, 244). This uncrossed boundary is also a practical one. Scholem urges Benjamin to draw consequences for the conduct of life from theoretical insights. This applies to banal matters—one ought not smoke—as well as the existential and political: Benjamin ought to commit to Judaism. Intense confrontations ensue, followed by reconciliation. A few weeks later, Scholem notes again, "I don't believe that since the prophets there has ever lived a man who has brought such a massive responsibility to completion" or that there is "something [in Benjamin] that is borderless, transcending all order,

---

4. Scholem, *Story of a Friendship*, 53, 49.

and that, by employing every effort, tries to order his work" (*LY*, 256). Scholem remains fascinated, even as he repeatedly describes Benjamin—and Dora, to at least the same extent—as decadent and mendacious. Taking distance, he proceeds to throw himself into his work, increasingly turning to his Zionist friends. Yet what he has received from Benjamin remains with Scholem as a mission and future project.

Scholem never concealed the abysses in this relationship, including his excessive expectations, his erotically charged relation to Dora, and his disappointment regarding the fact that the deceased Fritz Heinle was and remained *the* friend for Benjamin. In his story of their friendship, Scholem describes disappointment and reciprocal bitterness. This is due not least to his sense that Benjamin's attitude toward society was cynical, whereas—one can read between the lines—the Benjamins perceived Scholem as a moralist who wanted to convince Benjamin of Zionism by all means. Remarkably often, Scholem cites the letters that Dora wrote to him in the name of her son, Stefan:

> You are wrong in what you write, dear Uncle Gerhardt. I believe you really know very little about my Papa. There are very few people who know anything about him.... You, dear Uncle Gerhardt, still think that one has to do a great deal. Perhaps I shall also think that way when I am a grown man, but now I think more like my Mama, that is, not at all or very little; and so all this to-do and the great excitement over everything seems much less important to me than which way the wind is blowing. But I don't want to be smart-alecky, for you know everything much better. That's the whole trouble.[5]

In the years that followed, the two friends held each other at some distance. Even from this distance, however, Benjamin remained a central point of orientation for Scholem, who dedicated *Major Trends in Jewish Mysticism* to his friend. As we have seen, Benjamin fits the role of the modern prophet for Professor Scholem, who contributes decisively to Benjamin's reception and reputation, in part through an extremely influential portrait, as we will see below. Presumably it is precisely the distance from Benjamin that is crucial for Scholem's continued development. Looking back, Scholem once said that he had learned from Walter Benjamin: "'When you cannot say something perfectly, it is better to be silent.'"[6] Indeed, after getting to know Benjamin, Scholem's own writing takes on a new "tenor" of the prophetic and a certain "seclusion" of its own. If one cannot—and does not wish to—express oneself clearly and directly, one must do so indirectly.

---

5. Scholem, *Story of a Friendship*, 68–69. On Dora's perspective on her relationship with Scholem, see Weissweiler, *Das Echo deiner Frage*, chapter 3.

6. Bergmann, *Tagebücher und Briefe*, vol. 2, 264–265.

Scholem's shift in strategy led first and foremost to the rejection of the youth movement and its confessional, declaratory discourse, which he himself had used recently. At the beginning of 1918, he writes that he is "completely indifferent to the whole so-called youth movement; I do not believe that it is possible, and my work extends to the *matter*... and not the investiture. The whole youth movement is a German swindle. I want to be a Zionist and nothing else, not a 'moved youth.' I forgo my youth" (*Br I*, 136–137). Forgoing youth means forgoing public expression as well. Scholem no longer wants to write programmatic articles like the one on ideology. He distances himself from his own past—for example, from the *Blau-Weisse Brille*, which had been a "unworthy servant of Zionist language," too frivolous and too close to the "literati" (*T I*, 471).

This rejection reaches its conclusion in an open letter to Siegfried Bernfeld from 1918, entitled "Leave-Taking." Unlike in the essay "Jewish Youth Movement," published a year earlier, in "Leave-Taking" Scholem does not counter the existing youth movement with a demand for radicality, wholeness, or Zion. Instead, he rejects youth altogether: "It can no longer be fought against, but only seen through. It cannot be refuted, it can only be overcome" (*Br I*, 462). Scholem continues to argue on the level of language. The language of youth is actually no language at all but "chatter" without content: "one can interchange everything with anything and nothing changes" (*Br I*, 463). Youth speaks constantly, yet the fact that it cannot stay silent shows its true speechlessness: "People who cannot keep silent ultimately also cannot speak with one another. They do not understand each other, for their language has neither limit nor foundation, it is chimerical" (*Br I*, 463). Because youth lives in the world of chatter, where all demands have already been anticipated in imagination, communication is impossible, and it is thus necessary "to restore language to youth" (*Br I*, 463). Silence is now the only possibility, for it is the "only path of this overcoming that cannot be perverted" (*Br I*, 462). The path into silence for the sake of language is at once the path into loneliness: "Community requires loneliness: it is not the possibility of wanting the same thing together, but only communal loneliness that establishes the community of Zion; the source of our heritage is the communal—indeed, in a monstrous sense, identical—loneliness of all Jews" (*Br I*, 462). If there can be no visible community of Zionists here in Germany, Scholem writes to Bernfeld, it is necessary to have in mind a "secret society representing the only possibility of a lonely community that will be realized in concealment" (*Br I*, 465).

This text seeks to establish a politics of expression that is Zionist in Scholem's sense, centered on an "eloquent silence," a silence that is not only cessation of speech and not—or not only—retreat into personal "purity" but also a polemical and political act. Out of the rhetoric of radical negation comes reflection on rhetoric and reflective rhetoric, the formulations of which follow in paradoxical figures that are highly characteristic of Scholem's writing at this point: restitution of language through silence, restoration of community through loneliness. Is he merely shifting from the tautology of ideology (Zion is Zion) to the other pole of rhetorical possibility? His polemic makes sense less through these paradoxes than through its ascetic gesture and in the values that it suggests to the Zionist—"silence, work, and recognition, purity, stringency, and sacrifice" (*Br I*, 465)—as well as in its own manner of appearance, through its apodictic style.

Along with "silence" and "loneliness," "work" plays a decisive role for Scholem. The "Leave-Taking" letter, a verbose plea for silence, purports to focus on work: "What I can say here is not the positive, which indeed can only be made visible as the grounds of my negation. Work is oral teaching, and from this nothing can be put down in writing as method; it is only the *methodos* of my silence that I want to, and have to, pronounce here, not in order to proselytize..., but in order to testify to a youth that receives, unfolds, and passes down Zion and the teaching in silence" (*Br I*, 462). "Work" as "teaching" is central to Scholem's thought in these years, containing at once an ascetic and a religious element, apparent in the allusion to tradition with which he gains new legitimacy. He no longer speaks in the name of a coming youth but rather in the name of "teaching" and "tradition." This can no longer be simply pronounced, however. In order not to be perverted, work can only be accomplished in silence. If Scholem wants to be the legitimate speaker of tradition, he has to speak in silence, and this is what he attempts in his letter to Bernfeld. Silence plays a large role in Scholem's statements on tradition for reasons that go beyond philosophy of language, related to his recognition of his own problems of legitimate expression in the literature of tradition: "All Jews are incapable of saying the final word within written and writable language. This is linked to commentary" (*T II*, 200).

As a consequence of this emphasis on work and tradition, Scholem's argumentation within Zionism grew less and less "radical" after 1919. When he did take a position in public debates, he spoke out against the rejection of heritage in the name of "renewal," "naturalness," or "life." In 1919 he defended Bialik's revaluation of the Halachah against Brenner's charge that religious tradition had nothing more to say to modern life. Three years later, he initiated a collective protest against developments in the Jewish hiking association Blau-Weiss, which was drawing ever closer to the right wing of the German youth movement. More often, however, his position became invisible.

FOUR

ESOTERIC ZIONISM
Politics and Language

IN 1921 SCHOLEM WRITES TO Robert Weltsch and Hans Kohn that his conception of Zionism has become "an utterly nonrevolutionary notion of Zionism . . . since it refers to a stratum where there are no revolutions" (*LL*, 120). Social problems are no longer decisive for him, and the "revolutions of the spirit" that Scholem had once demanded of himself, at least, are now inessential compared to the "deep continuity of the Teaching" (*LL*, 121). His Zionism precludes "as irrelevant, if not pernicious, the expression '*revolutionary* Zionism' . . . ; in reality, it disqualifies the entire political sphere in which the revolution is rightly regarded as essential. Even if Zionism were a revolutionary undertaking, it would have to exercise double or triple caution in avoiding such terminology" (*LL*, 120). The last sentence with its negated subjunctive is highly characteristic. Scholem does not let matters rest with the assertion that Zionism is nonrevolutionary, instead proceeding to stress that one must separate it from revolution. Zionism and revolution are both fields with their own logic, but only as long as one is able to keep them apart. Zionism will not simply overcome politics; the two seem to remain standing side by side. Scholem also discusses the notion of revolution in a "Note on Bolshevism," asserting that the historical legitimacy of revolutionary action is independent of its outcome: "Revolutions fail. But this is never and can never be an *argument* against them. Again and again, revolutions transmit to generations the silent teaching of the unambiguity of history" (*T II*, 556). This does not apply to Judaism, however: "Revolution is where the messianic kingdom is to be erected without the teaching. Ultimately there *can* be *no* revolution for the Jews. Jewish revolution is only reconnection to the teaching" (*T II*, 556).[1]

---

1. See "Notiz über den Bolschewismus," *T II*, 556ff. In 1938, after the disappointment in Palestine, Scholem writes a note about the impossibility of a permanent revolutionary

For a time, Scholem discusses the relationship of Zionism and politics in quite a contradictory manner. With his emphasis on "teaching," Zionism at first seems to become entirely incomprehensible. In 1918 he writes with some confusion that he no longer knows what Zionism is: "Certainly I know it on the penultimate level: to give the Jewish people *form* [*Gestalt*]. But on the final level—perhaps there *is* no Zionism at all. There is religion that looks *entirely* different than Zionism" (*T II*, 145). Yet Scholem remains uncertain, above all because he is simultaneously starting to have doubts about what religion is. As of 1918, he stresses that he adheres to the absolute authority of religion and yet does not accept religion as binding for his own way of life, for "so long as the messianic realm has not come... I will not accept any sort of authority over my actions besides those that we erect on an anarchistic and free basis" (*LL*, 101).

In part 2, I will explore the role that this "religious anarchism" plays in Scholem's theological reflections. Politically, referring to a (deferred) religious authority implies that profane political action can be granted its own right with respect to religion. As long as religion is not binding—as long as the messianic realm does not yet exist—concrete political action remains necessary. Scholem gains a positive attitude toward politics in the narrower sense of tactics, power struggles, and the party system, precisely those aspects of Zionism that he had vehemently rejected in the phase of "ideology." This becomes very clear in "Politics of Zionism," a text from 1920. Scholem emphasizes that propaganda can be a legitimate tool and that radicality does not befit Zionism: "The Zionist bourgeoisie is a legitimate medium of esoteric Zionism, and radicalism is the swindle of the defrauded fraudsters" (*T II*, 625). Unlike a few years earlier, Zion is no longer cast as an authentic metapolitical location from which contradictions are ultimately sublated. As a result, it is better to feign being bourgeois than to simulate radicality. During this time, Scholem even considers whether "Zionist literature ought to be seen not as betrayal but as an effective defensive action for the invisible, if looked at from within" (*T II*, 486–487).

Here, as well, there seem to be two scenes—the visible and the invisible— each with its own logic. Scholem formulates this explicitly in "Politics of Zionism": "The political sphere is the one in which actions are basically construed as means.... *Within* the political sphere there can be *nothing* that leads out of it; one must not even *sense* that there is something else" (*T II*, 624). Zion is indeed

---

movement: "There is a permanent revolutionary *movement*—*before* victory!! But not afterwards! Victory is the turning point that changes perspectives, just as the hiker arriving at the top of the pass sees an entirely new landscape ahead of him. What *is* still there is important and problematic as always, but no longer of any desired *length* in its course" ("Schwindel der Revolutionen," 1).

still the aim of Zionist politics but no longer the object: "The politics of Zionism is directed at the realization of the unmetaphorical present of revelation (Zion). Zion must *not* appear in it. To speak of Zion is to betray it" (*T II*, 624–625). Zionist politics is still about more than mere politics, but this "more" can no longer be pronounced; it is only "secret teaching": "Preservation of distance is the highest political symbol" (*T II*, 625).

Again, one can clearly see Scholem's need to draw limits and his need for "order" instead of "confusion." This need increases with the ascetic turn, as one could generally define asceticism in terms of an enhanced need for form. Zionism is not *allowed* to be revolutionary, and even if it were, it would not be allowed to speak in a revolutionary way. Transgression of the limit between spheres is now the main focus of Scholem's polemic, as, for example, in the previously cited letter to Weltsch and Kohn: "You probably take the confusion of religion and politics for something great, I take it for misfortune. I think that the only reasonable sense of Jewish politics, if there is such a thing, would be to facilitate our rebirth in an invisible sphere, through systematic generation and advance of a certain appearance; the group of revolutionary Zionists did its best to let this rebirth freeze to death in the cold light of the public" (*Br I*, 217–218). Scholem thus reformulates the problematic relationship of politics and metapolitics in Zionism. Yet his imploring tone also makes something else clear: the relationship of religion and politics cannot be thought of as pure separation, for despite their essential difference, the two tend to mix with one another. For Scholem, religion and politics are not simply two different things—they can also jeopardize one another. His push for separation is a reaction to the corrupting confusion that is always possible, given that religion and politics both participate in the sphere of language.

Scholem already relates political questions to questions of language in "Leave-Taking," and in the following years it becomes even clearer that his politics is a politics of the word. He notes in 1919, after reading some political pamphlets by Büchner and Weitling: "The most elaborate sociological study of the means of production can't explain the most meager phenomenon and riddle of language. In each text lurks countless linguistic armies, lined up and half asleep, and the most curious operations are at work in language and in its relationship to the outside—what is commonly called its *influence*" (*LY*, 310). Scholem implies that it is possible to understand this dimension of politics with recourse to the linguistic dimension of religion. The "political word" emerges as the "unfolding of the canonical word"—that is, as the "mirroring of an expressionless world that was nonetheless language and word in an explicit world that is no longer either. This is my linguistic explanation of politics" (*T II*, 473).

Scholem's considerations regarding the linguistic character of politics appear to have a concrete point of departure. In 1917 he translated the *Yizkor* book, a memorial volume for the first Jewish settlers who had fallen in defense of their settlements. This book played a decisive role in the formation of a heroic mythology of the Zionist struggle, triggering several significant controversies.[2] Scholem soon became skeptical of this project, asking himself whether "mystification of violence" and death are not ominously operating in the book; he disclaimed the book not out of pacifism but because of the "ongoing, despicable mixture of spheres" (*T II*, 143). In its title, the book is oriented by traditional lamentation of the dead, yet it contains something entirely different than actual lamentations—namely, "the childish delight that 'he was ours'" (*T II*, 144), or ideological appropriation. The whole ideology of heroic death thus remains on the level of phraseology: "In Germany people speak in catchphrases and have no courage to do more, in Palestine people *die* for catchphrases. What is worse?" (*T II*, 144).

The juxtaposition of legitimate lament as a form of tradition and the catchphrase as a form of traditionless speech is visible in a series of other texts as well—for example, a short text entitled "The Truth" from April 1923: "This is what we find lacking in the Zionists: this inability to lament the lost youth of their people, their true misfortune. The security of a common future blocks their view into the abyss of mourning that gapes in the middle of all Jewish history, at the heart of all Jewish phenomena" (*T II*, 712). For Scholem, Zionism is no longer a turning toward the future, nor is it simply reconnection with a great past that is given in tradition. Instead, in this connection as well, there is something missed, belated, and failed. Not to be bypassed, this must be articulated, and Zionism must "raise ... the emotion and the grief that lie behind the grimaces of the eastern and western ghettos into a formative, unbending, healing force" (*T II*, 712–713). If lament articulates what is lost in a legitimate manner, the catchphrase illegitimately preempts what is anticipated.[3]

The reevaluation of religion and politics also leads to a reevaluation of messianism. In a text from 1919/1920 entitled "The Teaching of Zion," Scholem

---

2. See Frankel, "The 'Yiskor' Book of 1911." On the history of the translation, see *FBJ*, 88–90.

3. On the danger of the catchphrase, see also a drafted letter to his Socialist brother, Werner: "If one of these days you ever gain power (which is a good possibility), then the entire lack of purity, demagoguery, and all the evil you have gratuitously injected into workers (who trust you) through your rapid-fire clichés will present a terrible obstacle *against* any serious work. Nothing is more pernicious for a community than demagoguery. Because you have fed people an impure language, rotten ideology, and self-righteousness *à tout prix*,

writes: "the deepest conceivable recognition of Zionism consists in the limitative recognition that Zionism is also and precisely at the deepest level *not* a messianic movement.... The redemption that Zionism brings is not messianic redemption; redemption and thus Zionism would be messianic only if Zionism's claim were to produce and realize the teachability of the teachings" (*T II*, 622). Messianism itself, the metapolitical factor of Zionism, may not be used as a catchphrase—that is, it may not be deployed for political effect. Scholem already recognizes this danger before his immigration to Palestine or his engagement with Sabbatianism. He distances himself on the one hand from the reduction of religion to politics (redemption is social renewal) and on the other hand from the subsumption of politics under religion (Zionism is a messianic enterprise). Again, it is a matter of separation of that which is connected, a tension that determines Scholem's own expression: he refers to the recognition of Zionism's unmessianic character as "deep," only to be expressed esoterically. The exoteric statement that Zionism is no messianism would be wrong in a certain sense; this would be a purely political statement that does not describe Zionism as a whole. Characteristically, Scholem writes to Albert Baer: "One of the few sentences that I am prepared to pronounce on the positive content of Zionism is that Zionism is not a messianic movement—and I am not pronouncing it here!" (*T II*, 632). There is no categorical difference to be made between religion and politics in order to describe Zionism. There is only a precarious line to be drawn over and over again anew.

As a result, Scholem has to speak about his Zionism in a way that is at once messianic and unmessianic, just as the "secret teaching" is at once the precondition of Zionist politics and yet cannot feature in those politics. This is only possible in a discourse that is itself broken, always only expressing one part, and his reflections must therefore take on esoteric or ironic form. In "The Teaching of Zion," this is expressed in the paradoxical address—"For the students I do not have" (*T II*, 621)—and in the unclear status of the text: Is the text itself the "teaching of Zion," or does it only speak about this teaching?

Scholem writes in his memoir that the years from 1919 to 1923 "meant basically the end of my inner development toward that concretion of being that I had dreamed about."[4] By this point, Scholem has a legitimate position and a

---

instead of preparing them..., your regime—lacking a foundation—will unavoidably drown itself in a sea of blood" (*LY*, 319–320). Scholem was also clearly influenced by Karl Kraus's critique of the press: see "Über Journalismus, neuhebräische Dichtung und Musivstil" (*T II*, 586–588).

4. Scholem, *Von Berlin nach Jerusalem*, 140.

language of his own. He no longer needs to emphatically emphasize his own location, and he requires neither visions nor ideologies in order to imagine himself as a Zionist. Ascetic self-limitation and work have led to a new "substance," new speech, and new authority, aptly reflected in a remark by Franz Rosenzweig about Scholem:

> His Judaism is *only* a cloister for him.... As a result he became *speechless*. He only has the gestures of admiration or rejection, really only the *gestures* and only *these* gestures.... Indeed, at the price of being cloistered or reclusive he purchased that which we will earn: one must believe him, without being asked.... He is *really* "without dogma." One *cannot* catechize him. I have never before encountered this in a Western Jew. He is perhaps the first person there is to have really already returned home. But he returned *alone*.[5]

It is true that isolation, restraint, and polemical authority condition each other for Scholem, yet it is only from Rosenzweig's—entirely polemical—perspective that he is "speechless." He may refuse dialogue, but he retains the forms of indirect expression and authoritative verdict. His lack of dogma also finds expression in his guiding metaphor, no longer that of a (dogmatic) standpoint but rather a limit or border (*Grenze*) that has to be continually maintained and crossed at the same time. In "The Teaching of Zion," Scholem writes: "hovering between doubt and deed, and the task of letting this hovering itself become something essential in the realization of theocracy, define our heretical lives" (*T II*, 622). To be a Zionist means to live at the limit, and if Zionism on the whole is a revocation of confusion, the "impurity" of most Zionists lies in "living outside of this renunciation and not wanting to live within it" (*LY*, 313). Limits had been important for Scholem all along: the *Scheidelinie* against Europe, the difficult delimitation from Buber, the limit between religion and politics, and also the limit between doubt and faith. It is always a matter of making the position at the limit or border productive: "One can say that the border is the main agent of my being. I magnify my own powers. This is dangerous business" (*LY*, 222).

Moments of despair and traces of crisis remain present in these formulations, but now they are ascetically managed and internalized in such a way that they can become intellectually productive. For example, in "Zionist Despair" from the summer of 1920, existential and religious despair are transformed into

---

5. Rosenzweig, *Briefe und Tagebücher*, vol. 1, 704. Brocke ("Franz Rosenzweig und Gerhard Gershom Scholem") shows that this remark was intended to protect Rudolph Hallo from Scholem's influence.

a "theory" of the limit. The stable and productive despair of Zionists is differentiated from wild despair: "Zionist despair *never* leads to suicide, which is contrary to its regulations" (*T II*, 638). Resolute suicide is detached from despair that ironically withdraws itself. The "potentiated" ironic despair of Zionism remains formative and distinctive for Scholem and could be considered essential to the particular quality of his later prose, at once radical and restrained, sharp and serene. The text still has a confessional tone, but its author withdraws more and more from the reader's vision, following the logic of asceticism and esoteric Zionism. For the "spheres" of religion and politics that must not be mixed are always also spheres of the word. To write in different spheres always means writing on different levels, with different forms of address; it means writing "esoterically," if one understands this not as communication of the hidden but rather hidden communication. Scholem's "esotericism" is less a style of thinking than a practice of writing, an art of dealing with his own texts. Symptomatically, although Scholem makes fewer and fewer esoteric notes in later years and certainly no longer intends to draft a "system of philosophy," he meticulously saves his youthful notes, making transcripts and also using them again in his book on Walter Benjamin as well as other writings. Thus, his writing no longer aims at the acquisition of a "language that cannot be misunderstood," which, once gained, would be able to express identity with infinite plasticity. Instead, Scholem produces a series of texts that can only be continued with effort, in private. It is precisely this restraint, this refraction in self-expression, that institutes his individual expression in a particular way. Putting the brakes on manic writing, it serves to counterbalance self-expression that dangerously reflects on itself. Where there had been something self-tormenting and deliquescent about Scholem's diaries at the beginning of this phase, they now gain form.

Asceticism protects Scholem from the dangers of the catchphrase as well as the performative magic of "Zion," which are nevertheless set aside and archived rather than abandoned. "Passion and silence—that is the Zionists' secret" (*T II*, 210). Radicality and secrecy mutually maintain one another, and the price of this balance, the price of the ascetic ethos in general, is the impossibility of direct confession. In "The Teaching of Zion," Scholem writes, "Zionism cannot be helped until in the first place every possibility *for public avowal* is taken away. No one should have the right to find an *organ* for conversion" (*T II*, 478). Within Scholem's development, and in his political writing, a near reversal is taking place. Originally, his Zionism was above all else an avowal, a formula that made it possible for him to even approach Judaism again: to be a Jew was to be a Zionist, to be a Zionist was to speak of Zion. Now, Zion has completely disappeared from this speech, and to speak of Zion is to betray it. Zionism is "internalized," and so it must also be esoteric, veiling itself. While Scholem does take a certain pleasure in this masquerade, it has also become an inner necessity. When Hugo Bergman suggests to him in 1947 that he might speak for himself rather than yet again speaking as a historian about the statements of others, Scholem expresses doubt as to whether this would ever be possible for him: "I no longer believe in direct 'messages,' nor can I find among the 'messengers' anyone who could have brought some blessing. I tend to believe that it is precisely this naïve appeal to others ... that lies behind the failure of such attempts" (*LL*, 340–341).

FIVE

VICTORY'S DESPAIR

Reality and Crisis

IN THE AUTUMN OF 1923, Scholem immigrated to Palestine, and two years later he became the professor of Jewish mysticism at the Hebrew University of Jerusalem. He had arrived. He concludes his memoir at this point, having reached a seemingly stable position and achieved the fulfillment of his youthful yearnings.[1] However, his memoir also already reveals that his arrival in the Yishuv was far from unproblematic and his judgment on the politics of interwar Zionism deeply skeptical.

At the end of 1924, a year after his immigration, Scholem outlines the main themes of his disappointment in a short text:

> Oh God—this was not what we wanted. Inwardly we believed in the fullness of the heart, and here we are being killed by this thin, petty bourgeois mentality [*Kleinbürgerklichkeit*] that binds a Chaluz with a Klausner—I cannot forget his tirades, which I had to listen to in 1923 in Petah Tikva, when I happened into a lecture he was giving. And why? *Because the drying up of language has parched our heart*.... We came and thought we were plunging into the fullness of a sea..., but we are only wading in the mud of chatter.... *Metaphysically* we have lost in the country the battle that Zionism won in the world.[2]

---

1. On Scholem's arrival, see Zadoff, *From Berlin to Jerusalem and Back*, part 1. Referring to *From Berlin to Jerusalem*, Scholem writes in 1977, "I do not think there will be a continuation. It gets much too difficult. It is also much easier... to write critically about the circumstances of one's own youth than about the difficult developments in the Land of Israel in the last fifty years" (*Br III*, 166).

2. Scholem, "Der Zionismus wird seine Katastrophe überleben," 1. On Scholem's engagement in Brit Shalom, see Zadoff, *From Berlin to Jerusalem and Back*, chapter 2.

Instead of a renewal of Judaism, Scholem finds only narrowmindedness, only chatter instead of living language, and only victory in the world instead of metaphysical victory—these three themes are repeated again and again in his notes. The mixture of religion and politics that Scholem had already criticized in Germany was taking place continuously and to a massive extent in the Yishuv, which was undergoing a decisive transitional phase in the early interwar period. Social institutions were being established and ideological conflicts coming to a head—for example, between left-wing and right-wing Zionism and between secular and religious interpretations of Israel—in ways that remained at least partly alien to Scholem, who had constituted his position under much more relaxed ideological conditions.

Scholem criticizes the Socialist Zionists, long represented in the Yishuv, and above all revisionist Zionism, the emergence of which he sees as a symptom of a more general crisis for the entire Zionist movement: "Since the Revisionists have so unmistakably come into the inheritance of the Zionist apocalypse as true utopians, the inner exposure of Zionism has become clear."[3] He continues to speak out publicly against the mixture of religion and politics as it comes to light. In 1929, in response to reproaches that the peace policy of Brit Shalom betrays the hope for complete redemption, Scholem counters: "I, a member of Brit Shalom, am opposed . . . to mixing up religious and political concepts. I categorically deny that Zionism is a messianic movement and that it is entitled to use religious terminology to advance its political aims. The redemption of the Jewish people, which as a Zionist I desire, is in no way identical with the religious redemption I hope for for the future" (*JJC*, 44). As he did already before his immigration, Scholem differentiates here between religion and politics while also emphasizing that politics is not "entitled" to draw on religious language. This can only be propaganda and pretense: "The Zionist ideal is one thing and the messianic ideal is another, and the two do not touch except in pompous phraseology of mass rallies, which often infuse into our youth a spirit of new Sabbatianism that must inevitably fail. The Zionist movement is congenitally alien to the Sabbatian movement, and the attempts to infuse Sabbatian spirit into it has already caused a great deal of harm" (*JJC*, 44).

In private reflections, however, Scholem concedes that Zionists as yet have not grasped the force of religious tradition. According to him, they have only looked forward, and they have never succeeded in linking this "vocation" with "reflection" on the past: "The Zionists who never became aware of the dialectics of their situation have compensated themselves for the absence of historical

---

3. Scholem, "Nach fünfzehn Jahren: Selbstbetrug?," 2.

success with the coarsening of their intentions down to tangible measure. . . . Yet the *coarser* the concepts become, the more emphatically the reality of the next years will ensure their dissolution."[4] Scholem seems to be saying that the difficulties in establishing the Yishuv, in particular increasingly difficult communications with the Arabs, have finally led to the "brute" nationalism of the Revisionists, drowning out concrete difficulties with verbose proclamations. What is new in these deliberations is that Scholem thematizes not only the metapolitical dangers of this approach (the betrayal of "invisible" Zionism) but also the very concrete political risk to the Yishuv: an alliance of Zionism with British imperialism or the revisionist politics of Jewish force would ultimately lead to Zionism's demise.

Alongside the mixture of religion and politics, Scholem sees a more general threat to Zionism in its own success. In his first notes after immigration, he discusses how victory in the world has hindered victory in the Land of Israel. Two years later, in 1926, he writes about this in the text "The Victor's Despair," which expands on Ahad Ha'am's skepticism toward the political orientation of Zionism. The "original sin" of Zionism is the *"anticipation* of our victory": "Whoever preempts his victory in the spiritual loses the power to gain victory in the corporeal. We were not only dreaming, our utopias themselves, the beautiful hours when we thought we were daydreaming, they sucked up our best strength: we prevailed too early, for we are victors in the *visible* world of intelligence before we were victors in the invisible world of the demons who threaten the language of our rebirth, won in assemblies."[5] The problem is precisely not the profanation of utopia but the reverse: utopian dreaming has made political victory impossible, and the spiritual thus threatens the corporeal. In Scholem's view, victory has occurred in the wrong place—namely, the "visible world of intelligence," by which he seems to mean the sphere of propaganda, in which religion and politics are bastardized: "The abyss on which Zionism treads is *dreadful*: it has been shown that 'propaganda' is a power that could be invoked to help us, and like all ghosts, it no longer worked. Now that we can no longer be silent, our 'propaganda' prevents us from winning."[6] Zionism has remained metapolitically successful, achieving renewal of the Diaspora in a certain sense but losing its force in the process, reaching its aim only by using religious heritage for political purposes. Indeed, because it prevailed in the Diaspora, "Zionism once again ensured the existence of Judaism for one or two generations. This was a victory that we had

---

4. Scholem, "Nach fünfzehn Jahren: Selbstbetrug?," 3–4.
5. Scholem, "Die Verzweiflung des Siegenden," 1.
6. Scholem, "Die Verzweiflung des Siegenden," 1–2.

not thought about at all, victory on a field on which we did not even want to fight. Yet this victory cost Zionism the best of its strength."[7]

As these arguments demonstrate, Scholem does not meet the crisis unprepared—he has recourse to a developed rhetoric—yet his position shows a marked shift. In Germany, Scholem still recognized the possibility of an ironic use of propaganda and the disguise of a citizen. He spoke "in the name of" an invisible movement, as the one who understood the situation without being in it. In the Yishuv, there is no longer any such space of remove, and Scholem acknowledges that "we" have entered into a crisis. His skepticism increases from year to year. In the short text from 1924, Scholem still stresses the *critical* situation of Zionism: *this* is the time "when hearts must decide if they want to give up the Zionism that means the preparation of the eternal for the Zionism of the Jewish state, which is catastrophe."[8] Not much of the pathos of this pointed moment remains in the course of different revisions and paraphrases. Two years later, Scholem declares, "the Zionism that brought us here has become a farce."[9] In the last surviving text from 1930, also quoted in a long letter to Benjamin, he writes: "We misjudged the invisible forces of history. But can an error be mended? Is not irrevocability the true seal of the historical?"[10] Scholem almost seems to be writing in retrospect, looking back at something that has already lapsed. The title "After Fifteen Years: Self-Deception?" suggests that the Zionism that has served as a clear guideline since his youth has once again led him back into the "self-deception" from which he sought to free himself.

When there is no longer any positive, clear option, one's own actions become pointless: "It is not about saving oneself, but rather perishing decently: to leap into the abyss, the abyss between victory and reality, Zionism and existence, in order to close it. But we have no language. For this reason our sacrifice will be in vain."[11] It seems that the position at the limit of religion and politics no longer appears productive even to Scholem himself. It has not led to longed-for clarity but quite the opposite:

> In our youth we stood in the center and everything was ordered for us, but since we stepped out of the center . . . , we are blinded by an ambiguous light: politics in its effect on our life. In the center there is no politics, and without

---

7. Scholem, "Um was geht der Streit?," 16. "Dubnow . . . won along with Zionism, that is the paradox of the Zionist movement" (ibid., 17).
8. Scholem, "Der Zionismus wird seine Katastrophe überleben," 1.
9. Scholem, "Heute, vor 3 Jahren . . . ," 1.
10. Scholem, "Nach fünfzehn Jahren: Selbstbetrug?," 1.
11. Scholem, "Die Verzweiflung des Siegenden," 2.

> succumbing to messianic temptations, we were certain of the religious concept of our task. This has changed. And yet we are also not standing in the foreign dimension from which our movement could already be seen as complete in itself.... But where are we standing? This cannot be grasped in concepts, and that is an objection. We are seeking to influence the external from a reality that is not yet unfolded, a secret reality. This is a mystical yet futile endeavor, and the knowledge of fighting a losing battle is not fruitful—at least not beyond cognition.[12]

The old terms of the ascetic ethos are still present, but they can no longer be placed into any positive constellations, remaining fragments in space. There are still paradoxes, but they have no more productive force; they do not provide clarification and do not point to the future: "We remain standing as esoterics of an old style. Our physiognomy will remain ambiguous and confusing."[13]

Scholem's disappointment upon arrival in Palestine is perhaps most evident—and best understood—in his attitude toward language. As already mentioned, strong advocacy for Hebrew plays a decisive role in his self-understanding as a Zionist, contributing to crucial differentiation from other Zionists. In 1919, in a somewhat poetic account of the most recent phase in his development, Scholem writes: "At that time, we knew Hebrew to be the only way. The flow of words failed where the venerable stuttering of the old vocabulary set in, renewing us" (*LY*, 281). "Zion" is no longer necessarily the real Yishuv or merely an abstract ideal, but it is the place where Hebrew will be spoken. This expectation is not fulfilled, however. On the contrary, Scholem writes to Kraft already in 1925, "I suffer catastrophically from linguistic conditions" (*LL*, 137). In 1933 he also discusses with Benjamin "the suspect nature of a renewal that tends to manifest itself mostly as hubris and linguistic decay."[14] Much later, Scholem says that he did not learn his "dialectics" from a textbook but rather through the "contradictions in the constructive processes here [in Eretz Yisrael]: the inner contradictions of the revival of the secular language and the silence overpowering the language" (*JJC*, 36). The issue of language makes it clear that Scholem's immigration did not allow him to uphold the speaker position that he had previously acquired, even though the ending of *From Berlin to Jerusalem* suggests that this was the case. According to his memoir, Scholem was able to express himself in Hebrew, even though his pronunciation was colored by a Berlin accent. There

---

12. Scholem, "Nach fünfzehn Jahren: Selbstbetrug?," 4–5.
13. Scholem, "Nach fünfzehn Jahren: Selbstbetrug?," 4.
14. Scholem and Benjamin, *Correspondence of Benjamin and Scholem*, 66.

is enthusiasm in his account of belonging to the "first generation in which Hebrew moved from the book into spoken language," with attention to "Semitic syntax and beautiful word choice..., before a generation after them initiated the process of downfall through which spoken Hebrew became an Indo-European language."[15] He observes this process "with mixed feelings: happy because of the progress of our language and sad about the price that we have paid for it."[16]

As we will see in part 2, language plays a central role in Scholem's theoretical reflections on Judaism, as a kind of spiritual principle in which Judaism is realized. Beyond its philosophical and speculative roots, his notion of language is directly linked to questions and discourses of linguistic policy with practical relevance for the renewal of Hebrew in Palestine. Scholem's disappointment is more than just the predictable impact of an elitist intellectual hitting the ground of reality. His disappointment is linked to the concrete situation of language in the Yishuv. The project of the "revival" of biblical Hebrew involved a significant change in the Jewish language system; the sacred language of Hebrew, still common in the Diaspora, became the language of a new literature and then slowly also became the spoken language of the Yishuv.[17] In the decisive second phase, negotiations *about* language took place primarily *in* language, with debates about literature and the revival of Hebrew taking place in a Hebrew that incorporates the multilayered linguistic tradition of biblical, rabbinic, and medieval Hebrew as well as linguistic and literary forms of Yiddish and modern European languages.[18] We can take the work of Haim Nahman Bialik as an example. One of the most important poets of modern Hebrew, Bialik also offers theoretical reflections on the renewal of Hebrew that are highly significant for Scholem, who knew Bialik personally.

Bialik wants to renew the Hebrew language from within; he polemicizes against the invention of new words for expressions from other languages. Instead of a bilingual dictionary, in his view one should use a monolingual dictionary or, better still, a compendium of classical texts. Language cannot be manipulated artificially; it has to grow on its own. His Romantic faith in language goes hand in hand with modern linguistic doubt, as demonstrated

---

15. Scholem, *Von Berlin nach Jerusalem*, 90–91.
16. Scholem, *Von Berlin nach Jerusalem*, 91.
17. On the construction of living and dead languages, see Harshav, *Language in the Time of Revolution*, esp. 113–133; Rabin, "The National Idea and the Revival of Hebrew."
18. See also Alter, *Hebrew and Modernity*, as well as *The Invention of Hebrew Prose*, especially on the connection between a synthetic Hebrew that brings together different phases of language and modern realism.

by his 1915 essay "Revealment and Concealment in Language," which shaped Scholem's view of language. Here, Bialik describes language as a cycle: new words emerge in language, they are uttered, and then they pass into self-evident use. After this has happened, speakers no longer notice the deep significance that the words once possessed, "without their having any conception of how shaky is their bridge of mere words, how deep and dark the void is that opens at their feet, and how much every step taken safely partakes of the miraculous."[19] Once they become self-evident, words become a "dividing wall" against the richness of reality, but the stability of this wall is illusory: "If we were to strip all the words and systems completely bare to their innermost core, in the end, after the last reduction, we should be left with nothing in our hands but one all-inclusive word. Which? Again, the same terrible 'what?' behind which stands the same X, even more terrible—the nothingness."[20]

For Bialik, the power of words is founded in a nihilistic abyss of meaninglessness that becomes evident in speech. This is especially true of poetic speech, whose users are obligated "to introduce into language at every opportunity— never-ending motion, new combinations and associations. The words writhe in their hands; they are extinguished and lit again, flash on and off . . . , grow empty and become full, put off a soul and put on a soul. . . . The profane turns sacred, the sacred profane."[21] Bialik combines an avant-garde aesthetic of the alienation of language and linguistic doubt with the description of a synthetic style that actually sets old words into motion, bringing sacred expressions into new contexts. He outlines this procedure with thoroughly religious pathos; originally composed in biblicizing Hebrew, the text does what it says.

In place of a vocabulary or dictionary inventing new words for expressions of modern life, Bialik advocates for *kinus*, the ingathering of tradition. On the one hand, this refers to an anthology, typical for the invention of a national language. On the other hand, Bialik has constant recourse to religious language—for example, when he discusses the sealing of the canon. He emphasizes that the selection should be based on literary criteria alone while at the same time insisting that it should lay claim to cultural authority.[22] Bialik uses

---

19. Bialik, "Revealment and Concealment in Language," in *Revealment and Concealment: Five Essays*, 15.

20. Bialik, "Revealment and Concealment," 18, 21. The abyss can be described as a question: *"No word contains the complete dissolution of any question. What does it contain? The question's concealment"* (ibid., 16).

21. Bialik, "Revealment and Concealment," 25.

22. See also Rotenstreich, *Tradition and Reality*, 62ff.; Myers, *Re-Inventing the Jewish Past*, 133ff.

religious concepts to make this argument, especially in the essay "*Halachah and Aggadah*," which Scholem esteemed highly and translated into German.[23] The title alone contains two terms from rabbinic terminology of tradition, invoking the halachic (binding) aspect of rabbinic tradition as well as the aggadic (legendary) aspect, which is more free and open in form and content. In opposition to those who advocate for a modern Hebrew literature that would be a continuation of the Aggadah, Bialik stresses that both of these aspects belong together and that they are ultimately "two sides of a single shield.... *Halachah* is the crystallization, the ultimate and inevitable quintessence of *Aggadah*; *Aggadah* is the content of *Halachah*."[24] As in "Revealment and Concealment in Language," here, too, it is a question of a cycle of tradition, operating through a dialectics of freedom and form: "The value of *Aggadah* is that it issues in *Halachah*. *Aggadah* that does not bring *Halachah* in its train is ineffective. Useless itself, it will end by incapacitating its author for action."[25] True literature requires attachment, for it is "life in writing."[26] The meaning of this attachment remains open, however. Through such claims, Bialik charges literature with life, and literary confrontations gain in meaning and intensity as a result.

"Halachah und Aggadah" sparked intense contemporary controversy. Joseph Brenner accused Bialik of spouting mere theory when attention should be devoted to reality on the ground, a position corresponding to Brenner's own literary position. Unlike Bialik, Brenner did introduce new words and sentence patterns into the Hebrew language, explicitly aiming at a realistic mode of writing that tends to ironize Bialik's pathos.[27] Scholem aligned himself with Bialik in this controversy.[28] His view of Hebrew is essentially oriented by tradition, as demonstrated by his 1919 text "How Should One Learn Hebrew?": "The aim of learning Hebrew is not the ability to express oneself in this language ... or to understand what others express in terms of general meaning. Instead, it is a matter of penetrating Hebrew so that it becomes possible to grasp Judaism as identical in its spiritual essence to its linguistic essence. The *vision* of Hebrew is

---

23. See Scholem, *Story of a Friendship*, 101; *FBJ*, 146–147.
24. Bialik, "*Halachah* and *Aggadah*," in *Revealment and Concealment*, 46. Bialik uses a variety of metaphors for the reciprocal relationship between Halachah and Aggadah. Oral and spoken language relate to each other as thought relates to word, or word to deed, or like water to ice (ibid., 46), like lyric to epic (ibid., 58).
25. Bialik, "*Halachah* and *Aggadah*," 81. See Scholem's translation, *T II*, 577.
26. Bialik, "*Halachah* and *Aggadah*," 72. See Scholem's translation, *T II*, 572.
27. See Alter, *The Invention of Hebrew Prose*, 45ff.; Shaked, "Shall All Hopes Be Fulfilled?," esp. 780.
28. See *T II*, 102.

the aim, not its speech" (*T II*, 612). As Scholem sees it, Hebrew is less a means of expression—let alone communication—than the expression itself, less a tool than a medium that is essentially historical and essentially expressive of Jewish tradition. Thus, one should not begin by learning the spoken language—that is, modern Hebrew. One should rather follow along with historical evolution, first reading the Bible, then rabbinic writings, and so on. For Scholem, the language learned in this way would constitute a visible image of Jewish tradition, which would in turn generate a synthetic Hebrew in which the different contributing historical languages could still be perceived.

Scholem addresses these questions again in the brief essay "Notes on Hebrew and Learning Hebrew," written in September 1923, shortly after his arrival in Palestine. He emphasizes that the revival of the Hebrew language had already been the "uncanny point" of Zionism even before the war, but it was postponed: "This question . . . was shifted 'over there'—an apocalyptic concept at the time. Now the apocalypse has been transformed into a major business, we are 'over there' and we have to defend ourselves, and the Hebrew question mark . . . appears in a new form."[29] Scholem makes a distinction between written and spoken Hebrew, specifying that the crisis only affects the former: "Hebrew as a language of the book, of literature, is alive. It has a life that is still inwardly radiant, vast, and astounding, and in secularization it has retained the reflection and constant resonance of that revelation to which it owes its eternal life."[30] Written language, including modern Hebrew literature—Scholem refers to Mendele and Bialik—is thoroughly alive. In spite of its "secularization," it remains fulfilled: "This language has the fullness and reticence of true life, and to an extent that is shocking in today's world, it has conserved the honesty of metaphor and the renewal from a canon of language."[31] However, the situation is "entirely different when it comes to the spoken Hebrew that we encounter in Eretz Yisrael. . . . The spoken Hebrew here—not that of a select few, but the language you use to converse with your neighbors . . .—is not a language. It is, so to speak, the most complete Volapük that could be conceived for Jews from all over the world, for whom Esperanto is too distant, but it is not a language in which a world can live and weave. Many things contribute to this."[32]

Spoken language is therefore not a living language but rather a makeshift for communication. This is clearly an expression of cultural elitism that sees the very

---

29. Scholem, "Bemerkungen über Hebräisch und Hebräischlernen," 1.
30. Scholem, "Bemerkungen über Hebräisch und Hebräischlernen," 2.
31. Scholem, "Bemerkungen über Hebräisch und Hebräischlernen," 3.
32. Scholem, "Bemerkungen über Hebräisch und Hebräischlernen," 3.

use of language as misuse, but it is also more than this—namely, the experience of a political crisis reflected in language. For Scholem, the mixture of languages expresses danger, as suggested in this text by the argument that Hebrew has always lived off of its rich past: "This eternal life has endangered its temporal life, there can be no doubt about that."[33] It is not temporal life that endangers eternal life but the other way around, and this is what makes the situation political.

In a letter to Franz Rosenzweig bearing the title "On Our Language: A Confession," Scholem brings the endangerment and dangerousness of language into focus rather than its decline. Characterizing the situation in Palestine, he strikes an apocalyptic note: "A generation that takes over the most fruitful part of our tradition—its language—cannot, though it may ardently wish to, live without tradition. . . . Because at the heart of such a language, in which we ceaselessly evoke God in a thousand ways, thus calling Him back into the reality of our life, He cannot keep silent."[34] Crucially, Scholem stages a double threat, through the tradition inherent in language and through detachment from tradition:

> [The people] think they have secularized the Hebrew language, have done away with its apocalyptic point. But that, of course, is not true: the secularization of language is no more than a *manner of speaking*, a ready-made expression. It is impossible to empty the words so bursting with meaning, unless one sacrifices the language itself. The phantasmagoric Volapük spoken in our streets precisely defines the expressionless linguistic space which alone has permitted the "secularization" of language. But if we transmit the language to our children as it was transmitted to us, if we, a generation of transition, revive the language of the ancient books for them, that it may reveal itself anew through them, shall not the religious power of that language explode one day?[35]

In the political and linguistic context of the Yishuv during the interwar period, this text can be read in two ways. Either Hebrew has not been secularized

---

33. Scholem, "Bemerkungen über Hebräisch und Hebräischlernen," 2. "Whereas in living languages, this life of literary language crystallizes out of spoken language, and the depths of the linguistic are formed by contact with the spoken word, none of this applies to Hebrew up to the present. Its truest life is still the life fed by history (and not so rarely by the influence of living Yiddish)" (ibid., 3).
34. Scholem, "On Our Language," 99. Mosès interprets this text based on kabbalistic philosophy of language and Benjamin's theory of language. Mosès, *The Angel of History*, chapter 9.
35. Scholem, "On Our Language," 97. On this double danger, see Wohlfahrt, "Haarscharf auf der Grenze," 197ff.

as a language but rather transformed into an illusory language with no inner life and no silence, or this "secularization" never actually took place, and the apocalyptic content of language has only been hidden. Or both: sometimes the danger of being without language reveals itself, and sometimes it is the danger of language's apocalyptic content that is revealed. Nothing is decided yet, but Scholem's text derives its pathos from the fact that this cannot go on indefinitely: "As for us, we live within that language above an abyss, most of us with the steadiness of blind men. But when we regain our sight, we or our descendants, shall we not fall into that abyss?"[36]

Scholem's discussion of the "abyss" of language is reminiscent of Bialik's formulations from "Revealment and Concealment in Language," along with kabbalistic formulations: "Language is name. The power of language is enclosed in the name; the abyss of language is sealed within it. Now that we have invoked the ancient names day after day, we can no longer hold off the forces they contain."[37] It also has an immediate political significance with respect to the danger of the catchphrase. Scholem had addressed this danger in his youth, and he continued to address it later—for example, in the conclusion to his first study of Sabbatianism from 1928: "Especially in decisive moments, the messianic phraseology of Zionism is not the least of the Sabbatian temptations that could wreck Judaism's renewal, and the stabilization of its world out of the unbroken spirit of language."[38] Scholem's diaries make it clear that he sees a particular danger in the nationalistic catchphrases of the revisionist movement. If one equates the Zionist project—or even the idea of a Jewish state—with redemption, it is no longer possible to evaluate the situation realistically. If one continually speaks of the "Land of Israel" in the biblical sense, including all of Judaea, Galilee, Samaria, and Transjordania, there is no room for compromise.

"On Our Language" is organized around the abyss between these two dangers. Again and again, Scholem evokes this future, this "inevitable revolution": "When the day finally comes and the force shored up in the Hebrew language is unleashed, when the 'spoken,' the content of language, takes form once again."[39] This future reveals itself in the present as well: "As for us, we are seized with fear when, amidst the thoughtless discourse of a speaker, a religious term suddenly makes us shudder.... The day will come when the language will turn against

---

36. Scholem, "On Our Language," 97–98.
37. Scholem, "On Our Language," 98.
38. Scholem, "Die Theologie des Sabbatianismus im Lichte Abraham Cardosos," in *Judaica*, vol. 1, 146.
39. Scholem, "On Our Language," 99.

those who speak it. There are already moments in our own life when this happens, unforgettable, stigmatizing moments, when all the presumptuousness of our enterprise is suddenly revealed. When that day comes, will there be a young generation able to withstand the revolt of a sacred tongue?"[40]

In addition to expressing the historical danger of language and the dangerous nature of history—themes that will continue to determine Scholem's historical work—"On Our Language" is also a text about his own writing, its risks and its development. "Our" language, the language that Scholem so decisively desires, is a language that would allow for a true, pure, and complete community, a language that would give him the means to express himself, to be Jewish, and to speak in the name of Judaism. This language proves to be too precarious, however, threatened by the political danger of the catchphrase on the one hand and the dissolution or desiccation of language on the other. Thus, neither Zion nor "our language" remains as an unquestioned telos, and Scholem soon begins to reflect on other languages that he might need to use, first in order to publish his emerging research on the Kabbalah.[41] In 1930 he asks himself "whether it is right to write a book with which one wants to contribute something new in such a way that historians of religion and philosophers cannot read it" (*Br I*, 245)—that is, in Hebrew. As late as 1934, he writes to Moritz Spitzer, head of the Berlin Schocken Verlag, regarding his work on a foundational introduction to Jewish mysticism though its literary history and development of ideas: "Language remains the big problem here.... As you will easily understand, as a professor at the Hebrew University, I have great psychological scruples about seeing a foundational book in my field first published in German at this time and under present conditions" (*Br I*, 257). In his letter, Scholem goes on to suggest publishing the book both in German and in Hebrew, but neither of these editions was ever completed. The book heralded here appeared seven years later in a third language that had not even occurred to Scholem in 1934: *Major Trends in Jewish Mysticism*, translated into English from Scholem's German manuscripts by Georg Lichtheim. This third language, in no respect Scholem's own, may have provided the only way out of the dilemma of whether to write in German or Hebrew. More generally, in the years following World War II, Scholem let go of his longing for one language that would allow him to express himself fully and completely, instead establishing for himself different genres in different languages to write about the widely varied and often contradictory aspects of his intellectual project.

---

40. Scholem, "On Our Language," 98.
41. Weidner, "'Das große Problem bleibt hier die Sprache.'"

SIX

LOOKING BACK

Rewriting the Past

SCHOLEM'S CRITICAL—OR EVEN DESPAIRING—STATEMENTS ON Zionism from the 1920s and 1930s did not remain his final word on the subject. In later interviews and lectures on Zionism, he usually did not refer to a menacing crisis of Zionism but a "dialectic of continuity and rebellion," a "metamorphosis" of Zionism, or a "natural process of change."[1] This does not indicate reconciliation with actual political circumstances in Israel, on which Scholem took an increasingly critical position. Instead, it reflects his reaction to a break far more radical than the crisis of Zionism he had previously feared: the Holocaust.[2] Already in 1946, Scholem recognized that the Holocaust had profoundly changed the situation of Zionism, which up to that point had drawn its primary force from rebellion against exile: "This revolutionism was quite convenient to all of us, so long as there was someone against whom to rebel. Today, following the great disaster which has befallen our people, our situation has been tragically altered: the revolution finds itself in a vacuum from the national viewpoint; the nation is no longer the great reservoir assuring the continuity of that against which we rebel. Thus, we ourselves need to worry about both sides of the coin" (*PM*, 155). With nothing more to negate, Scholem's

---

1. Scholem, "Zionism—Dialectic of Continuity and Rebellion," 263, 275, 284.
2. See also Scholem's letter to Shalom Spiegel from May 8, 1945 (!), that victory had not actually been achieved. According to Scholem, what victory meant is that it would once again be possible to fight "for the good": "The wrestling match will start from the beginning; and the essence of our 'success' lies in the fact that it can begin at all" (*LL*, 324–325). On the Shoah as a break in messianic thought for Scholem, see Weigel, "Gershom Scholem und Ingeborg Bachmann," 614; Idel, "Zur Funktion von Symbolen," 64ff., 68ff.

texts on Zionism and Judaism become less sharp and less pointed. In his youth, he saw Judaism as a totality defined primarily by what did *not* belong to it. In contrast, in 1974, Scholem speaks of Judaism as an open organism with endless manifestations and unlimited possibilities: "There is nothing Jewish that is alien to me" (*JJC*, 42). The established intellectual sovereignty underlying this statement is also determined by the radical experience of a rupture of civilization, although Scholem does not often publicly address this experience. Prepared by his earlier ascetic turn, despair becomes increasingly interiorized, a secret not to be told.

Rarely polemical in his later works, Scholem does criticize the role of Orthodox Judaism as well as the movement of the Canaanites, who entirely reject Jewish heritage in their recourse to the prehistory of Canaan.[3] Scholem sees this as a radicalization of the Zionist rejection of exile and condemns it as "educational murder" (*PM*, 85). In his view, this falls outside the bounds of conflicting interpretations of history: "I am one of those who say that there is no conflict. It is obvious that we are all torch bearers. Except the Canaanites."[4] As a result, he also does not believe the prognoses that there will be a normalization of Israel that would diminish the force of the past; such prognoses underestimate "the tremendous power of reconstituting historical memory through the dialectical swings of the pendulum" (*LL*, 412). "It would seem to me closer to the truth to say that a crisis will, and must, develop. Indeed, perhaps even a life-threatening crisis.... That this crisis has erupted in earnest during our generation strikes me as a sign legitimizing the historical process we have witnessed. I am not saying that the Jewish people won't go under; yet a metamorphosis of tradition and of the forms its genius takes does not count as a disaster" (*LL*, 412). Crisis and the downfall of tradition are still possibilities, but now they are part of a general metamorphosis. Scholem stretches the rhetoric of intensification to include a recognition of diversity. In addition, his previous assessment of the aim of Zion gives way to a projection of space for Jews who remain on the move, a shift outlined in a letter from 1980: "This has convinced me of the utter falseness of my earlier definition of Zionism which I used to give until 1950: Zionism is a movement against the excessive travelling of the Jews. Could I have been wronger? So now I have another definition on which I hope to end my days: Zionism is the return of the Jews into their own history. Of course, one can say (as Fania does) that they don't seem to want it too much" (*Br III*, 216, written in English by Scholem).

---

3. *PM*, 93–99; Scholem, "Zionism—Dialectic," 284ff.
4. Scholem, "Zionism—Dialectic," 275. See also ibid., 278ff., 288ff.

Zionism is no longer a fixed goal, nor an abstract place, but rather the Jews' own history. As a result, it can be categorically distinguished from messianism: "The difference between Zionism and Messianism resides in the fact that *Zionism is acting within history, while Messianism remained on a Utopian plane*."[5] However, this distinction between history and utopia is not so simple, especially in Scholem's historical texts. As we will see, it is the tension between these two elements that drives Scholem's thought, leading him to say elsewhere that while it is "little wonder" that Zionism is accompanied by "overtones of Messianism," nevertheless "it is bound to history itself and not to meta-history; it has not given itself up totally to Messianism" (*MI*, 35–36).[6] Persisting in the rhetorical overtone of connotations and appositions, messianism does not disappear easily even where there seem to be clear distinctions, as in the distinction between history and metahistory. There is still something "more" to this, "a hidden core," "a mystical side" (*JJC*, 43, 44), a remainder of apocalyptic thought. Scholem points in this direction only vaguely: "It hasn't manifested itself. But one bright day it will do so. Perhaps we will be privileged to see it manifest itself. But meanwhile— well, that is why I have never dealt with this matter" (*JJC*, 45). Indeed, it is only in his historical texts that Scholem actually articulates these thoughts.

This viewpoint also determines Scholem's attitude toward Zionism's critics. On this point, too, he expresses himself rarely, almost reluctantly, and often with an apodictic refusal of dialogue. He counters Hannah Arendt's 1946 text "Zionism Reconsidered" with what he calls "a confession": "I am a nationalist and am wholly unmoved by ostensibly 'progressive' denunciations of a viewpoint that people repeatedly, even in my earliest youth, deemed obsolete. I believe in what can be called, in human terms, the 'eternity' of anti-Semitism" (*LL*, 331). Although his "political credo" remains "anarchistic," he insists that one cannot use anti-Zionist arguments to debate the dangers of Zionist politics, which he thoroughly acknowledges; instead, it is necessary to do so from the standpoint of Zionism. He therefore wonders "to what extent, from the position of your question, Zionism is still possible, that is, the opinion that proceedings in Palestine are in any case the decisive event of Jewish history for our

---

5. "Zionism—Dialectic," 269. See also "Zionism is rather a movement within the mundane, immanent process of history" (Scholem, "Judaism," in *Contemporary Jewish Religious Thought*, 507).

6. Scholem uses different formulations, sometimes speaking of "utopian return to Zion" (*MI*, 35) and elsewhere emphasizing that it is primarily a matter of conceiving a particular Jewish mission: "the return to Zion could be construed as the Jew's betrayal of their vocation to be a transcendent people—to be a people that is not a people, to quote Heine, a *Volksgespenst*" ("Judaism," 507).

generation" (*Br I*, 310). Zionism is no longer determined by its content (as renewal, for example) but only as the decisive event. Scholem is now an anti-anti-Zionist, so to speak, distrustful of dialogue, as demonstrated by his response when asked about George Steiner in an interview: "Let everyone do what he likes. It is not realistic to argue with him. A person who gives priority to his own private, personal troubles, and indulges himself in the creative opportunities of alienation—should go where he likes, and live to the best of his understanding."[7] Experience has made Scholem humble, as he notes in 1969: "Throughout my life I was tossed hither and yon by expectations and disappointments; expectations from the Jewish people in general and, in particular, from us who were at work in the land of Israel. I have come to know many phases of this process, from highest expectation to deepest disappointment, indeed despair; and I have gone through them myself. That has left me without any inclination to speak with any semblance of authority, which in this case could have been nothing but presumption and pretense" (*JJC*, 244–245). Scholem forgoes the semblance of authority that he so vehemently claimed in his youth. He does so based on experience, however, and this gives him a different kind of authority as well as other forms of expression. These include the writing of history, in which the messianic crisis remains central, as well as numerous essays on his contemporaries, German Jews, and German Judaism. In these essays, he interprets his own experience and communicates it in a manner that his public finds authoritative, at least for a time.

Scholem's essays on Germans and Jews played an important role in the 1960s. Moving the discourse forward, these texts gained an almost canonical character as authoritative interpretations of German-Jewish relations, providing clarification that formed the basis of nascent research.[8] This had two major consequences for his own intellectual project. On the one hand, through his extensive knowledge of the material, Scholem was able to assert a position of scholarly authority even outside the specific terrain of the history of the Kabbalah. On the other hand, he was able to give shape to the story of his own life, no longer matching the outline anticipated in his youth but nevertheless grounding his own story in history.

Once again, we can trace the beginning of this process back to a sharp polemic, in this case a polemic against the idea of a German-Jewish dialogue. In an

---

7. Scholem, "Zionism—Dialectic," 266.
8. See Rubin, "The 'German-Jewish Dialogue' and Its Literary Refractions: The Case of Margarete Susman and Gershom Scholem," and Voigts, "Das Machtwort: Scholems Position zum 'deutsch-jüdischen Gespräch.'"

open letter on the occasion of a festschrift for Margret Susman in 1962, Scholem takes issue with the idea that there has ever been a German-Jewish dialogue "in any genuine sense whatsoever, i.e., *as a historical phenomenon*. It takes two to have a dialogue, who listen to each other, who are prepared to perceive the other as what he is and represents, and to respond to him" (*JJC*, 61–62). The three reasons that he offers are crucially important for German Jewry, in his view. In his verdict, Scholem first points out a fundamental asymmetry: the Germans did not take any part in this dialogue; it was only the Jews who "spoke to themselves, not to say that they outshouted themselves" (*JJC*, 63). Second, and Scholem calls this the "salient point" of his argument, "the Germans, where they engaged in a dialogue . . . with the Jews at all, did so under the presupposition that the Jews were prepared to give themselves up *as Jewish* to an ever more progressive extent. One of the most important of the phenomena . . . is the fact that the Jews themselves were in large part ready to do this"; the supposed dialogue was thus "based on the expressed or unexpressed self-denial of the Jews, on the progressive atomization of the Jews as a *community* in a state of dissolution" (*JJC*, 66, 62). Third, retrospective talk of dialogue is an utterly perverse category of interpretation. It disregards the "fact that no dialogue is possible with the dead, and to speak of an 'indestructibility of this dialogue' strikes me as blasphemy" (*JJC*, 64).

In the context of West Germany in the 1960s, Scholem objects to the "introduction of sublime and solemn-sounding terms like *dialogue*" (*JJC*, 66) as well as the pathos that would belatedly dissolve Jews into German history—intellectual history above all. This objection is entirely justified and valid, with implications that are far from obvious, related not only to German-Jewish history but also to Scholem's own position. Particularly relevant are his views on the self-abandonment or "self-deception" of the German Jews, which Scholem repeatedly refers to as a central realization of his youth: "Our parents, to sum up the situation, thought they knew what they wanted, and in this they were not so much deluded about their surroundings—regarding which few of them entertained great illusions—but rather about themselves. . . . And it was because of these inner contradictions and chasms that they preferred ambiguity and obfuscation over clarity and had little use for those who wanted to throw light on the situation."[9] For Scholem, self-deception means more than deluding oneself about the nature of one's surroundings. It refers to a relationship with oneself that is characterized by a lack of clarity and a life that is shaped by the "contradiction between the wish to forget its own history as far as possible,

---

9. Scholem, "On the Social Psychology of the Jews in Germany," 32.

and the sentiments of wide circles who would not go as far as that and in whom the awareness of the contribution to their personal character of a history that differed basically from the German past, was still alive."[10] The fact that German Jews of the nineteenth and early twentieth centuries developed a hybrid sense of belonging has been widely confirmed by subsequent scholarship: most Jews in Germany wanted to participate in German society and culture while retaining aspects of Jewish particularity.[11] Scholem's notion of self-deception has further implications, for it is clear to him that this is a matter of *Jewish* self-deception and not only a question of doubled or split belonging in which one part—of oneself—pulls something over on the other. Scholem characterizes assimilated Jews neither simply as Jews nor as non-Jews but rather as Jews who only pretend to be non-Jews: "They are no longer even Jews, in the full sense of an unbroken historical consciousness, who speak here, but rather Jews in flight from themselves" (*JJC*, 69). Yet they still fly *from themselves*; they are still somehow Jewish even "at the pure nadir of complete alienation" (*JJC*, 63), and there is still a "component of Jewish feeling," a "piety" that binds them to the past.[12]

This description indicates that the Jewish lack of clarity must be understood in immanently Jewish terms. Jews do not flee from anti-Semitism or to the Germans; they flee from themselves. They do not become Jews through the gaze of others; they become Jews through their own Jewish belonging, even when this involves self-alienation. Scholem argues that the failure of assimilation is not an external fate but an internal crisis of Jewish existence, as expressed by his choice of "self-deception" as a central term. He thereby emphasizes his "conviction that the liquidation of the Jewish substance by the Jews themselves must in large part be held responsible for the fact that this dialogue did not come to take place as a historical phenomenon" (*JJC*, 68). As we will see, the notion of the self-destruction of Judaism in modernity plays a significant role in Scholem's historiography, and this position also plays a role in his own self-presentation. The "German" element should no longer appear in this presentation at all, for it is merely the murky starting point for self-deception, and it is necessary to shove off from this point in order to make it "from Berlin to Jerusalem." For Scholem, recognizing self-deception as such at an early stage, narrating the way out constitutes a sufficient response. In his essays on German Judaism as well as in his memoir, the destination—self-actualization, or

---

10. Scholem, "On the Social Psychology," 28.
11. On this dual objective, see Tal, *Christians and Jews*, 16ff.; Volkov, *Jüdisches Leben und Antisemitismus*, 131ff.; Meyer et al., eds., *Deutsch-Jüdische Geschichte*, vol. 2, 208ff.
12. Scholem, "On the Social Psychology," 20.

existence in "unbroken historical consciousness"—remains largely implicit as a virtual vanishing point.

Along with his own story, Scholem also invokes other images in contrast to self-deception. In his 1964 essay on Walter Benjamin—one of Scholem's first biographical essays—he stresses the "profound difference" between the many German Jews who "unquestioningly look upon themselves as forming part of German culture and tradition, as belonging to the German people" and those who did not "succumb" to this "lurid and tragic illusion" and who "wrote in full awareness of the distance separating them from their German readers" (*JJC*, 190): he names Freud, Kafka, and Benjamin. Scholem does not have much to say about Freud, and when he refers to psychoanalysis, he does so in a rather derogatory manner. Kafka is a central authority for him and the object of various aphorisms.[13] Of the three, Benjamin is the one to whom Scholem devotes a full portrait in this essay and later an entire book. Through the figure of Benjamin, Scholem can once again write about Germany and German Jews even after his verdict on German-Jewish dialogue—and after 1945—and in this way, he is also able to write about himself. He emphasizes that he is writing as a friend and that the image he presents of Benjamin, "though authentic in its way, has always been determined by personal decisions" (*JJC*, 174). Written ten years later, his book *Walter Benjamin: The Story of a Friendship* continues in the direction of autobiography.

By no means focused on Benjamin's Jewish belonging, the 1964 text constitutes a comprehensive portrait, an obituary written more than twenty years after Benjamin's death. Scholem offers the chronological story of their encounters while describing Benjamin as a person and as a thinker. In this telling, Benjamin appears as "a metaphysician pure and simple" (*JJC*, 178). Yet over the course of his life, he "forsook systematic philosophy to dedicate himself to the task of commenting on the great works, a task which at that time—with his prime interests still belonging to theology—he considered preliminary to commenting on sacred texts" (*JJC*, 181). He often did not communicate directly, cultivating "the esoteric thinker's stance," with a "peculiar aura of authority emanating from his thought, though never explicitly invoked" (*JJC*, 177). Precisely through his engagement with major works and his restraint in expression, Benjamin gained a particular language: "In his best works the German language has achieved a perfection that takes the reader's breath away. It owes this perfection to the rare achievement of blending highest abstraction with

---

13. See Alter, *Necessary Angels*.

sensuous richness and presentation in the round, and thus bears the hallmark of his notion of metaphysical knowledge. In a wonderful fashion his language, without abandoning depth of insight, closely and snugly fits the subject it covers and at the same time strives in competition with the subject's own language from which it keeps its precise distance" (*JJC*, 182–183). Benjamin's process of thinking in commentary continues even after his so-called turn to materialism. Scholem emphasizes "the discrepancy between his real mode of thought and the materialist one he has ostensibly adopted.... His insights are those of a theologian marooned in the realm of the profane. But they no longer appear plainly as such" (*JJC*, 186–187). This frequently instills his later works with "a shadowy and ambiguous element" (*JJC*, 187). Here, too, there are indications of self-deception; Scholem reproached his friend for this already in their intense epistolary confrontation in the 1930s.

It is only in the final, crowning section of his essay that Scholem turns to the "Jewish element" in Benjamin's thought, which forms a foundation even though it is often present "only in overtones" (*JJC*, 191). Benjamin relies "(instinctively, I almost added)" on "Jewish concepts" for orientation, with two "categories" serving above all as "regulative ideas" throughout his life: "on the one hand Revelation, the idea of the Torah and of sacred texts in general, and on the other hand the messianic idea and Redemption" (*JJC*, 193). These ideas demonstrate the intertwining of philosophy of language and philosophy of history that is so characteristic of Benjamin's thought. Scholem uses these elements to show how Jewish belonging is positively manifested even in the most extreme alienation and even when Benjamin no longer presents his "basic method"—that is, commentary on authoritative texts—as such: "I would characterize his latter-day thinking as a materialist theory of Revelation whose very subject no longer figures in the theory" (*JJC*, 194). Given these two main ideas, Scholem finally asks why Benjamin continues to refer "to the *utopian* category of religion, to Redemption and the messianic idea, whereas its *existential* (more aptly perhaps: its substantive) category disappears" (*JJC*, 194). As we will see in part 2, Scholem deals with this question himself in his reflections on the "nothingness of revelation."

In the intervening decades between his writing and the present, Scholem's interpretation of Benjamin's thought in terms of Judaism and theology has developed a long and significant reception history.[14] At the time of its publication, however, reception of his essay was relatively peripheral, since Benjamin was

---

14. Weidner, "Thinking Beyond Secularization."

primarily read as a Marxist. Whereas in the 1964 essay, Scholem characterizes Benjamin as a commentator of major works, a few years later he notes with some irony that Benjamin's texts seem to have themselves become "a kind of Holy Writ," especially for "young Marxists" (*JJC*, 198). Scholem also suggests a reason why this development was possible: "The gesture of the esoteric writer perceived in him by Adorno and me was that of the producer of authoritative sentences, and that, to be sure, also means, from the very outset and because of their essence, sentences lending themselves to quotation and interpretation" (*JJC*, 199). As further illustrated by the marginal notes in his personal library, Scholem criticizes and even ridicules the endemic citation of Benjamin's work in left-wing Marxist research in the 1970s for a delirious ignorance of context. As to whether the fascination with Benjamin was a trace of the memory of something authentically Jewish, or whether Benjamin served as the last medium of connection to Jewish history even in West German society, or whether it was all just a farce, Scholem remains silent.

Benjamin is not the only writer whom Scholem relies on to reflect on the afterlife of religion and the crisis of modernity. Particularly relevant in this context is his engagement with S. Y. Agnon, specifically with respect to Scholem's relationship to the fate of the Hebrew language, which—as we have seen—is crucial for his early texts. Already in his youth, Scholem saw Agnon as one of the most significant authors of modern Hebrew literature. Along with Bialik's essay "*Halachah* and *Aggadah*," he translated Agnon's story "The Tale of the Scribe," which revealed to him how it is possible for Jewish tradition to be carried on in the present, although he studiously ignored the ironic and subversive moments in Agnon's narration.[15]

In 1967 Scholem dedicates an essay to Agnon, with the telling title, "S. Y. Agnon—The Last Hebrew Classic?" Here, Scholem is considerably less enthusiastic yet far more precise regarding the ambivalence that Agnon represents, an ambivalence that replaces the former radical alternative of apocalyptic downfall or the loss of language. Particularly for German readers, Scholem emphasizes that Agnon's work must be understood against the backdrop of the development of the Hebrew language. From the outset, modern Hebrew is based on a paradox: "it fed on a language of predominantly religious tradition but strove for secular goals" (*JJC*, 94). Initially, this involved relatively little contact with spoken language. In Agnon's work, however, Hebrew literature was confronted with the development of spoken modern Hebrew. According to Scholem,

---

15. See Alter, *Hebrew and Modernity*, 12 ff., 140ff. On the biographical connection, see also Laor, "Agnon in Deutschland."

Agnon consciously faced the fact "that this metamorphosis of Hebrew [into a spoken language] involved a decisive loss of form" (*JJC*, 95). Scholem's take on this process and its attendant dangers is shaped by his own experiences: "When a language is no longer forged by the study of ancient texts and conscious reflection, but rather by unconscious processes in which the power of tradition is a minor factor, that language is bound to become chaotic. This chaotic quality of present-day Hebrew ... may one day become the vehicle of expression for a new genius, but by then that language will be essentially different in its means and potentialities" (*JJC*, 95). Speaking in terms of "loss of form" rather than profanation, Scholem no longer describes this process as dissolution, instead stressing the "anarchic vitality, the lawlessness and roughness of the new language" (*JJC*, 96). Agnon's mastery lies in his position at the "crossroads" of this development, from which point he was able to see in both directions, taking into account Hebrew as the language of the book as well as spoken Hebrew: "That is a position enabling a writer of genius to attain the rank of a classic.... He can become a classical master—but he will be the last of his line" (*JJC*, 95).

For Agnon, the form of religious tradition and the transmission of texts remains present. He writes in a synthetic style with deliberate, visible reference to traditional texts and forms, thus achieving a "language of extraordinary density" and "tension."[16] Scholem suggests that Agnon writes in a kind of sacred language that lends "luster" to profane objects as well: "For in this language, even the most profane is set into a sacred context."[17] Yet this sacralization is also ambiguous and incomplete: "At the same time, however, it makes the endless range of relationships of a Holy language and marked literary tradition into the object of a game that is not entirely simple but shot through with ironic lights, in which the Holy is profaned or at least secularized in manifold refractions."[18] It is not only adherence to traditional forms that generates the classical language of Agnon's early texts but also the ironic employment of those forms. This is not successful when he presents himself entirely as a traditionalist: "The author's dialectical attitude toward his own experience and toward his tradition ... has been abandoned, and that, I would almost say, is a great pity" (*JJC*, 116).[19]

---

16. Scholem, "Über einen Roman von S. J. Agnon," 331.
17. Scholem, "Über einen Roman von S. J. Agnon," 331.
18. Scholem, "Über einen Roman von S. J. Agnon," 331.
19. This remark is aimed particularly at Agnon's turn to Orthodoxy: "We observe a frenzied endeavor to save for posterity the forms of a life doomed to extinction. It is a somewhat sad spectacle, for one notices the intention and becomes annoyed" (*JJC*, 115). See Niewöhner, "'Ich habe keinen Garten und habe kein Haus,'" 86.

An imitator of classical form, Agnon is also its beneficiary and exploiter. For Scholem, this position at the limit is what makes his language into "the most beautiful Hebrew that has been written for centuries. It is the expression of a substance of language that lights up in an endlessly fractured richness of colors before approaching a decisive, creative, dangerous metamorphosis in return migration from the house of learning and from literature into the everyday."[20] As in "On Our Language: A Confession," Scholem's essay on Agnon is also defined by a moment of expectation that oscillates between radical change and indeterminacy. Ultimately it remains open whether the substance of language that lights up in crisis will be used up (or burned out) or whether this is only preparation for the actual metamorphosis. Moreover, Scholem notes in passing "that it is the shattering of this sacred context of tradition, and the movement of Hebrew from the house of learning into the language of infants, that determines the entire problem of Hebrew and its literature in the new Israel, which at the same time makes a mastery of the kind achieved by Agnon effectively impossible from this point forward."[21] Scholem's fundamental diagnosis of an abyss in the Hebrew language has not changed, but it has become less dramatic. With the great crisis already passed rather than still in store, the apocalyptic pathos of a coming catastrophe gives way to quieter, more melancholic tones.

Thus, retrospectively, we can see that Scholem did find a position to speak from, and he did reach the form of belonging that he sought. However, just as the route to this belonging was far more indirect than a simple spatial movement from Berlin to Jerusalem, so too is the result: to be a Jew, a Zionist, a scholar is less a clear standpoint than it is a permanent compromise, an act of improvisation determined by strong tensions and even contradictions. More often than not, these contradictions are obscured and rendered invisible by the powerful rhetorics that Scholem developed by writing in different discourses and genres. Indeed, the specific power of his writing derives from these tensions and obscurities that he employed in careful balance, which reveal to the reader all the complexity and richness of a twentieth-century Jewish intellectual life.

---

20. Scholem, "Über einen Roman von S. J. Agnon," 332.
21. Scholem, "Über einen Roman von S. J. Agnon," 332. In his acceptance speech for the literary prize of the Bavarian Academy of Fine Arts in 1974, Scholem highlights precisely this interplay of oral and written Hebrew: "Having migrated from the ancient books to the mouth of babes and sucklings, it has given way to an extremely vital language, characterized by an anarchistic lack of rules. Only by the confrontation between these two linguistic worlds will the Hebrew of the future develop, deriving its image from the fruitful experience of the meeting between them—a fertile, but also dangerous process" (*PM*, 22). Scholem's counterexample here is the degeneration of the German language during National Socialism.

PART 2

PRACTICING THEORY: SCHOLEM'S EARLY READING

"One cannot prove Judaism in any ultimate sense; you have to believe in it."
Not so. If Judaism is *the* truth, one must be able to prove it. (*LY*, 153)

Scholem's early diaries do not revolve exclusively around himself. He also grapples widely and extensively with general questions and philosophical problems, such as the essence of language or the nature of history, and with Judaism above all. With their markedly theoretical character, the diaries seem to have served as a workshop of ideas where the young Scholem could develop and record his various considerations. We can distinguish four different layers in his theoretical writings in the early diaries. First, there are notes on mathematics and systematic philosophy, employing the language of neo-Kantianism and—to some extent—logical calculus, mostly from 1916 and early 1917. Second, from early 1917 onward, there are many aphorisms, excerpts, and essays on what Scholem roughly projects as a "theory of Judaism." Here, he also engages with the work of Franz Joseph Molitor, Samson Raphael Hirsch, and other interlocutors. Third, late in 1917, likely stimulated by Walter Benjamin, Scholem uses the style and terminology of early Romanticism to write more and more "fragments" and collections of aphorism and theses on the theory of Judaism as well as philosophy of language and history. Fourth and finally, Scholem writes various more developed texts that attempt to condense his thought from a certain time, such as "On Lament and Lamentation" from January 1918, "On Jonah and the Concept of Justice" from the end of 1918, and "On the Kabbalah, Viewed from Beyond" from 1921, which already connects Scholem's philosophical speculations with his later philological study of the Kabbalah.

It is the third layer—the writing of fragments—that is probably the most typical of the young Scholem's writing, as it reveals a formal tension between perpetual problematization and questioning on the one hand and an apodictic tendency on the other. Continually rewriting his texts, Scholem ends up with succinct formulations. To cite but one example, he notes in the summer of 1918: "Commentary is legitimate interpretation" (*T II*, 198), a formulation that will resonate across his entire oeuvre, as in a late essay: "Not system but *commentary* is the legitimate form through which truth is approached" (*MI*, 289). Thus, with knowledge of Scholem's later writings in mind, his early texts are all the more fascinating, because they seem to be the source of many later considerations and formulations and because things that later appear in complex historical presentations are formulated here directly and without mediation.

These texts are anything but easy to understand, however. If we simply read them as precursors of later theses, we quickly find ourselves in an interpretive circle, explaining difficult passages through even more difficult passages. Moreover, this kind of reading overlooks the indeterminate, searching, and fragmentary form of the early writings, which resists systematization and foils expectations of internal coherence. As previously discussed, recent history of ideas has shown that the attribution of coherent beliefs or worldviews is just as problematic for the history of thought as the search for influences or the application of general labels such as idealism, irrationalism, or Hegelianism.[1] For a more productive reading of Scholem's early texts, we must focus precisely on their difficulties and the obstacles preventing straightforward understanding—that is, we must focus on their fragmentary and hybrid form. Bearing distinct traces of the work of thought, these are not merely scattered notes but often variations, versions, and revisions of the same text, with differences that allow for orientation and reveal the questions behind the many answers that Scholem gives. Indeed, it is only by reconstructing the questions behind the texts—their problematics—that one can develop a productive reading that goes beyond the attempt to pin down Scholem's views and

---

1. See the introduction to this book and also Weidner, "Reading Gershom Scholem."

opinions, seeking to understand his theoretical praxis.[2] His is essentially a practice of writing, experimenting with different idioms in order to work out for himself what he is able to say rather than simply capturing his thought in words.

Emphasizing the moment of praxis, one must also keep in mind that Scholem's theoretical reflections on Judaism are only one side of a larger project and only the reflex of a practical task that was his primary occupation in the early years—namely, gaining familiarity with the Jewish tradition. In his memoir, he writes of the decisive *"Erlebnis* in my relationship to things Jewish," when he learned to read the first page of the Talmud in the original: "It was my first traditional and direct encounter, not with the Bible, but with Jewish substance in tradition" (*FBJ*, 47). The enthusiastic fifteen-year-old Zionist from an assimilated family continued to pick up Jewish tradition in the years to come. Gaining necessary knowledge as he progressed, he learned Hebrew and read the texts of biblical, rabbinic, and later kabbalistic Judaism. This eagerness is characteristic of and specific to Scholem. On the one hand, differently than other philosophers of Judaism up to and including Cohen and Buber, Scholem did not begin his theoretical reflection only when he was already familiar with traditional heritage. For him, Judaism was not something given that could be subjected to reflection; the traditional path of learning and the modern path of theory unfolded simultaneously, with reciprocal influence. On the other hand, Scholem distinguished himself from many of his contemporaries through his explicit skepticism toward any attempts at direct appropriation of Jewish heritage. Neither existential determination nor systematic reflection could replace the knowledge of tradition, or, as Scholem writes in retrospect, this was "something that resisted conceptualization all the more emphatically the older I became; for it revealed a secret life, one which I had to acknowledge as being impossible to conceptualize, and which seemed portrayable only through symbols" (*FBJ*, 48–49). It does not suffice to understand tradition—one must also "have" it. Yet for Scholem, who acquired tradition as an already assimilated outsider, it is equally insufficient just to "have" tradition—one must also understand it in a way that makes this possession possible.

Reflections on tradition—and how to relate to tradition—are thus an essential component of Scholem's early writings. Due to the semantic ambiguity of the term, and the fact that it tends to play only a marginal role in modern

---

2. On theoretical praxis and problematics, see Althusser, *For Marx*, chapter 6, and *Philosophy and Spontaneous Philosophy of the Scientists*, chapter 3.

philosophical thought, "tradition" offers fertile ground.[3] Not only can "tradition" signify the active process of *traditio* as well as the passive *traditum*, but it also functions differently in different contexts: in cultural theory, it can refer to the knowledge handed down by society (in contrast to invention); in hermeneutics, it can describe the reception history of classical texts (in contrast to rupture); in history, "tradition" can refer to oral tradition as opposed to written sources; in philosophy, it represents prejudgment as opposed to the autonomy of reason; and in theology, tradition may stand in contrast to reason but also to revelation. "Tradition" has the connotation of the anteriority of something transmitted as well as the simultaneity of the eternally valid. The semantics of the obligating gift are inscribed in tradition as the obligations of "heirs" with respect to their ancestors. Tradition can be conceived in juridical terms as the (contractually regulated) transfer of property and also as the biological and genealogical relation of reproduction. Conversely, like religion, tradition can also always mean something general, as a cultural or anthropological universal, and something particular, as the tradition of a particular community.

Tradition is therefore a nodal point linking Scholem's general reflections to his thoughts on Judaism. Theoretical as well as practical, tradition is indeed a condition of possibility of Scholem's theorizing. He wants to write not only *about* tradition but also *in accordance with* tradition. The concept of tradition is all the more fitting because it can describe both the tradent's self-description and the outsider's concept of this process, both the historical process and the claim to an unbroken lineage, both continuous change and eternal stability. This oscillation is what makes the concept fruitful in attempts to invent tradition as well as in attempts to inscribe oneself into tradition or to find a position from which the acquisition of tradition might be conceived as possible. As we will see, this undertaking is paradoxical to some extent and semantically productive as a result. If tradition is conceived as prereflexive, the idea of a theory of tradition runs into some problems: if being "in" the tradition is the precondition of being Jewish, the very act of "entering" the tradition becomes a problem. Scholem's texts reflect these paradoxes and render them productive through theoretical work. Never satisfied with his formulations, Scholem is always revising, supplementing, and varying what he has written. His early

---

3. On the history of the concept, see Shils, *Tradition*; Eisenstadt, *Tradition, Change, and Modernity*, esp. chapters 7–9; Prickett, *Modernity and the Reinvention of Tradition*. See also the critical distinction between "tradition" as a cultural-anthropological universal, "traditions" as specific cultural symbolic orders, and "the tradition" as a legitimizing authority with claim to truth, in Ricoeur, *Time and Narrative*, vol. 3, chapter 7.

texts become legible as experimentation with the semantic potential of the concept of tradition (written/oral, timeless/temporal, canon/commentary) as well as with semantics that are typical of Jewish tradition (as in the idea of an oral Torah, with all its internal contradictions). Step by step, Scholem thus develops a poetics for his own theoretical writing, which he increasingly understands as "commentary." In addition to writing about tradition and in accordance with tradition, this is a matter of writing *as* tradition, taking the form of commentary, citation, and indirect discourse.

In the following chapters, we will analyze this project, focusing on its paradoxes, contradictions, and shifts. These moments in their ambiguity contribute decisively to Scholem's intellectual figure—at times even more so than the "solutions" that he finds to the problems he confronts. Roughly tracing the chronology of his thinking, we will discuss his early engagement with critical philosophy; his first attempt to formulate a theory—namely, a theory of the language and poetry of lament; his engagement with the phenomenology of tradition; his adoption of the early Romantic idea of fragments and paradoxes as a specific mode of writing; his attempt at a theory focused on prophecy and messianism; his explicit theological reflections about the notion and nature of revelation; and finally his conceptualization of "philology." The latter not only acts as a bridge between his theoretical and historical interests, which we will discuss in part 3, but also reveals the extent to which this bridge rests on the rhetorical and poetic foundations of specific forms of writing.

SEVEN

LANGUAGE AND TRUTH

First Steps

IN THE SUMMER OF 1917, Gerhard Scholem writes in a letter to Werner Kraft that "preoccupation with Hebrew and reflections upon the foundations of mathematics have driven me to meditate upon the nature of language" (*LL*, 52). His diaries contain many such remarks. For example, he notes that the principle of the affinity of roots in the Hebrew language represents the order of the world, or that mathematical definitions are not tautologies, as Fritz Mauthner claimed (*T I*, 17–18, 421, 139). After reading Mauthner's *Contributions to a Critique of Language* in 1916, Scholem underscores the metaphoricity of language: "It is practically self-evident for language to speak in similes, in symbols: what is recognized usually cannot even be said other than in symbols.... The core cannot be said: nature, for nature is unspeakable, it can only be suggested image by image" (*T I*, 264). A little later, he articulates a contrast between the parabolic nature of language and the imagelessness of mathematics: "Mathematics is entirely objective, it does not know a single simile, and in no mathematical book ... does one find the words 'as if.' Here, language has surmounted itself: it states what is, without a detour" (*T I*, 265). As Scholem himself emphasizes in retrospect, his approach to the topic derived from two perspectives that stand in marked tension with one another: "The linguistic-philosophical element of a conceptual language wholly purged of mysticism, as well as the limits of the latter, seemed clear to me.... In those days I fluctuated between the two poles of mathematical and mystical symbolism."[1] This polarity determines his thinking on language in an enduring manner, and it is also decisive for his initial reflections on Judaism. As he later writes, there is "only

---

1. Scholem, *Story of a Friendship*, 61.

one proof for Judaism: language," but, as this note continues, "this insight is a paradox as long as it is not developed" (*T II*, 213).

Scholem's engagement with language is a first attempt to endow his intellectual habitus with theoretical dignity. As we have already seen, he is striving for his own language during this time, and he draws on what he is engaged in: learning the Hebrew language, reading Hebrew literature, and studying mathematics. However, this does not mean that we can reconstruct a theory or philosophy of language that would constitute the foundation of Scholem's later philosophical and historical statements. For one thing, theory emerges for him as a reaction to certain thoughts, experiences, and influences, and for another, this is by no means a stable process. Often incoherent and contradictory, his statements fulfill their function and develop their richness precisely as a result of their conceptually undetermined, rhetorically overdetermined form.

In Scholem's diaries, there is an initial focus on mathematical reflection. He emphasizes the autonomy of mathematics in particular, polemicizing against a normative or foundational "philosophy of mathematics": mathematics is of "highly philosophical significance, but is not capable of, or accessible to, philosophical critique" (*T I*, 259). More radically: "If a starting point in mathematics remains the only possible starting point to found the concept of science, then *mathematics must examine itself*; 'philosophy of mathematics' should not be done" (*T I*, 264). Contrary to his phenomenological teachers Bruno Bauch and Paul Linke, but also contrary to Cohen, Scholem argues for the capacity of mathematics to control itself through the formalization of its concepts into a logical calculus. In a seminar presentation given in the fall semester of 1917, he defends the calculus of the *Begriffsschrift* developed by Gottlob Frege against a phenomenological philosophy of mathematics.[2] Scholem pinpoints the significance of formal notation, arguing "that language is a thoroughly unsuitable means of expressing logical relationships" and in the "endeavor to allow thought to speak in its own language, not one that is imposed on it. This language is not a phonetic language. Only the symbol can come into consideration for its communication" (*T II*, 109). In this context as well, Scholem emphasizes the limitedness of natural language as compared to its "symbolism," but here he means artificial notation with mathematical symbols rather than metaphorical language. Such formal notation makes up a language beyond language to the extent that it is mute: "The languages of symbolism are silent" (*T II*, 110).

---

2. Along with Frege, Husserl's antipsychologistic foundation of logic is a significant factor in Scholem's reservations regarding a mysticism of language in Landauer's sense and in his general aversion to psychology. See, for example, his critique of psychologism in *T II*, 110.

With the conception of the symbol as script, Scholem departs from the level of semantics and common notion of the symbolic as developed, for example, by Mauthner—he is no longer asking what signs mean but how they are written and read. At the same time, a nonsemantic moment is thereby related to natural language—its phonetic nature—along with a dynamic of sounding and hushing that will become central to Scholem's thoughts on language in history. Lacking in simile and sound, the language of mathematics only serves as a limiting case. This is why, in conclusion to his seminar presentation, Scholem emphasizes that there are areas "that cannot be reached by logical calculus.... Indeed, this will be all objects whose inner linguistic principle cannot be exhausted by the teaching of signs, such as religion or history" (*T II*, 111).

It seems that this presentation did not particularly resonate with Frege's seminar. Tellingly, Scholem's own attempts at a "mathematics of mathematics" are not formalized, instead taking the shape of a material ontology with formulations wavering between Platonism, phenomenology, and neo-Kantianism without settling on a distinct use of terms.[3] Scholem's ideas also often pass over into other areas, as at the end of his presentation or when he insists that not only mathematical symbols but also the central concepts of his contemplation of Judaism should be understood unsymbolically: "The Torah *cannot* be a symbol..., for a transmission of the truth is by its nature unsymbolic. Justice is not a symbol" (*T I*, 434).

At the same time, the interpretation of mathematics as a form of notation makes Scholem extremely critical of the "mystical" interpretation of mathematics that was widespread among his contemporaries—for example, Gustav Landauer. For Scholem, both mathematics and mysticism are of the highest dignity, for, "excepting mysticism, only mathematics can know something in its essence" (*LY*, 112). However, he does not tire of emphasizing the "great contrast: mathematics only *can* speak nakedly and without simile, mysticism only in image and simile" (*T I*, 265). Here, his approach differs crucially from Romantic Kabbalah reception, as is especially apparent in his critical reading of Novalis: "He wanted to link both [mysticism and mathematics], and speak of mathematics symbolically; the fact that he thereby ended up on a purely mystical path proves the impossibility of this attempt" (*T I*, 265).[4] Mysticism

---

3. Consider, for example, Scholem's shifting distinctions between idea (*Idee*), concept (*Begriff*), and essence (*Wesen*) (*T II*, 141ff.) or his indecision as to whether mathematics is to be understood analytically or synthetically (*T I*, 139, 382, 467; *FBJ*, 97).

4. See also Scholem's major critique of Novalis, whose "final aim is great, pure, and true: the relation of all things back to theory, but he only reaches it in that he actually strips the

and mathematics might be similar, but they represent different modes that are not to be confused.

Scholem speaks quite often of different "spheres" or regions, and he envisions a "doctrine of order" (*Ordnungslehre*) that would delimit these spheres to avoid confusion between them. According to this doctrine, the language of mysticism or the language of mathematics does not refer to something else, as in a simile, but rather first and foremost to itself; these languages are *terminologies*—as conceived in the context of logical calculus—to the extent that their meaning is determined by the conventional reference of its terms to one another. The notion of a terminological language becomes just as important for Scholem's theoretical reflections as for his treatment of kabbalistic texts. As we will see, unlike his predecessors, Scholem does not take these texts to symbolize something different but insists that they should be deciphered from their reciprocal reference. The notion of spheres or orders also refers to a philosophical project that emerged in the summer of 1917 alongside Scholem's linguistic-theoretical considerations: "The mathematical theory of truth cannot achieve what I thought at first: a metaphysics," Scholem notes: "Only complete metaphysical security could guarantee the accomplishment of our theory, if, at the decisive point—in the question of the essence of the *allocation* of truth to mathematical structures and to being—the theory is not to become symbolism, which it is indeed striving to overcome . . . in a deeper sphere" (*T II*, 26).

In September 1917, Scholem registers an "important experience in the pure heights of the idea" (*LY*, 183). Having read Kant's *Prolegomena to Any Future Metaphysics*, he sees a challenge in the "enormous question marks" that Kant attaches to the possibility of metaphysics: "and I *know* that metaphysics is possible and is the beginning of philosophy. . . . Someone may come and say, 'these metaphysical views of yours are all well and good, but regrettably I must refuse to test them,'" because "the fundamental categories you use in both metaphysics and the normal sphere aren't at all *explained* here. Rather, it has meaning only by enabling experience" (*LY*, 183).

Philosophical considerations played an important role in Scholem's notes from the outset, as he read Mauthner, Buber, Nietzsche, Kierkegaard, Simmel,

---

idea of science [*Wissenschaft*] of its autonomy, and in that he thus foists something else onto it . . . that *he* calls mysticism. . . . Yet by identifying all things in this way . . . , one robs oneself of insight into the coincidence of orders that are different" (*T II*, 254). Kilcher emphasizes the significance of Novalis but ignores Scholem's critique and thus overstates Scholem's aesthetic approach to the Kabbalah (*Die Sprachtheorie der Kabbala*, 336ff.).

and others. Thus, the "important experience" of the *Prolegomena* is not equivalent to the shock that reading Kant provoked for so many philosophical adolescents. Unlike for Heinrich von Kleist, for example, it is not the objectivity of experience that is called into question, as Scholem had already learned skepticism from Mauthner and Nietzsche. Reading Kant pointed Scholem to another, more methodical problem: How is philosophy possible after skepticism? According to Kant, every metaphysics, even a skeptical metaphysics, becomes entangled in transcendental appearance when using its terms in fields that can no longer be related to possible experience. "Metaphysical" propositions therefore threaten to be simply objectless (or antinomic). As Kant himself already noted, this raises the question of the possibility, status, and systematic structure of philosophy in an entirely new way.

Kant's questioning of the legitimate use of metaphysical propositions left a lasting impression on Scholem, not least of all because it led to a joint project with Walter Benjamin at a time when the two were growing closer. In keeping with contemporary attitudes, both friends called for Kant's thinking to be surpassed. As Benjamin writes to Scholem, one must preserve "what is *essential* in Kant's thought," but "I still do not know at this point what this 'essential' something consists of and how his system must be grounded anew for it to emerge clearly."[5] The two agreed to pursue these questions together by reading Hermann Cohen, the most important neo-Kantian of the day.

Cohen, too, aims at a revision of Kant. Above all, he wants to overcome Kant's concept of a simply receptive sensibility. In his *Logic of Pure Knowledge*, Cohen explicitly refuses "to let a doctrine of sensibility precede logic. We begin with thought. Thought may have no origin other than itself, if its purity is to be unrestricted and unclouded."[6] For Cohen, limiting experience to sensibility restricts the autonomy of human reason and the "purity" of thought. Removing limits on the concept of experience is attractive to Benjamin and Scholem to the extent that "nonsensible" experiences of aesthetic, religious, or metaphysical nature are no longer excluded from the definition of experience. In addition, Cohen's polemic against intuition (*Anschauung*) and immediate sensibility is also appealing to Scholem because it enables him to express his aversion to

---

5. Benjamin, *Correspondence*, 97. On Benjamin's reading of Kant, see above all Deuber-Mankowsky, *Der frühe Walter Benjamin und Hermann Cohen*; Fiorato, "Unendliche Aufgabe und System der Wahrheit," and "Die Erfahrung, das Unbedingte und die Religion."

6. Cohen, *Logik der reinen Erkenntnis*, 12–13. For broader context on the idea of overcoming Kant, see Köhnke, *Entstehung und Aufstieg des Neukantianismus*, 404ff.; Ringer, *The Decline of the German Mandarins*, esp. chapter 2.

Buber's *Erlebnislehre* in philosophical terms. Especially in *The Concept of Religion in the System of Philosophy*, the first of Cohen's major works that Scholem read, there is a sharp criticism of feeling as a source of knowledge and basis of religion.[7]

Instead of limiting experience to sensibility, Cohen relates it to the discursive dimension of thought, modeled in the form of a series of questions tracing back to Platonic dialogue: "The concept is a question and remains a question; nothing but a question. The answer, too, that it contains, must be a new question, awaken a new question. This is the inner methodical relationship that exists between question and answer, that every question itself must be an answer; thus, each answer can and must also be a question. . . . No solution can count as definitive."[8] This logic of question and answer will become central to Scholem's thought, implying a notion of "dialectics" fundamentally distinct from that of Hegel. It also leads to a rethinking of the concept of origin (*Ursprung*), which for Cohen does not refer to something primary and simple—as in a sort of primary intuition—but rather a particular kind of question that supposedly original evidence must pose to itself. Origin always refers to the *problem* of origin: "The supposedly original identity of being is replaced here by the 'problem' from which the identity in question first emerges as 'idea.'"[9] This problem is original to the extent that it is the final basis of referral. It is the question: "What is 'what is'?"—the question of the concept itself implied in every judgment—or the "problem of the problem."[10]

Scholem employs a similar figure of thought: "Judaism can only be raised to a higher power once: in philosophy. Philosophy is the autonomous answer, not to the question posed by Judaism, but answer as theory of the question" (*T II*, 333). Overall, both Scholem and Benjamin sharply criticize Cohen, particularly when it comes to the interpretation of Kant. Let us take as an example Cohen's treatment of space in his commentary on Kant's *Critique of Pure Reason*. According to Cohen, what is intuited (*das Angeschaute*) is not given, but rather

---

7. See, for example, *T II*, 86ff., especially the polemic against Schleiermacher, 94ff.
8. Cohen, *Logik der reinen Erkenntnis*, 378. See also the description of concepts as question marks (ibid., 16) and as questions (ibid., 30) and the description of the question as the "lever of origin," "foundation of judgment," and "basis of foundation" (ibid., 3–4).
9. Fiorato, *Geschichtliche Ewigkeit*, 28.
10. See Fiorato, *Geschichtliche Ewigkeit*, 34. Cohen's notion of origin "forms the demonstration of the impossibility of a definitive encounter with being in the pole of essence. As the most extreme gesture of discursivity that butts against its own limits, the judgment of origin (only) represents final, 'self-ironic' evidence of thought, which—without seeking refuge in the intuition of essences—discovers its own abysmalness" (ibid., 31).

it is "space ... that constructs external objects."[11] He transfers the model of geometric construction onto objectivity as such, thereby significantly deviating from Kant, for whom geometric construction is a special case that cannot by any means stand for experience on the whole. Neither a construction nor a concept, for Kant space is a pure form of intuition to be distinguished from the categories of reason.[12]

Although Cohen's book is presented as a commentary, not once does he mention this radical difference between his approach and that of Kant. Furthermore, the problematics of surmounting the Kantian duality of sensible intuition and rational concept become clear in this context. For Kant, the distinction between intuition and concept has an important *critical* function, allowing us to distinguish "rational" and "rationalizing" conclusions—that is, those in which the categories of reason are related to possible intuition—from those in which this is no longer the case and which consequently threaten to become mere speculations.[13] With similar intentions, Cohen substitutes Kant's attachment of experience to sensibility with the attachment to science and its progress on the one hand and insistence on the ethical dangers of materialism and pantheism on the other. While the latter argument does play a role in Scholem's theory of Judaism for a time, he strictly rejects the former: "Cohen's fundamental idea that only sees nature and knowledge in the 'given' fact of science. This tastes indigestibly positivistic and is surely false" (*T II*, 170). Thus, highlighting Cohen's consistent misinterpretation of Kant, Scholem and Benjamin's reading ended in disappointment.[14] The project of a renewal of metaphysics on the basis of Kantian thought became problematic, and the insufficiency of Cohen's interpretation ultimately came to represent

---

11. Cohen, *Kants Theorie der Erfahrung*, 7. See also ibid., 26, 104, on construction in experience. This interpretation is ultimately based on Cohen's pronounced Platonism. See also Köhnke, *Entstehung und Aufstieg*, chapter 5.

12. See Kant, *Kritik der reinen Vernunft*, B 40ff., and B 741ff. Scholem, too—albeit in an uncertain manner—addresses the question of whether mathematical judgments are analytical or synthetic (e.g., *T I*, 275, 382) and criticizes Cohen's interpretation on other points as well (see, for example, *T I*, 261, 276; see also *Von Berlin nach Jerusalem*, 74).

13. See Köhnke's critique: because Cohen does not specifically deal with dialectics, he loses sight of the critical move and does not recognize the function of bonding reason to experience; Cohen's Platonism and his claim to say the "same" thing again "better" prevent him from understanding the particularity of Kant's thought formation (Köhnke, *Entstehung und Aufstieg des Neukantianismus*, 273ff.).

14. In a letter to Ludwig Strauß from December 1918, Scholem emphasizes that his "complete and here certainly absolute rejection" does not apply to "Cohen's figure and existence" as a Jew nor to his three-part *System der Philosophie*, but rather to the "*interpretative*

an insufficiency of philosophy as such. Yet even after this disappointment, Kant remained the paradigm of philosophy for Scholem, albeit from an at least partially neo-Kantian perspective.

Three aspects of this Kantianism can be discerned in Scholem's later writing, as philosophically restrained as it may be. First, Scholem displays great reservations regarding conceptual speculation. This is particularly apparent in his critique of Hegelian Marxism, which he judges not only based on its materialist fundamental assumptions but also on its category of the totality of society, which for him leads "utterly into the abysmal," as it will not be redeemable in concrete research and will therefore always "expire in the purely speculative."[15] Second, Scholem regularly emphasizes the critical moment of reason, as, for example, in a late interview: "The instrument of Reason developed in man largely on the critical, destructive side.... In the area of construction, Reason has had relatively few successes.... Reason is a dialectical tool that serves both construction and destruction, but has had more notable successes in destruction" (*JJC*, 31). What is constructive is something different, "something moral" (*JJC*, 32), but this other thing transgresses philosophy as he sees it. Third, Scholem seems to identify philosophy with autonomous, systematic thought. He views Rosenzweig's claims to transcend idealism with a new kind of heteronomous thought as "theology" (*PM*, 202). His disappointment in neo-Kantianism did not result in a turn to a new, noncritical, or "positive" philosophy, as it did for Rosenzweig and the other "new thinkers" of the interwar period. Instead, it prompted him to take up forms of thinking and writing that he no longer considered to be philosophical.

Cohen" (*Br I*, 180). See Scholem's criticism of the "method of obtaining unfounded objectlessness on false pretenses" (*T II*, 275); in Cohen's work, "the reality of the objectless is proven out of the *demand* for methodical unity" (ibid.): Cohen's critique is "a mystification, not mysticism" (*LY*, 264). See also *Story of a Friendship*, 59ff.

    15. Scholem, ... *und alles ist Kabbala*, 22. Scholem writes to Adorno regarding *Negative Dialektik* that mediation through societal totality plays "the role of a deus ex machina"; it is a "thoroughly metaphysical thesis in itself..., that there is such total mediation as the basis of explanation of every phenomenon," a "basis of belief that one must grant to you" (*Br II*, 178).

EIGHT

LAMENTATIONS
Thinking Language

ONE OF THE MOST SIGNIFICANT texts from this period is the manuscript "On Lament and Lamentation," written by Scholem in December 1917, at a time when he was still working on a mathematical theory of truth. While the critique of Cohen still lay ahead of him at this point, isolated figures of Cohen's thought already played an important role. Above all, this text can be understood as a response to Walter Benjamin's "On Language as Such and on the Language of Man" and thus as the beginning of the two thinkers' symphilosophizing, which would prove decisive for Scholem. Written as an epilogue to his translation of biblical lamentations, the text is closely related to his engagement with the Hebrew language and the appropriation of heritage. In several respects, it is a fitting first point of intersection for the different threads in Scholem's intellectual development. At the same time, the short text of less than six print pages shows how Scholem compresses various ideas into a single expression that for him is at once theoretical and existential. On the one hand, in the manuscript he "laid out things in the epilogue that come from the extreme depths of my heart" (*LY*, 201), and he calls the text "a description of my inner state" (*LY*, 212), indeed a *"confession"* (*LL*, 71). On the other hand, it is a first attempt to systematically articulate his own thought as well as his own experience with Jewish heritage and to make a genuine theoretical statement.

In August 1917, Scholem writes to Werner Kraft that Benjamin's work on language "'merely' set out to accomplish an unspeakably important task: to clarify terminology" (*LL*, 51). However, Scholem notes, "absolutely fundamental elements are still missing from the work—for instance, a discussion of the nature of symbols in language ... and the theory of signs and of script, which in my opinion lead to the deepest levels possible, for they raise the most decisive questions for mathematics and the philosophy of religion" (*LL*, 51). Scholem's text is an attempt to provide these missing pieces. At most, Benjamin points in this direction by mentioning a "doctrine of signs" without which "any linguistic philosophy remains entirely fragmentary," in addition to introducing the distinction between language as the "communication of the communicable" and "symbol of the noncommunicable," closely related to the relationship of language and signs. Benjamin does not expand on this, however.[1] Scholem picks up on the familiar terminology of symbol and mute speech, pursuing Benjamin's reflections on the nature of language and especially of silence, which plays a large role in his notes during this time. For example, in the fall of 1917, Scholem states: "One of the deepest truths of language is how speaking passes from silence to silence, with language lurking between them as the medium of silence" (*LY*, 189). As later formulations make clear, this can certainly also be understood as a critique or at least continuation of Benjamin's work: "The spiritual essence of man is language, but language *must* encompass silence, otherwise it is untrue" (*LY*, 216).

Benjamin's text starts with the maxim "Every expression of human mental life can be understood as a kind of language."[2] Benjamin develops this insight through the paradigm of the creation story, in which the original language of names as well as the derivative language of judgment can be situated. Scholem opens his text "On Lament" in a manner that is hardly less general—"All language is infinite"—only to immediately specify that the language of lament and the language of God are differently and more deeply infinite than other languages, because while the infinity of language is always constituted by a limit or border between what is revealed and what is kept silent, the infinity of the language of lament "remains throughout on the border [*Grenze*], exactly on the border between these two realms. . . . It is not symbolic, but only points toward the symbol; it is not [objective (*gegenständlich*)], but annihilates the object."[3] Scholem takes up Benjamin's distinction between the communicable and noncommunicable in language and implements it in a different paradigm, that of lament, by drawing on the conceptuality of silence, script, and symbol. Linguistic, philosophical, and poetological considerations are thereby intertwined, with each other and with theological figures of thought such as that

---

1. Benjamin, "On Language as Such and on the Language of Man," in *Selected Writings*, vol. 1, 73–74. See Menninghaus, *Walter Benjamins Theorie der Sprachmagie*, chapter 1.
2. Benjamin, "On Language as Such and on the Language of Man," in *Selected Writings*, vol. 1, 62.
3. Scholem, "On Lament and Lamentation," 313, translation slightly modified.

of revelation, which Benjamin only touches on. Scholem calls out the need "to recognize two polarities as identical: silence as a source of language, and Revelation as the source of language" (*LY*, 216).

In terms of philosophy of language, the figure of the limit or border (*Grenze*) is key for Scholem in several respects.[4] On the one hand, the text repeatedly alludes to the border between sound and soundlessness, language and script, and speaking and silence. Lament gives expression to the soundless in language. Benjamin designates names as the language of language, insofar as the designative dimension of language is originally manifested in the name and the act of naming. In contrast, lament seems to reveal the noncommunicable and expressionless, which is likewise a dimension of language: "And therefore lament can usurp any language: it is always the not empty, but extinguished expression, in which its death wish and its inability to die join together. The expression of innermost expressionlessness, the language of silence is lament."[5] Lament divests speech of meaning, dissolving the meaning of words or even emptying them of meaning, representing a kind of "death drive of language."[6] For Scholem, lament permanently loses its object. It is "volatile [*labile*] language," which cannot remain intact: "Language in the state of lament annihilates itself, and the language of lament is itself, for that very reason, the language of annihilation [*Vernichtung*]. Everything is at its mercy. It repeatedly attempts to become symbol, but this must always fail, because it is border."[7] Scholem also defines the destructive movement of lament in terms of its objective side, designating mourning as its object. Not a communicable object itself, mourning is a symbolic condition of all things.[8] As the language of silence, lament is also pure language, in which the linguisticality of language manifests itself just as unbrokenly as in the language of names. If the language of silence is also pure, it also has an inner relationship to truth, or what Scholem calls teaching: "Teaching encompasses not only language, but also, in a unique way, that which lacks language [*das Sprachlose*], the silenced, to which

---

4. On Scholem's use of topological imagery and its Kantian implications, see Ferber, "A Language of the Border."
5. Scholem, "On Lament," 316.
6. Hamacher, "Bemerkungen zur Klage," 90.
7. Scholem, "On Lament," 313, 314.
8. "Mourning is a condition of each thing, a state into which everything can fall.... Of course, mourning lies wholly in the realm of symbolic objects: it denotes for each thing the first order of the symbolic" ("On Lament," 315). Scholem is oriented by Benjamin's description of mourning as an expression of the muteness of nature. See Benjamin, "On Language as Such," in *Selected Writings*, vol. 1, 72–73. See also *T II*, 615–616.

mourning belongs."⁹ This relationship between teaching and silence will prove decisive for the dialectics of esoteric tradition that Scholem is beginning to work out here.

While Scholem conceives of lament as a limit *in* language, he also considers it in contrast to other languages. Its counterpart is not the language of joy, which does have an object, as Scholem emphasizes at the outset of the essay. Indeed, lament cannot be answered in human language, because it has no definite object: "There is no answer to lament, which is to say, there is only one: falling mute [*das Verstummen*].... Only One can answer lament: God himself, who through revelation evoked it [i.e., lament] out of the revolution of mourning."¹⁰ This, too, shows that we are dealing with pure language, pure to the extent that it has no definite object and does not designate any definite negation but rather the withdrawal of the nameless—and it is thereby oriented toward the future: "So long as the inviolability of silence is not threatened, men and things will continue to lament, and precisely this constitutes the grounds of our hope for the restitution of language, of reconciliation: for, indeed, it was language that suffered the fall into sin, not silence."¹¹

Scholem also thinks of lament in poetological terms, with reference to the biblical lamentations commented on by this text. The Book of Lamentations begins with a lament for Jerusalem:

> How deserted lies the city,
> once so full of people!
> How like a widow is she,
> who once was great among the nations! (Lam 1:1, NIV)

The verse begins with a hopeless situation for the desolate city, and fragmentary similes underscore the incommensurability of disaster ("With what can I compare you?" Lam 2:13). Syntactically, these announcements do not even make up a full sentence, let alone an argument. The lamentations break out of comprehensible communication into mere recitation and rhythm. "Monotony is the deep linguistic symbol of expressionlessness.... Each word appears only to die"; lament is thus only pure to the extent that it is movement: "only the ever-recurring force of the border phenomenon prevents lament from becoming stable, which means nothing other than symbolic babble."¹²

---

9. Scholem, "On Lament," 316.
10. Scholem, "On Lament," 316.
11. Scholem, "On Lament," 319.
12. Scholem, "On Lament," 318, 319. See Mintz, *Hurban*, esp. chapter 1.

However, lament does not remain on the border. In this essay and elsewhere in his notes, Scholem stresses that although lament is "mythic" and therefore devoid of any future, Judaism was able to integrate it through teaching, with hope (*T II*, 391). In a particularly significant passage, he states that it is the integration of a "prophetic element into lament—for such is hope" that allowed lament to be included in Jewish literature: "After the word was annihilated, in the end, from the ashes of the burning of lament arises the new messianic word. Without this, lament could never have found and maintained a place among the Jews, for its lack of consolation would have destroyed it [*ihre Trostlosigkeit hätte sie zerstört*]" (*T II*, 391). Again, it is the annihilating character of language that dissolves meaning and gives rise to new hope. Hope is necessary, for otherwise "it" would have been destroyed. The "it" here is ambivalent, as the "sie" in the German sentence could refer to either lament or the Jews. This ambivalence suggests that hopeless lament would destroy itself and also destroy Judaism. The breaking apart of poetic form could also be destructive, as lamentation might find no return, yet hopelessness is not the final word. Continuing to lament, the desolate city of Jerusalem gains her own distinct voice, and this voice enters into dialogue with the Lord:

> Her fall was astounding;
> there was none to comfort her.
> "Look, LORD, on my affliction,
> for the enemy has triumphed" (Lam 1:9)

According to Alan Mintz, lamentation "can be understood as a record of man's struggle to speak in the face of God's silence."[13] This struggle undergoes a decisive transition from desolation to address, with powerful poetological implications. Scholem stresses that lamentation is also poetry: "*Every* lament can be expressed as poetry, since its particular liminality between the linguistic realms, its tragic paradox, makes it so."[14] Indeed, the move from loss and desolation to the acquisition of a voice—and the move from solitude to dialogue—has a long poetic tradition in the genre of the elegy, which grapples with the question of how the subject should speak in a moment of loss or how loss can be transformed into poetic voice.[15] The elegiac voice addresses loss with words, but these words are always in danger of being lost: "The infinite

---

13. Mintz, *Hurban*, 42.
14. Scholem, "On Lament," 317.
15. See Weidner, "'Movement of Language' and Transience"; Barouch, *Between German and Hebrew*, 23–75.

tension that inflames each word of lament, ... the infinite force with which each word negates itself and sinks back into the infinity of silence, in which the word's emptiness [*Leere*] becomes teaching [*Lehre*], but above all the infinity of mourning itself, which destroys itself in lament as rhythm, prove lament to be poetry."[16] The focus on the single word that is "inflamed" in lamentation likely relates to Hölderlin, an important reference point for Benjamin as well as for Scholem. In his notes, Scholem writes that Hölderlin led a Zionist life among the German people and that he holds an absolute authority alongside the Bible: "Hölderlin and the Bible are the two only things in the world that can never contradict each other" (*T II*, 347). Hölderlin gave the elegy a distinctive place in the philosophy of history, as his elegiac poetry represents the absent gods to humans. At the same time, he developed a poetics that focuses on the single word and tends to dissolve syntactic junctures, thereby revealing the essence of the word, so to speak.[17]

Thus, for Scholem, poetry is essentially lamentation, and this becomes explicit in other literary judgments. In Mörike's *Nolten the Painter*, there sometimes appears a "silence ... that seems to call up lament," but "pure lament is not heard in this book; the error that it is founded upon is the opinion that one can lament without having spoken" (*T II*, 193). Scholem criticizes Rilke's *Notebooks of Malte Laurids Brigge* even more sharply for being full of ghostly ambiguity and perverting lament in order to resist the mythical order of law (*T II*, 294ff.). He also remains skeptical of most Hebrew poetry for its subjectivism: "Therefore, the modern 'lamentations' of lyric are not lamentation in the deepest sense.... Pure, contentless lamentation belongs to the community" (*T II*, 389). In his diary notes more than in the essay "On Lament," Scholem makes it clear that it is ultimately the nation or the people who speak in lamentation: "There is no individual who laments, who lamented lamentations [*der die Klagen klagte*]. The lamenting ego is only and uniquely the national ego. The people lament and are allowed to lament according to authenticated laws, no individual has the right to do so. This constitutes a problem in Job and a difficult paradox in the third lamentation.... Wailing

---

16. Scholem, "On Lament," 317–318. "Lament is thereby conceived as a very complex figure: as the death of language in the form of a repetitive, symbol-oriented movement of its extinguishment, as a repeated articulation in which anything symbolized is extinguished, annihilated" (Weigel, "Scholems Gedichte und seine Dichtungstheorie," 31). I am also grateful to Sigrid Weigel for her suggestions in conversation regarding Scholem's understanding of aesthetics.

17. See Weidner, "Reading the Wound."

women are the people as such" (*T II*, 388). True community is a lamenting community, a community that would be able to relate to its past. On the other hand, however, this means that the poetry of the nation must engage in lament and therefore must operate at the dangerous border of falling silent. For Scholem, the political moment of lament as the language of the people is highly problematic, as already discussed in the context of his translation of the *Yizkor* book in chapter 4.

In a manuscript dated April 1923, Scholem highlights danger as well as the gulf between his idea of the political and politics as practiced. Entitled "The Truth," the text states that what Zionists truly lack is the ability to lament: "The security of a common future obscures the view into the abyss of mourning that gapes in the midst of all Jewish history, in the heart of all Jewish phenomena" (*T II*, 712). This thought prefigures Scholem's despair regarding the "victory" of Zionism after his immigration (see chap. 5). In 1923, however, Scholem still expresses high hope in lament as such: "When Zionism will have learned how to lament, it will be more than a hope: it will have gained redeeming power over our souls" (*T II*, 712). The restitution of language may yet be possible, the past may yet return, and there may yet be a form in which to relate to this past not merely as antiquarian memory nor as expected future but as a life of lament— a life at the border of language and silence. As already mentioned, one of the functions of the reference to the elegiac mode in his writing is the quest for a voice that operates at this border. This is a crucial quest for the young Scholem, who wants to speak with a distinctively Jewish voice while realizing how difficult this is under the conditions of modernity.

NINE

TRADITION, TEACHING, DOCTRINE
A Jewish Form of Truth

NOT ONLY A LINGUISTIC AND literary problem for Scholem, lament is always also a political issue. Lament relates to the people, to Zionism, and especially to Jewish history. It is a form of this history and thus also a form of teaching, a focal point for Scholem as well as Benjamin in their youth. "Teaching" (*Lehre*) also has a double meaning, connoting both "doctrine" and "education." It is a philosophical category, as evident in the discussion of Cohen, but it also stands for entirely practical problems that both Benjamin and Scholem dealt with in the context of youth movements; for Scholem at least, it also comprises the complex meaning of Torah. The overdetermination of the term unfolds in discussions between the two friends as well as in a number of metaphors and figures of thought that will resonate in Scholem's later texts.

Responding to a polemic of Scholem's against the Jewish youth movement, a September 1917 letter from Benjamin exemplifies how theoretical categories can be developed out of practical questions:

> The teacher does not actually teach in that he "learns before others" [*vor-lernt*], learns in an exemplary way. Rather, his learning has evolved into teaching, in part gradually but wholly from within.... I am convinced that tradition is the medium in which the person who is learning *continually* transforms himself into the person who is teaching, and that this applies to the entire range of education.... Knowledge becomes transmittable only for the person who has understood his knowledge as something that has been transmitted. He becomes free in an unprecedented way. The metaphysical origin of a Talmudic witticism comes to mind here.[1]

---

1. Benjamin, *Correspondence*, 93–94.

Benjamin thus construes education as an immediate and infinite medium of "teaching" or "tradition." While the one who educates and the one who is educated are contained within this medium, they are also free to act in it. According to Benjamin, "It is so difficult to speak about education because its order completely coincides with the religious order of tradition"; as is often the case in Benjamin's writing, this difficulty is condensed into an ingenious image: "[Teaching (*Lehre*)] is like a surging sea, but the only thing that matters to the wave (understood as a metaphor for the person) is to surrender itself to its motion in such a way that it crests and breaks."[2] Teaching as a medium is thereby "broken": transmission cannot take place continuously, and recourse to the past is not simply conservative return. It always newly actualizes itself in the break—a figure of thought so important that it will play a central role in Benjamin and Scholem's correspondence regarding Franz Kafka twenty years later, as we will see below.

Scholem takes up this idea from Benjamin, also describing "teaching" as a "medium, in which the one who is learning is transformed into the teacher" (*T II*, 302). At the same time, Benjamin's formulations reflect conversations with his friend, and the reference to Talmudic wit reveals that these considerations are addressed to Scholem. Tradition already plays an essential role in Scholem's reflections, as in the 1918 essay "On Lament": "That lament can be transmitted belongs to the great, truly mystical laws of the peoplehood [*Volkstum*]."[3] During this period, his reflections likewise revolve around the relation of freedom and boundedness: "In the unity of loneliness and bonding, of loneliness and community, is to be found the deeper unity of freedom and history, all within the concept of the Teaching, of tradition. He who wants to pass on tradition must live both alone (for how else will he know the tradition?) and in community (for how else could he transmit tradition?)" (*LY*, 191). Scholem is also trying to reformulate his old, metaphysical determination of religion: "Is it really true that 'religion is the consciousness of the Order of things'? ... How does one go from this to tradition? Can a consciousness (also in a mystical way) be *taught*?" (*LY*, 194).

The question of how the truth can be learned is an eminently practical question for Scholem, related to the question of how to think of tradition in order for it to represent a continuum between those with knowledge and those without, and between traditional Jews and Jews with an assimilated background such

---

2. Benjamin, *Correspondence*, 94, translation slightly modified. See also McCole, *Walter Benjamin*, 76ff.; McCole interprets Benjamin's entire work in light of the problem of the appropriation of tradition.

3. Scholem, "On Lament," 317.

as himself. His contemplation of tradition is also contemplation of what he himself is doing. The specificity of his position lies in the fact that he is simultaneously within a community and lonely: because he is within the tradition even as he confronts it, he has at his disposal a double register in which to speak about tradition.

In addition to Benjamin, Scholem develops these concepts in dialogue with other interpreters of Judaism. As is often the case when it comes to tradition, the interpreters are not those who live their lives within the tradition as a matter of course but those who explicitly devote themselves to its examination. For Scholem, two thinkers play an especially important role: Franz Joseph Molitor (1779–1860), who was in many respects a typical nineteenth-century German counter-Enlightenment thinker, combining freemasonry, philanthropism, theosophy, Christian Kabbalah, and Catholic Romanticism with a polemic against rationalism, materialism, and Protestantism; and Samson Raphael Hirsch (1808–1888), the founder of German neo-Orthodoxy, whose polemical position against an understanding of Judaism as a confession Scholem shared and whose stress on the traditional form of life deeply impressed Scholem even though he never adopted an Orthodox way of life himself.[4]

Scholem read Molitor's multivolume *Philosophy of History, or, On Tradition* in 1916 with enthusiasm and later declared that it was Molitor who had pointed him to the "address where the secret life of Judaism . . . seemed to have once dwelt" (*Br I*, 471).[5] Not only does Molitor provide a more or less accessible exposition of the basic ideas of Kabbalah, but he also emphasizes the epistemological significance of tradition and the tension between esoteric and exoteric transmission that will become essential for Scholem's understanding of both tradition and history. Molitor's presentation of the Kabbalah is embedded in theological speculations regarding tradition as a divine intervention to help fallen creatures that require "stimulation and aid."[6] Scripture alone is not sufficient here, for it lacks "all concrete determination and individual specification" and is "subject to every kind of misinterpretation": "The orally pronounced word, as well as practice and life, must therefore be the constant companions and interpreters of the written word; otherwise the written word remains an

---

4. On Scholem's engagement with Molitor and Hirsch, see also Weidner, "Self-Deception and the Dark Side of History: Gershom Scholem's Mythology of Counter-Enlightenment."

5. See also Scholem's long reference to Molitor in "Revelation and Tradition as Religious Categories in Judaism," in *MI*, 285.

6. Molitor, *Philosophie der Geschichte*, vol. 1, 3. On Molitor, see also Kilcher, "Franz Joseph Molitors Kabbala-Projekt vor dem Hintergrund seiner intellektuellen Biographie."

abstract concept in the mind, lacking all life and concrete content."[7] Counter to Enlightenment book knowledge and the Protestant scriptural principle, Molitor relates life to tradition.

This also means that tradition has a life of its own. Rather than Mosaic law, it is the secret transmission of mysticism that forms the "living soul" and "deep center of the entire life" of Judaism as well as "the living principle of the entire progressive development of Judaism and its higher development into Christianity."[8] Tradition transmits the Hebrew language itself, most notably the vowel signs that are absent from written scripture. Whereas biblical criticism holds that vocalization first occurred with the Masorah in postbiblical times, Molitor stresses that it had been transmitted orally: the "vowel and accent signs existed, but, as noted, only in the hidden so to speak; they only emerged where it was necessary."[9] On the one hand, the Torah had to be handed down unvocalized, for it "would have lost its endlessness for intuition [*Anschauung*] through a definite punctuation and word division, and thus it would have become a definite individual, ceasing to be the one and all."[10] On the other hand, however, scripture without vocalization would have been deficient: "How can one believe that the godhead trusted correct reading and meaning merely to the easily changed word, without linking that word to certain signs, and thereby giving tradition a secure ladder and firm basis.... Religious grounds thus speak to the original age of the vocal signs."[11]

For Molitor, the Masorah—and thus the entire Kabbalah—is not the ever-new interpretation of a text but rather the faithful retention of an authentic, original meaning in another medium, as along with a profane moral and legal tradition, there is an inner secret teaching for the initiated. Familiar from the Enlightenment, in this context the idea of a *duplex religio* relates less to the rationality of content than to the mode of transmission.[12] What is specific is the

---

7. Molitor, *Philosophie der Geschichte*, vol. 1, 6. For the polemic against the Protestant scriptural principle, see, for example, ibid., 48–49.
8. Molitor, *Philosophie der Geschichte*, vol. 1, 38, 43, 12.
9. Molitor, *Philosophie der Geschichte*, vol. 1, 387.
10. Molitor, *Philosophie der Geschichte*, vol. 1, 367. The vowelless scripture was "entirely fit to actively and vitally preserve the spirit, as long as the spirit remained in its simplicity, and to protect it from sinking into dead letters" (ibid., 369).
11. Molitor, *Philosophie der Geschichte*, vol. 1, 385–386.
12. Enlightenment *duplex religio* primarily had the political function of conveying the simultaneity of the true yet politically inopportune rational religion and the religion of the masses. See Assmann, *Religio Duplex*. On the Romantic reception of this figure of thought, see Schulte, "Kabbala in der deutschen Romantik."

close connection of the two religions, through which the "inner" can only appear in the medium of the "outer," for it is *only* the vowel signs that remain hidden, whereas the consonantal scripture is completely overt. As a result, esoteric tradition always exists in Judaism only *within* exoteric tradition: "Everywhere in the pagan religions, the esoteric is sharply separated from the exoteric.... In Judaism, however, the esoteric was only faintly parted from the exoteric, and a simple, graduated transition opened from the one to the other. The Jews did not recognize any closed-off mysteries in the sense of the pagan peoples.... As a result, uniquely and singularly, Judaism was capable of progressive development, out of which the salvation of Christianity was prepared."[13] This passage shows how Molitor's theological construction is closely interwoven with his thinking of history, and it also provides entry into the historicity and textuality of the Jewish tradition, especially the Kabbalah. First, although it is authentically Mosaic, this transmission is now embedded in a history through its interaction with exoteric Judaism. Second, Molitor thereby offers insight into the specific *form* of traditionalist literature—namely, commentary. As the esoteric tradition does not contain new truth but rather unfolds what is implicit, the book commentaries are "not themselves symbolic" but "merely the explanation of the symbol," and the books of this tradition are "without all mystical form, and in them everything is unbound and free. Therefore, these books are not true scriptures, but rather merely notes that are made into general tidings."[14] The commentaries are actually abbreviations, and as Molitor points out, "most manuscripts are so full of abbreviations that they cannot be understood without a key."[15]

Molitor's traditionalist interpretation of the Kabbalah represents somewhat of an exception for the nineteenth century, when the general assumption was that the Kabbalah pronounced *new* truths, concealed in the garb of old letters for reasons of dissimulation. For instance, Adolphe Franck's 1843 *The Kabbalah, or, The Religious Philosophy of the Hebrews* gives a more modern, critical, and historical account of the Kabbalah than Molitor does, yet it loses sight of the organic relationship between Jewish mysticism and normative Judaism. For Franck, it is only due to "habits of prudence" that the kabbalists continue to refer to the Torah; the form of the text is "a gross exterior under which was hidden a mysterious meaning," and the mystical interpretation of scripture is a "means of assuring themselves of full liberty without openly breaking with

---

13. Molitor, *Philosophie der Geschichte*, vol. 1, 201.
14. Molitor, *Philosophie der Geschichte*, vol. 1, 53–54.
15. Molitor, *Philosophie der Geschichte*, vol. 1, 81.

religious authority; and, possibly, they felt the need of doing something to assuage their consciences."[16] Indeed, the kabbalists "obeyed the impulse of their intelligence only. The ideas they introduced into the sacred books . . . , these ideas are entirely their own, and constitute a system truly original and truly grand."[17]

Whereas for Franck, the kabbalists wrote allegorically, Molitor wants to take the Kabbalah seriously as a tradition capable of truth. His close connection between philosophy of language, philosophy of history, and apologia for the Kabbalah quickly drew Scholem in, turning him into a traditionalist, at least polemically. Whereas in August 1916, before reading Molitor, he had referred to the Bible as an "arsenal of divine longing and divine security" and as a work of "religious *Übermenschen*" (*LY*, 132), he now corrects himself: the "divinity" of the Bible does not lie in its "humanity" but "far, far deeper. It is *not* in myth, but in its view of history" (*LY*, 145). Further, "Judaism is the embodiment of history, and because Judaism is the *absolute* truth, it follows that the Bible and the Torah are divine. For this reason, one can employ the Bible as a proof" (*LY*, 145). With this perspective, Scholem also gains another angle to polemicize against Buber's *Erlebnislehre*: "you cannot 'experience' if you do not know God's work, God's actions. God's actions, however, constitute the 'Tradition,' the Torah. And the Torah is not just the Pentateuch. The Torah is the essence and integral of all religious tradition" (*LL*, 37). In addition, Molitor and the concept of tradition provide support for Scholem as he grapples with historical critique of the Old Testament: "In the end, historical skepticism can be overcome only through the Jewish conception of Tradition. *Judaism is the embodiment of history.* Judaism also supplies the historical standards that can truly be applied to everything" (*LY*, 144). Thus, Judaism does not *have* a history, it *is* history, but this history itself is at once the "unfolding of the Torah": "The equation History = Torah perhaps expresses this essential issue: Torah is History. The history of the Torah is the inner history of the world, with the historical process playing itself out in the unfolding of the Torah. *Historiography is the science of the inner laws of the Torah* (which is a history, to be sure, yet to be dealt with and explored). Molitor had an inkling of this, but he saw it Christologically, whereas one must see it as a Jew. *This would be a genuine ideology of Zionism*" (*LY*, 143).

---

16. Franck, *The Kabbalah*, 77, lviii, 141–142. Franck speaks quite disparagingly at times of the "oddness, affectation and habit, which in the Orient so often abuse allegory even to subtlety" (ibid., 147).

17. Franck, *The Kabbalah*, lix. On idealistic interpretations of the Kabbalah, see also Idel, *Kabbalah*, 8ff.

As this passage demonstrates, it does not escape Scholem that Molitor ultimately relies on a Christological view of history that he himself vehemently rejects, particularly in a note on "Zionist life" from 1919/1920: "There is only one thing that this life in all of its orders is implacably and inexorably opposed to: every Christology. Here lies the death of our substance. Zionism is the mute, terrible war against this" (*T II*, 623).[18] As we will see in his interpretations of messianism and prophecy, Scholem will continue to conceive of history in relation to truth without referring to a mediating figure such as that of Christ for the Christian Kabbalah.

Scholem also found an entirely different path to tradition, a more Jewish path focused on entirely different aspects of tradition. On this path, his most important interlocutor was the founder of neo-Orthodox Judaism, Samson Raphael Hirsch, who opposed attempts to reform Judaism or adjust Jewish life and practices to modernity, especially to the surrounding German bourgeois society of the nineteenth century. Hirsch once famously asserted that legitimate reform means that "we have to educate and elevate our generation toward the heights of the Torah, but not lower the Torah to the level of the times."[19] He became a powerful moral and political critic of Enlightenment universalism and secularism, claiming that it is possible to be both an observant Jew and a citizen in the modern world—as encapsulated in the formula *Torah im Derech Eretz* (Torah with the way of the land). Vehemently refusing to separate the kernel from the shell within Judaism, Hirsch argued against limiting Judaism to a rationally graspable idea. Even the abstruse commandments "express convictions in symbolic form" that are no less important than the actual precepts: "The care given to so-called trifles is no more ridiculous and no less reasonable than... attention to clear, intelligible diction or legible handwriting."[20] Hirsch's own exegeses in the Pentateuch commentary thus draw on the plenitude and abundance of detail in midrashic exegesis, which his contemporaries dismiss as contemptible Talmudic nitpicking. Beyond contributing to the tradition, Hirsch reframes it—for example, comparing Talmudic exegesis with natural science: "Moreover, just as the phenomena of nature remain facts

---

18. In discussion of Bloch's *Geist der Utopie*, Scholem also polemicizes against Bloch's Christology. In a letter from 1920, Scholem writes that all of Bloch's distortions of Judaism in this book are "only emanations of the central Christology that is foisted upon us here. To conceive of *corpus Christi* in *any* sense as the substance of our history is not possible for me" (*Story of a Friendship*, 109).

19. Hirsch, *Nineteen Letters*, 242. On Hirsch, see also Breuer, *Modernity within Tradition*.

20. Hirsch, *Nineteen Letters*, 183–184.

even though we may not have found their causes or interrelationships, and just as their existence does not depend on the results of our investigation—rather, the reverse is true—so, too, the commandments of the Torah are law even if we have not yet uncovered the cause and interrelationships of even a single one, and our fulfillment of the commandments in no way depends on the results of our investigation."[21] He reproaches classical as well as modern philosophy of religion for starting from the wrong side: "People should have taken a stand within Judaism and asked, 'Inasmuch as Judaism makes these demands upon us, what must be its view of the purpose of human life?' ... Instead, they took their stand outside Judaism and sought to adapt it to their viewpoint."[22]

Scholem was attracted to Hirsch because "never in his life did it occur to him to say Judaism and ..." (*T I*, 434), and he studied Hirsch's commentaries with great intensity and admiration from 1915 to 1918. Hirsch's striving for totality was just as appealing to Scholem as the aspiration to approach Judaism through the intensive reading of sources rather than from a modern philosophy. For Scholem, Hirsch was the only Jew of the nineteenth century to recognize that "the theory of Judaism is *not* the theory of an idea" (*T II*, 316). Taking the place of this idea is an emphasis on tradition and an altered view of the Torah. Early on, in light of Hirsch's mode of symbolic interpretation, Scholem speaks of his "internal tendency toward Jewish mysticism" (*T I*, 414), even referring to Hirsch as "Judaism's last mystic" (*T II*, 316).[23] But Scholem is also skeptical. Even when he concedes that "the driest 'juristic' deliberation in the Talmud is religious" (*LY*, 145), he takes offense at the teaching of divinity in halachic discussions: "For this is the upshot of the doctrine of sacredness: that one doesn't concede to the human spirit the capacity of making independent normative judgments about life. For this reason, in order to secure recognition, everything that supposedly has the force of law is connected up with God" (*LY*, 133). Most importantly, Scholem does not take the step of accepting the Orthodox way of life. Hirsch emphasizes again and again that the commandments are not only the expression of symbols but that they are to be enacted, and one must take the meaning of the commandments for one's own life as a starting point.[24] Scholem hesitates, however, musing about a more

---

21. Hirsch, *Nineteen Letters*, 272n.
22. Hirsch, *Nineteen Letters*, 266.
23. Schweid is right to emphasize the "ambivalence in feeling and thought" of Scholem's relation to Orthodoxy (*Judaism and Mysticism*, 157).
24. Hirsch, *Nineteen Letters*, 181. As we have seen, Hirsch derives the possibility of his symbolic exegesis from the *validity* of individual commandments.

complex relationship between action and knowledge and also between history and the present—a decisive qualification that I will discuss in further detail below.

Much later, in a confrontation with Hirsch's successor Isaac Breuer in 1934, Scholem is far more critical of Hirsch, arguing that Hirsch's symbolic exegeses ultimately only serve to read bourgeois virtues and familiar ideas into the text of the Torah by means of the "most unrestrained allegorizing (which, as was customary then, mistakenly considered itself symbolism)," and "which logically and earnestly forbade itself access to mysticism and genuine symbols (in which not just any old 'ideas' are realized, but something which cannot be expressed or carried out)" (*MI*, 332).[25] Scholem calls this retreat "Kabbalah-phobia"—that is, the decision "to abrogate any deeper speculation which in a new and positive way might have led back to that world of the Kabbalah" (*MI*, 321). In the end, this is why Hirsch's program of *Torah im Derech Eretz* also led to assimilation: "The slogan, which was supposed to strengthen the Jewish backbone of the pious in a changed world, contributed more than any other to breaking it for him" (*MI*, 329).[26]

Despite his reservations, Scholem was able to learn from Molitor as well as Hirsch what it means to connect the question of the capacity for truth in language and teaching with the question of tradition. This led to a series of texts in which he relates his philosophical reflections on truth and language to questions of tradition. He argues against Hirsch that the question of the divinity of the Torah is only the "shell" for the "problem of truth" (*LY*, 152): "The Torah is not a law, just as Judaism is not religion. Torah is the transmission of God and divine things; it is the principle of the gradual rediscovery of the truth that is hinted at in writing but whose understanding has been lost" (*LY*, 153). The truth of the Torah thus becomes a special case of a general problem of truth. Indeed, in the Torah, the relationship of language and truth even "appears least problematic: as the language of God it must necessarily be the language of truth, of *every* truth" (*LY*, 149).

---

25. Hirsch's "symbolism" and his "separatism" were his "means of violence." "In a way that is not free of brutality, Hirsch *forced* what history denied him" (*T II*, 316).

26. This critique comes in the context of Scholem's polemic against Breuer, especially against his metahistorical claims. For Breuer, the Jew "wants to be a Jew and nothing but a Jew—but in a long, and certainly extremely dubious interpretation of the theocratic claim to sovereignty, he is forbidden to exist within the realm of secular history" (*MI*, 331); at the same time, the "triumphant re-entry of Kabbalah into orthodox thought" becomes manifest here (*MI*, 333).

Scholem expands on these thoughts in November 1916 in a longer note of around four print pages, with the title "On the Talmudists' Method of Research." The problem of purely analytical, logical thinking is that while it could lead to "continuously new truths," this "infinity would be indifferent, in human terms" (*T I*, 438)—a thought that vaguely resonates with the Kantian critique of pure speculation. Thought therefore requires a "regulative instrument": "This instrument is the Torah. With the Torah the problem of the relationship of language to truth does not need to be raised, or in any case is easily solved because the Torah is assumed to have arisen from the divine center" (*LY*, 155). Through this regulative instrument, Talmudic exegesis distinguishes itself from mere arbitrariness and speculation, and thus it can also be designated as true experience in the Kantian sense: "for Talmudic Judaism the Torah has been in the spiritual realm... what the physical world is for modern science: a place in which everything has a meaning, where nothing gets lost, and whose study—with the help of certain basic assumptions and regulative instruments—can go beyond logical schemata to produce an unending series of factual truths" (*LY*, 156). Here, Scholem transfers Cohen's notion of the continuum of experience onto exegesis, applying an epistemology that is more advanced in a certain sense. Whereas Hirsch grounded exegetic procedure in the positive validity of individual commandments, Scholem concentrates on the nexus of experience as an infinite process that obeys the "law of the *constancy of truth*" (*LY*, 156). The idea that the Torah "arises" in the divine realm also relates to Cohen's concept of origin, though Scholem does not offer further explanation of what he means by this. For now, as he emphasizes again and again, it is infinite connection that replaces recourse to the divinity of the Torah: "Seen absolutely, the Talmudic method of research, which *logically* does not build on the divinity, but rather on the *truth* of the Torah, must be able to establish itself without the foundation of the *Torah min hashamayim* [the Torah is from heaven], except that this would be infinitely difficult, indeed impossible in our time, because the absolute truth whose possession would be a requirement does not seem to be found yet" (*T I*, 441).[27]

Here, the term "Torah"—which Scholem always employs emphatically during this period—is meant to link exegesis to philosophy, as he also explains in a letter from August 1917. On the one hand, he understands Torah as "the principle according to which the order of things is fashioned," which he also refers to as "the language of God," but on the other hand, he characterizes it as "the

---

27. Translator's note: Hebrew words in citations from Scholem have been transliterated throughout.

network or embodiment of Jewish traditions," claiming that it is "recognizable in the traditions of men" (*LL*, 54). He proceeds to argue that while Torah in the sense of tradition is not "identical" to Torah in the sense of spiritual principle, it "*coincides*" (*Br I*, 89). Yet he does not clarify his meaning, and the critical question of the legitimacy of reading truth from the Torah occupies him again a short time later in the essay "On Lament." To further unfold this question, Scholem employs a different rhetoric—namely, that of paradox and irony.

TEN

PARADOX

Fragments of a System

PARADOX IS ONE OF THE most important figures of thought in Scholem's writing. His early crises revolve around the "gaping paradox in the life of a committed Zionist" (*LY*, 91), and—as explored in part 1—paradoxical formulations of communal loneliness or polemics of silence lead him to his own position. In his later texts, he repeatedly describes the paradoxical constitution of the Kabbalah, evident in its pointed formulations as well as in conceptions such as the sanctification of exile in *zimzum* or "redemption through sin" in Sabbatianism. Exploring paradox as a theoretical category and mode of writing in his early notes, Scholem also engages with other thinkers of paradox, primarily Søren Kierkegaard and German early Romantic thinkers such as Friedrich Schlegel and Novalis.

In Scholem's diaries from 1914 to 1916, Kierkegaard is one of the most frequently mentioned names.[1] Scholem styles himself after Kierkegaard's image: "In thinking about myself, I'm always comparing myself to him" (*LY*, 31), and he pronounces Kierkegaard a Jew (*T I*, 108), with a "faint trace of Old Testament humanity" (*LY*, 132). Rather than anthropological concepts such as fear and sin, Scholem finds Kierkegaard's dialectics of communication and of faith most significant. Faith is neither cognitive recognition nor immediate feeling for Kierkegaard but rather an absolute relationship to oneself, which by itself cannot be developed or imparted: "The paradox of faith is this, that there is an

---

1. Scholem read (at least in part) Georg Brandes's Kierkegaard book (*T I*, 41ff.), Kierkegaard's *The Instant* (ibid., 108, 245), *Concluding Unscientific Postscript* (ibid., 108), *Stages on Life's Way* (ibid. 145, 232, 237), *Philosophical Fragments* (ibid., 154), and *Fear and Trembling* (see *Br II*, 199–200).

inwardness which is incommensurable for the outward."[2] The paradox here is not that faith is somehow mystically ineffable but that it asks for the very expression that destroys it. Thus, it calls for a specific form of expression that can be found in paradox: "The 'how' of truth is precisely truth. It is therefore untruth to answer a question in a medium in which the question cannot arise."[3] Communication about faith is deeply ambiguous, and rather than synthesis, Kierkegaard's dialectics leads to a "thoroughly analyzed and conscious ambivalence, sufficiently dialectically conscious of itself to not reject what it arises from and what nourishes it: doubleness.... One can call this ambiguity that is Kierkegaard's element a nihilistic vacuum, or one can call it the space of the simple that never develops."[4] Even when Kierkegaard appeals for the "leap" into faith, this faith is always linked with doubt and demonic desperation.

Kierkegaard's ambivalence is crucial for Scholem from the outset. Retrospectively, he relates that in his youth he lived "on the razor-thin border between religion and nihilism" (*Br I*, 471). Indeed, there are various statements on doubt and desperation in his diaries—for example, from the end of 1914, after reading Kierkegaard: "I would like to pray, but can't.... I can't utter the thing that always brings me back to Kierkegaard: his *Credo, quia absurdum est*.... I can't even say *I believe*. No, I can only hope" (*LY*, 31). Elsewhere he writes: "Over the past century the old heaven has been so completely torn to bits that it's now gone forever" (*LY*, 47), and further: "God is insufferable" (*LY*, 60). Scholem no longer has any desire to study, and he wants to "break the habit" (!) of running to the synagogue (*T I*, 87). In addition to his inability to pray, Scholem speaks of his fear of the Bible and cites Kierkegaard's self-stylizing in *Stages on Life's Way*: "He was a thinker, but didn't pray; a preacher, but didn't believe; he could help many others, just not himself" (*LY*, 31).

Scholem emphasizes Kierkegaard's doubtful and demonic side, thereby distancing himself from existentialist Kierkegaard reception among Jews who stress the moment of individual decision. Scholem rejected this tactic already when discussing the youth movement: "Leaping over the chasm is no solution to the problem. We can't leap" (*LY*, 59). In his discussion of Kierkegaard as well, Scholem puts tradition in the place of decision or experience: "At the very core of Judaism lies the belief that there is a [tradition (*Überlieferung*)] from God, and this is something no modern man can grasp. This is the point that Kierkegaard never understood, which comes out clearly in his brand of

---

2. Kierkegaard, *Fear and Trembling*, 79.
3. Kierkegaard, *Concluding Unscientific Postscript*, 270.
4. Nordentoft quoted in Deuser, *Kierkegaard*, 15.

Christianity. I erred grievously when I believed that Kierkegaard had been a Jew" (*LY*, 145–146).[5] More than simply the answer to the question that Kierkegaard poses, tradition is itself implicated in the dialectics of communicability. This problem remains central for Scholem. In 1947, in response to Hugo Bergmann's suggestion that he should speak about religion directly, not as a historian, Scholem writes: "I no longer believe in direct 'messages,' nor can I find among the 'messengers' anyone who could have brought some blessing. I tend to believe that it is precisely this naïve appeal to others... that lies behind the failure of such attempts" (*LL*, 340–341). Not only a rhetorical mask, Scholem's indirectness of communication also has its own dialectics: "I live in despair and can be active only out of despair" (*LL*, 341). Here, too, the ascetic ethos of keeping silent is deeply ambivalent, for while desperation stands behind irony, behind desperation stands irony once again.[6]

In Scholem's youth, engagement with Kierkegaardian dialectics coupled with his interest in the theory of "teaching" led to the adoption of a new idiom involving the concepts and forms of the German early Romantics. In this he followed Benjamin, who in 1917 and 1918 was working on his dissertation on the early Romantic concept of art criticism. In a letter from the summer of 1916, Benjamin already suggests to Scholem that "romanticism seeks to accomplish for religion what Kant accomplished for theoretical subjects: to reveal its form. But does religion have a *form*?? In any case, under history early romanticism imagined something analogous to this."[7] Benjamin thus reads the early Romantics in a transcendental framework in order to carry out the expansion of the Kantian concept of experience beyond science.[8] Similarly, Scholem uses the Romantics' ideas to relate the problem of tradition to epistemo-critical questions and to a pointed concept of mysticism that will be essential to his later interpretation of the Kabbalah.

We have already seen how Cohen dissolves Kant's notion of intuition and positions the continuum of (scientific) experience in its place. Benjamin attempts

---

5. Translation slightly modified.
6. See also Ernst Simon's interpretation of this silence as a "form of indirect communication in the sense of the young Kierkegaard," in which "the partial silence of indirect communication... [is] to be understood as God's silence, and thus as a declaration to God" ("Über einige theologische Sätze," 162).
7. Benjamin, *Correspondence*, 89.
8. Benjamin's dissertation strives to "break as harshly as possible with depraved notions of the 'Romantic' in the sense of a formless poetry of the unconscious or the dark nightside of experience" (Menninghaus, *Unendliche Verdoppelung*, 52). See also Steiner, *Die Geburt der Kritik*, 17ff.

to think this infinite continuum of experience with the early Romantic notion of reflection. Similarly to Cohen, Benjamin does not want to accept any foundation in original sensible passivity, instead conceiving of reflection as immediate: "Only with reflection does that thinking arise on which reflection takes place. For this reason, we can say that every simple reflection arises absolutely from a point of indifference. One is at liberty to ascribe to this indifference-point of reflection whatever metaphysical quality one likes."[9] Reflection is medial in the same way that language is medial: it is not a tool applied to what is already given but a field in which objects first come to appear. Thus, Benjamin speaks of Romantic theory on the whole as a theory of the medium of reflection.[10]

Consequently, reflection is also infinite: it has no exterior that limits it. Benjamin is careful to distinguish this observation from Cohen's central notion of infinite progress. It is an "axiomatic presupposition" for the Romantics "that reflection does not take its course into an empty infinity, but is itself substantial and filled," and the progression of reflection "is not at all what it is understood by the modern term 'progress.' . . . Like the entire life of mankind, it is an infinite process of fulfillment, not a mere becoming"; Benjamin apodictically links this distinction to "Romantic messianism," but he is not able to develop this in his dissertation.[11] His thinking on reflection as "fulfilled" in the sphere of art resurfaces in the final section, in reference to Goethe's notion of an "ideal" of art: "Just as, in contrast to the idea, the inner structure of the ideal is discontinuous, so, too, the connection of this ideal with art is not given in a medium but is designated by a refraction."[12] For Benjamin, fulfillment does not represent an

---

9. Benjamin, "The Concept of Criticism in German Romanticism," in *Selected Writings*, vol. 1, 134. Menninghaus calls this a "reinterpretation of reflection from a form of mediate and disjunctive thought to *the* form of 'immediate' and 'intuitive thought'" (*Unendliche Verdoppelung*, 32), pointing to the "polemical absence of Schelling" in Benjamin's dissertation (ibid., 54), which systematically excludes the question of the basis of reflection.

10. Benjamin introduces the term "Reflexionsmedium": see *Gesammelte Schriften*, vol. 1, 36–37; "The Concept of Criticism," in *Selected Writings*, vol. 1, 132. The concept of the medium is already present in the theory of language developed in Benjamin's essay "On Language as Such," where language is defined as medial, immediate, and endless. See Benjamin, "The Concept of Criticism," in *Selected Writings*, vol. 1, 62–74. See also Weber, *Benjamin's -abilities*, esp. chapter 4.

11. Benjamin, "The Concept of Criticism," in *Selected Writings*, vol. 1, 129, 168, 117. "Benjamin could not have more blatantly exposed a core of his presentation to the randomness of arbitrary acceptance" (Menninghaus, *Unendliche Verdoppelung*, 37).

12. Benjamin, "The Concept of Criticism," in *Selected Writings*, vol. 1, 179. This refraction means that the works cannot "attain to" their archetypes; "they can resemble them only in a more or less high degree" (ibid., 180).

achievement deferred to the future, nor the complete imparting of what is to be achieved in reflection, but rather a moment of break, of difference.

Scholem takes up this theory of the medium of reflection for the sake of "recapturing the dignity of knowledge as an immediate relationship" (*LY*, 194)—that is, in order to continue the philosophical project of overcoming Kantian dualism. While this project is accompanied by parallel aesthetic reflections for Benjamin, Scholem relates the notion of the medium to religious tradition, as already indicated in the text on lament. Operating within and by means of this tradition, he tries to resolve philosophical questions while at the same time gaining a new understanding of tradition.

In the summer of 1918, Scholem writes the short text "On Talmudic Style," picking up on his argumentation from "On the Talmudists' Method of Research" while no longer reading midrashic exegesis as experience in the world of the Torah but as infinite reflection and thus as a medium in the sense of Benjaminian early Romanticism. He starts with the predominance of the *question* in the Torah: "The Talmud is based on the only legitimate kind of question: the medial," which "knows no answer, that is, its answer must essentially be a question again," for which reason the Talmud has "powers of any height, which never leave the medial" (*T II*, 311–312). Scholem adopts Cohen's model of experience as the infinite exchange of questions and projects it onto tradition, stressing the infinity of the process, which cannot be limited from the outside. Any "attempt at an answer within Jewish orders (for example, in *real* dialogue) is a priori determined to fail. Thus, ultimately Jewish philosophy of religion exists... only on a foreign basis. In Jewish terms, the *system* of the *answer* is the purely demonic. The answer is the magic that is forbidden" (*T II*, 312).

Along with questions, silence plays a central role here. In Scholem's account of lament, language is related to silence. In his theoretical reflections, as in his polemics against the youth movement, Scholem links silence to teaching: "The sphere of the teaching knows only *one* foundation and requirement: that of silence" (*T II*, 197). Yet silence is no longer simple, passing again and again into expression: "To the extent that the Teaching relates to consciousness, *the Teaching is passed on in silence*. The passages in which the Teaching breaks through silence are double points of the Teaching. It is there that the Teaching's relationship to *life* becomes dialectical" (*LY*, 194). Like lament, it is figured by a border that it continuously transgresses. In another formulation, Scholem writes: "Teaching is transmitted in (not through) silence" (*T II*, 204). Thus, considerations on the relationship of esoteric and exoteric tradition are negotiated in the language of communicability. In the essay, these considerations are also related to Jewish traditional literature: "In Talmudic style, the art of keeping a secret ... has become material content. Not what is said, but what is kept silent [*das Verschwiegene*] is the actual transmission in it" (*T II*, 311). Another way of expressing this dialectics is through the idea of abbreviation, shaped by Molitor: "The abbreviation is the transition to silence, in that script as abbreviation no longer expresses anything.... Within script, the abbreviation abandons the literary. It becomes the merely signifying, and in the *Siddur Ya'avetz* it finally becomes the interpret*able* as such. In this work, whose abbreviations no one can read, the principle of abbreviation operates ironically ad absurdum" (*T II*, 331).[13] In these formulations, Scholem is already developing his notion of the infinite interpretability of scripture, which will be highly significant for his reading of the Kabbalah as well as his later theological reflections. This notion has a strong political orientation, for if such a mute script lies at the heart of what is transmitted, "the disaster and misery of Jewish history is that the silent tradition was lost the moment men forgot how to be still" (*LY*, 265).

The adoption of ideas from early Romanticism also has a significant impact on the form of Scholem's thought, for the "theory of Judaism" that he has in mind can no longer be a "system of answers." Rather than dogmatism or *Ordnungslehre*, it has to be a theory of the question itself, as he articulates already when reading Cohen: "Judaism can only be raised to a higher power once: in philosophy. Philosophy is the autonomous answer, not to the question posed by Judaism, but answer as theory of the question" (*T II*, 333). Scholem's theory would thus be a reflection that determines the problem (the origin) of his object of study, and philosophy would not solve the problem of Judaism—similarly to the Talmud, which never offers a response—but it would allow for the formulation of the "problem of the problem." The implication is that philosophy will be something more than a philosophy of the Talmud—namely, a Talmudic philosophy that takes its place as a question in the continuum of questions.

Yet what is this unformulated problem of the Talmud that is up for investigation? It seems to be the question of the "fulfillment" of reflection pointed to by Benjamin in his rather enigmatic statements about Romantic messianism and Goethe. With respect to the Talmud, it would be this fulfillment that distinguishes Talmudic reflection from the bad infinity of mere speculation. In "On

---

13. See also Scholem's distinction: "Talmudic abbreviation is the sublimation of an acquaintance, the kabbalistic is the sublimation of a stranger. The secrets that one does not know have no names, only an abbreviation" (*T II*, 331). At the same time, Scholem also reflects on other formal phenomena of transmission, for example, the mosaic style that he designates as "commentary in the text," founded in the "mystical paradox ... that transforms the canonical word into the poetically (*traditionally*) determined" (*T II*, 356).

Talmudic Style," this is expressed in the question of the borders or limits of the Talmudic. Even if the medium of the Talmud is infinite, for Scholem it still relates back to "canonical style, which is that of the Bible," and unlike Talmudic style, this cannot be reflected or "raised to a higher power" (*T II*, 312). As he did with lament, Scholem compares the language of the Talmud to another form of language. One way to think of this is to conceive of oral teaching as "commentary" on the written Torah: "Commentary is the inner form of oral teaching, only accomplished in this teaching. Commentary is legitimate interpretation: in the end, there can only be commentary on the Bible, the *absolute* written work" (*T II*, 198). Through this relation to the canonical, commentary is not the infinite process of mere speculation or casuistry but an actual experience that has its own substance and fulfillment. Like the relationship between idea and ideal for Benjamin, this fulfillment turns out to be extremely strained and discontinuous.

Reception of early Romanticism is significant not only in how it relates to the shift of Kantian questioning toward religion and history but also in how it changes the form of Scholem's theoretical writing. This change proves remarkably productive. Beginning in the fall of 1917, Scholem's diaries become more extensive, and he also writes numerous general fragments—partly in his diaries, partly in separate collections such as "Short Notes on Judaism"— which clearly follow the pattern of early Romantic fragments. Differently than in German idealism, the figure of the "reflection of reflection" is more than speculative—and thus constructive—for the early Romantics. It is also critical, posing the question of how a post-Kantian philosophy could even be presented. For Friedrich Schlegel, "the communicability of the true system can only be a limited one; this can be proved a priori."[14] In their attempt to be systematic and unsystematic at the same time, Schlegel's fragments are critical engagement with systems thinking avant la lettre: "It is equally fatal for the spirit [*Geist*] to have a system and to have none. Thus it must resolve to combine both."[15] Benjamin explicitly characterizes this fragmentary writing as "mystical," arguing that Schlegel uses a "mystical terminology" to seek "a noneidetic intuition of the system, and he finds this in language. Terminology is the sphere in which his thought moves beyond discursivity and demonstrability."[16] Fragmentary

---

14. Schlegel quoted in Benjamin, "The Concept of Criticism," in *Selected Writings*, vol. 1, 139.

15. Schlegel, *Werke*, vol. 2, 173 (Athenäums-Fragment no. 53).

16. Benjamin, "The Concept of Criticism," in *Selected Writings*, vol. 1, 139–140. Schlegel's comment on limited communicability shows "how consciously Schlegel felt himself to be a mystic even in his early period" (ibid., 139).

writing can thus be understood as an experimental form that is a "reflection of reflection" of a philosophical system not yet at hand.

As we will see, Scholem has further recourse to the model of mystical terminology when he begins to reflect on the Kabbalah (see chap. 14). Initially, he employs mysticism in philosophical terms, for instance when he describes Kant as a "mystic of the greatest style" (*Br I*, 169), whose "mythical objectivity" leads him to an "undesired anticipation of an order related to the Romantic" (*T II*, 315). Above all, the discussion of mysticism and the form of the fragment allow Scholem to shift into a different praxis of self-fashioning. He no longer sees himself as an ideologue of Zionism, much less as its myth-bringer, but rather as an esoteric critic. Reflecting in December 1918 on why he finds writing so difficult, he notes, "I think not in thoughts but in systems," and for this reason he cannot produce anything: "I am a composer of symbolic literature comprehensible only to myself. . . . But I would transmit the system of philosophy (which is certainly paradoxical) only as an eminently Jewish paradox" (*LY*, 287).[17] Precisely because tradition is a medium for Scholem and not a system of answers, fragments can take their place in this medium. They themselves are questions raised to a higher power, and as questions, they, too, can be handed down. Lonely writing that is only comprehensible to itself thus becomes part of tradition, and the paradox that it can be handed down but not communicated makes it all the more Jewish.

This paradox reaches a zenith in "95 Theses on Judaism and Zionism," which Scholem composed in the summer of 1918 as a birthday gift for Walter Benjamin. Apparently meant to invite joint discussion, this gesture was also an attempt at rapprochement in a moment when the relationship between the two friends—who had been living together for three months at that point—was going through a problematic phase. The ninety-five mostly short sentences make up approximately five print pages, ranging over a wide variety of themes, from linguistic and historical theory, to the theory of Judaism and Jewish tradition, to the critique of false Zionism. For example:

1) Judaism is to be deduced from its language.
2) Teaching is the sphere of double negation.

---

17. Here, too, the theory of the fragment has a critical function with respect to systematic presentation. Resistance to communication is particularly apparent in the theory of *Witz*, which is a "warning against what is ultimately Christian" (*LY*, 287). See also: "The joke [*Witz*] is the Torah that was already taught before the days of the Messiah, . . . its totality is torso, in essence, ironic totality. . . . In the form of the joke the transmit*able* [das Tradier*bare*] is transmitted" (*T II*, 368–369).

3) "He gave us teaching in the sign and elucidated it in tradition."
4) Strictly speaking, the rationalists only claimed that the divinity of the Bible lies in its humanity.
5) History is the term for the inner law of teaching.
6) Samson Raphael Hirsch denies the evil *instinct*.
7) Religions relate to each other as languages, without being languages.
8) "The just ones prepare the earth as the site of the divine."

...

15) "In teaching, there is no before and after."
16) Written tradition is the paradox in which Jewish literature essentially unfolds.

...

21) Zion is no metaphor.
22) Tradition is the absolute object of Jewish mysticism.
23) Samson Raphael Hirsch is the last kabbalist known to us.
24) The law of Talmudic dialectics is: truth is a constant function of language.
25) Jewish humor is the self-overturning of teaching.
26) No man has the right to be a Zionist for a reason.
27) Teaching is the medium in which the one who is learning is transformed into the one who is teaching. Scholars are the pupils of the wise.
28) In teaching, there is neither subject nor object. Teaching is a medium.

...

31) Commentary, i.e., legitimate interpretation, is the inner form of teaching.
32) Spoken, oral teaching consists of questions.

...

58) Teaching is transmitted in silence—not through silence.
59) Where teaching breaks through silence, its relation to life becomes dialectical. The outward history of teaching is based on this. (*T II*, 300–304)

At first glance, this text seems to confirm that the young Scholem's writing already contains the metaphysical germ of his entire thinking. A reader of

Scholem's later works can easily recognize central topics in this early text: the central role of tradition, the tension between spoken and written language, the strong notion of commentary, and so on. With minimal mention of the Kabbalah, we seem to see Scholem's thought in a "pure" form here, devoid of its historiographical veil.[18] Upon closer inspection, however, the theses appear deeply obscure. The twenty-second thesis—"Tradition is the absolute object of Jewish mysticism"—confirms that the young Scholem already sees a close connection between tradition and the Kabbalah, but it is not clear what exactly he means by "tradition," let alone "absolute object." Every individual thesis invites reference to others, suggesting systematic coherence. Any attempt to pin down this system quickly leads to frustration, however, as different possible connections open into a labyrinth rather than providing clarity. While the twenty-second thesis seems to refer back to the sixteenth thesis, the precise relation between the two is far from clear: Is tradition mystical in itself or only to the extent that it is subject to the paradoxes of a written tradition? Furthermore, we do not know whether "tradition" and "teaching" are synonymous or how they relate to each other if not. Finally, we could ask ourselves whether the twenty-third thesis follows the twenty-second thesis only accidentally, or whether it comments on its predecessor. The twenty-third thesis in turn refers back to the sixth, and so on. Despite their clear appearance and apodictic tone, the theses are by no means a system of definitions; more often than not, obscure terms are explained by other terms that are no less obscure.

At this point, it is helpful to consider the genesis of Scholem's "95 Theses" in older diaries and manuscripts. Compared to the clear-cut, generalized formulations of the final theses, these original drafts refer to specific situations. For example, take the fifty-eighth and fifty-ninth theses. As we have seen, these theses were first drafted in "Leave-Taking," Scholem's polemical letter against the Jewish youth movement, which in his view substituted talking for learning. If we keep this context in mind, we can roughly understand what Scholem means. However, can we be sure that this context still applies? In the form in which it is presented within "95 Theses," the thesis is devoid of any context and thus seems to have a general meaning, specified at most by the other theses. By

---

18. Only the seventy-sixth and seventy-eighth theses refer to the Kabbalah: "76. The Kabbalah calls God, the infinite, nothing as well. This is the true path of Jewish mysticism, leading to Hermann Cohen.... 78. The Kabbalah states: every language consists of the names of God" (*T II*, 305). In general, biblical and rabbinic context is much more prominent than the Kabbalah in "95 Theses." On the methodology of reading these fragments, see also Weidner, "Reading Gershom Scholem," as well as chapter 13 in this volume.

cutting the theses out of their original contexts, Scholem enacts a form of semantic closure that is typical of poetry: the terms used here have meanings that are both specifically rich and highly ambiguous. We can observe the same effect in the more theoretical theses—for example, twenty-four and twenty-eight. Scholem's similar formulations in longer, more argumentative texts such as "On the Talmudists' Method of Research" reveal how he grapples with different vocabularies and arguments. Yet in their thetic form they present themselves not as questions or problems but as answers—albeit answers to which we seem to lack the questions, more suggestive than discursive.

In other cases, a preliminary version of the thesis contains an important specification that is omitted in the final version, as in a predecessor of the very first thesis: "There is only *one* proof for Judaism: language. This insight is a paradox as long as it is not developed" (*T II*, 213). Or "Judaism must be able to be accessed from its language. This is the idea of Hirsch's Pentateuch commentary" (*T II*, 212). Even the citations from traditional literature or rabbinic sources are reduced; the fifteenth thesis—"'In teaching there is no before and no after,'" a quotation from the Babylonian Talmud (Pesachim 6b)—was originally followed by an explanatory comment: "That is, teaching is a medium" (*T II*, 206). Once again, the explanatory second sentence is omitted, thereby cutting off the relation to another term ("medium"), which is now only implied. As a result, the relation among the final theses remains vague. Their cohesion consists less in explicit relations or conjunctions than in the repetition of keywords such as "teaching" and "tradition." Moreover, due to their thetic form, their order also seems to be contingent: every reader can rearrange the theses differently, thereby coming to a different result. The procedures of condensation thus also result in a weakening of the systematic or syntactic structure.

Shifting perspective, it is helpful to focus on the form of "95 Theses," as it is their form that complicates understanding. While the logical syntax and thematic coherence is weak, a certain unity is generated by the recurring pattern of the thesis, and through title and date, which locate the text as a distinct utterance in time and space (even if the total of ninety-five should not be taken too seriously, as Scholem uses the number seventy-three twice, and there are actually ninety-six theses). The early Romantic fragment seems to be more significant than the literary paradigm of the Lutheran theses in terms of impact on Scholem's writing. As we have already seen, this form ironically refers to a totality that is impossible to express directly. The theses are clearly also modeled on classical rabbinic literature consisting mainly of "theses": rabbinic and midrashic texts often present themselves as collections of aphorisms by different sages, the meaning and order of which is often only implicit and difficult to conceive. The significance of this form for Scholem's aphorisms is revealed by his citation of such sayings—for example, in the third, eighth, and fifteenth theses. Here, more than writing *about* tradition, he writes tradition, copying and thus transmitting traditional sayings. The ease with which these sayings stand alongside his own aphorisms demonstrates that the latter are also in keeping with tradition, imitating the authoritative, succinct, and sometimes obscure sayings of the sages.

Thus, in addition to the direct, designative relation to tradition, there is an indirect, mimetic relation of formal resemblance at work in the text, implying a fictional moment: Scholem writes *as if* he were part of the tradition. In other words, the literary techniques explored above—the condensed and even paradoxical form of the thesis, integration of traditional citations, authoritative style, interrelation of different terms, lack of context and order—transform descriptive writing about tradition into a performative act that produces what it describes. More precisely, the text becomes descriptive and performative at the same time, thus undergoing an essential overdetermination. This is most clearly demonstrated by the sixteenth thesis: "Written tradition is the paradox in which Jewish literature essentially unfolds." First and foremost, this refers to historical tradition and the paradox that in Judaism the oral Torah is written down and even canonized. Second, the thesis refers to Scholem's problem of entering tradition from the outside, the paradox of writing as if he belongs to tradition. Finally, it refers to itself: by taking a traditional written form while at the same time confessing to be mere writing, the sixteenth thesis does what it describes, which is made possible by the terse form of the thesis and its elision of context.

Scholem's "95 Theses" thus constitutes a literary enterprise, an implicit attempt to inscribe himself into tradition. The theses' primary function is also to develop and practice a language that will enable Scholem to make this move, involving a set of terms—"tradition," "commentary," "paradox," "teaching," and so on—and the relations among them. However, this language and the form of the thesis also have their functional limits. As noted, such theses generate little coherence, and they can be continued indefinitely. To achieve closure, the text requires a specific situation and, above all, an addressee. Scholem's theses are addressed to Benjamin and thus linked to the project of their symphilosophy, a joint discussion in which the unity could have been realized. Yet Benjamin did not prove to be the reader that Scholem hoped for. He was not responsive to this gesture offered during a period of reciprocal estrangement, and the planned discussion of the theses never took place. After a couple of days, Scholem took the text back and kept it among his papers; the project of a theory of Judaism became more and more of a memory or an archive of ideas to be realized in another form, with isolated formulations and terms interspersed into later texts. But first, the failure of the thesis project led him to take up a form that he had already used in "On Lament and Lamentation"—namely, commentary on a biblical text. For lack of discussion with his friend, Scholem sought out another counterpart: the prophet Jonah.

ELEVEN

PROPHECY AND MESSIANISM
Rethinking History

AS WE HAVE SEEN, SCHOLEM'S project of learning the Jewish tradition did not begin with an encounter with the biblical texts but with the Talmud, in line with a more traditional Jewish education. Nevertheless, he also studied biblical text alongside Hebrew grammar, traditional commentaries, and modern Protestant biblical criticism. In the decisive years of 1917 and 1918, he was particularly engaged in studying the prophetic books, which were heavily contested among his contemporaries. Whereas liberal Jewish exegetes such as Hermann Cohen read the prophets as teachers of a social morality, Protestant exegetes either held fast to a conservative Christological interpretation—according to which the prophets announced the coming of Christ—or read them progressively as demagogues and charismatics who radically broke with the society of ancient Israel. What is at stake here is primarily the interpretation of messianism, which also determines much of Scholem's later conception of Kabbalah, as we will see in chapter 17.

Messianism is present in Scholem's writing from the outset. As we have seen, there was a time when Scholem imagined himself as messianic myth-bringer to the Jews, but he soon gave up on that idea. However, he returned to the category of messianism in discussions with Walter Benjamin, who declared messianism to be the core of Romanticism—albeit without elaborating on what he meant by this. Scholem's notebooks reveal that this was a topic of intense conversations between the friends—for example, in the fall of 1917, when Scholem notes: "The greatest image of history is to be found in the idea of the messianic realm. (History's endlessly deep relationship to religion and ethics arises out from this thought.) Walter once said that the messianic realm is always present, which is an insight of *stupendous* importance—though on a plane which I think no one since the prophets has achieved" (*LY*, 192). Here, speculation is no longer focused on the Messiah but on the "idea of the messianic realm," no longer as a person but as an "image of history." The meaning of the continuous presence of the messianic realm remains vague. Nine months later, in the summer of 1918, Scholem writes that he is "thinking a lot about the metaphysics of time in Judaism.... Hebrew grammar, Jewish history, the prophets, and encompassing them all, the Torah: these are my quarries" (*LY*, 254). He formulates a series of aphorisms on messianic time, some of which feed into the theses discussed above—for example, the notion that the "eternal present" is Judaism's temporal concept and that the time of Judaism is divided into four times: "The time of lament, historical time, the time of revelation, and messianic time are the most essential temporal orders of Judaism" (*T II*, 305). The meaning of these remarks only becomes clear in a text written a few months later, which Scholem read to Dora and Walter Benjamin in the fall of 1918: the approximately ten-page manuscript "On Jonah and the Concept of Justice." Alongside the text on lament, this is among the most important of Scholem's youthful writings, and it requires an in-depth reading.

The first thing to note is that the text takes the form of commentary, to which Scholem always already attributes a special significance. The texts comments on the biblical Book of Jonah, which seems to play the same kind of role that the imagined dialogue with Benjamin played for "95 Theses," giving the text structure and allowing Scholem to gather different ideas about messianism previously sketched in his diaries. To begin, his commentary emphasizes that the Book of Jonah is an extremely unusual prophetic book. While the other books of the prophetic canon largely consist of the words of the prophets, the Book of Jonah contains no prophecies at all, composed instead of a plot that is not without humor. Jonah receives the divine mandate to prophecy God's judgment on the city of Nineveh, and after some initial hesitation, he carries out this mission. Whereas biblical prophets deliver their prophecies in vain more often than not, Jonah is immediately successful in impelling Nineveh to repent, such that God does not enact judgment. Disgruntled, Jonah complains to God that God knew in advance that Jonah's prophecy would not be fulfilled and therefore hesitated. God causes a kikayon plant to grow to provide Jonah with shade but then causes it to wither. When Jonah becomes angry once again, God asks the rhetorical question that ends the book: "You have been concerned about this plant, though you did not tend it or make it grow. It sprang up overnight and died overnight. And should I not have concern for the great city of Nineveh...?" (Jonah 4:10–11).

Scholem's interpretation commences with attention to this atypical form. As the Book of Jonah does not contain any prophecies, it reflects the problem of prophecy in "mediumistic transparency," and thus it is the "very key to understanding the prophetic idea": "It presents the theory, one might say, for that which the other books deliver in detail."[1] This theory is indirectly communicated "to inaugurate a problem" in the structure of the book, the meaning of which Scholem emphasizes with a graphic depiction, a diagram that he refers to as a "symbolical representation, which is more than a simile."[2] Above all, the diagram accentuates the symmetry of question and answer, which is already familiar to us: "Every such inauguration expresses itself in a question, and precisely in this the highest education is achieved. The teacher educates through questions, not through answers."[3] The Book of Jonah poses questions in two ways. On the one hand, the book as a whole does not give an answer but shows a problem, thus presenting a question. On the other hand, questions also play a central role within the book, especially the closing question. God himself is the teacher: "That God himself gives the prophet instruction is the ultimate expression of the idea that the education in question here is truly the central and decisive education"; both aspects, divine education *in* the book and the form *of* the book represent instruction, encompassed for Scholem by a particular idea: "The object of this instruction is the idea of justice."[4] To develop the idea of justice, it is necessary to clarify the relationship between questions within the book and the question of the book itself.[5]

Instruction does not occur directly, through what is said, but indirectly, through the narrative. At first glance, this narrative also seems atypical for prophecy: the recalcitrant and hesitant Jonah is far from being a good example of a prophet. Yet precisely this feature is the key to the prophecy, according to Scholem. The conclusion in particular makes it clear that while Jonah misunderstands his assignment and thus prophecy, his misunderstanding is what allows the reader to understand prophecy. What constitutes Jonah's misunderstanding of the prophecy? Scholem hardly deals with the first part of the book—Jonah's evasion of the divine mandate—concentrating instead on his appearance in Nineveh and the consequences of that appearance. According

---

1. Scholem, "On Jonah and the Concept of Justice," 356, 353, 354.
2. Scholem, "On Jonah," 354.
3. Scholem, "On Jonah," 354.
4. Scholem, "On Jonah," 354.
5. Scholem emphasizes the significance of the speech *act* in the book of Jonah: "Command and question are the two antithetically oriented absolute acts of language's positing that enclose the entire domain of language asymptotically" ("On Jonah," 355). As categories of utterance, they are also set in relation to justice: "The positing of the question is the verdict of justice ...; the Book of Jonah ends with a question" (ibid., 358).

to Scholem, Jonah mixes up two understandings of prophecy—namely, judgment and foresight on the one hand and admonishment and warning on the other. Chapter 3, verse 4b, expresses this with a deeply rooted double meaning: "'Forty days more and Nineveh *is* overturned,' which from Jonah's standpoint is meant as a statement of fact, from God's standpoint as a warning."[6] Jonah believes that he is proclaiming a judgment of future events, but his true function is to admonish and warn so that the doom he prophesies does not actually come to pass. His success reveals what Scholem calls the "prophetic irony" that if the warning is effective the foresight is false, and vice versa.[7] For as mentioned, the common fate of biblical prophets is that their predictions of doom are ignored so that the negative outcome does occur, and the unheeded warning proves ineffective. With its unwilling, misunderstanding prophet and perfectly attentive audience, the Book of Jonah seems to present a reverse of the usual prophetic situation.

Scholem figures this misunderstanding in moral and legal terms: "Jonah takes the standpoint of the law, and from this side he is indeed in the right; God takes that of justice."[8] In a diary entry from the summer of 1916, two years earlier than the Jonah text, Scholem addresses this difference: "It is extremely important that in the Hebrew *mishpat* [law] and *zedakah* [justice] have entirely different stems. *Mishpat* is something human, *zedakah* divine. God's *mishpat* cannot reveal itself (Isaiah 58), but only his *zedakah*" (*T I*, 392). Here, justice is at the center of his attempts to understand Judaism: "The *essence of Judaism* is justice. A divine category.... In Judaism one does not have faith, but is just" (*T I*, 392). In fact, the biblical concept of justice—or righteousness, as *zedakah* is usually translated—does differ essentially from the idea of distributive justice in Greco-Roman legal thought: whereas the latter is represented by the blind Justitia giving to each his own part, biblical righteousness is represented by the master or ruler who helps those in need, as in the proverbial widows and orphans.[9] Rather than something formal, biblical righteousness designates a relationship of care and fidelity that initiates and upholds a state of just order, a relationship that unites both God and man and humans among themselves.

---

6. Scholem, "On Jonah," 357.
7. Scholem, "On Jonah," 356.
8. Scholem, "On Jonah," 357.
9. See the classic account in von Rad, *Old Testament Theology*, vol. 1, part II, D3. See Schmidt, *Gerechtigkeit als Weltordnung*, esp. 172–173, 181–182; justice is understood as a state of salvation that is to be restored if violated. See also Koch, "Sädaq und Ma'at," 55ff.; Assmann and Janowski, *Gerechtigkeit: Richten und Retten in der abendländischen Tradition und ihren altorientalischen Ursprüngen*.

It is by divine righteousness that God upholds his promise of salvation and thereby makes human righteousness possible, as broadly discussed and also problematized in prophecy. Calling human beings to justice and fidelity to God, the prophets simultaneously pose the question of the extent to which God still upholds his promise to "unjust" Israel and the question of how the world can be transformed into a just place.

Scholem suggests that these are precisely the questions addressed in the Book of Jonah. Jonah is formally in the right, and thus he cannot be refuted, but he can be indirectly instructed about God's saving righteousness that goes beyond retribution. The book's instruction is indirect insofar as it can only be presented through the interdiscursive logic of different speech acts and viewpoints. None of these speech acts in itself comprises justice. God does not proclaim justice; justice reveals itself through the threat of annihilation: "In the act of repentance, the law is overcome and the judgment is not carried out.... This, and nothing else, is the meaning of justice in the deepest sense: that judgment *is* allowed, but the execution of it remains something entirely different."[10] Jonah's legal viewpoint is too rash, for God's Word does not coincide with its lawful implementation. The deferral that God grants to Nineveh is what makes the prophetic proclamation into a proclamation of justice, and thus a revelation, as Scholem notes in an addendum to his theses: "Deferral [*Aufschub*], one of the central ethical orders, contains the basis of duration, the *being* of justice" (*T II*, 533). The concept of deferral plays a central role in his reflections on the difference between law and justice, which is not completely abolished but held in deference as a difference: "The Torah knows the death penalty; Talmudic law does not question it but enacts the idea of deferral by imposing an extraordinary burden of proof.... Through such a burden judgment is rendered practically impossible. The underlying idea, however, always remains the same: judgment is possible, its execution is not possible."[11]

Deferral thus breaks apart the identity of judgment and execution—a feature that Benjamin later explores as characteristic of a mythical understanding of law in his essay "Critique of Violence." For Scholem, the fact that judgment is not sublated in the process fundamentally differentiates Jewish justice from

---

10. Scholem, "On Jonah," 357.
11. Scholem, "On Jonah," 358. The requirement to do good deeds for those in need that is specific to the Jewish conception of righteousness is also understood by Scholem in terms of deferral: the poor are not to be judged differently than the rich, but judgment is to be deferred, and this deferral becomes manifest in good deeds: "Deferral that has become action is justice as deed" (*T II*, 528).

Christian love: "Love is the annihilation of judgment, justice that of the execution; one who loves does not judge. Justice and the law complement each other and coincide; love and the law exclude each other."[12] The Christian sublimation of judgment causes the dialectics of justice to disappear, splitting into law and mercy. At the same time, justice is not only the still-pending fury of a justice to come, an infinite task. In a note elsewhere, Scholem describes this purely future-based understanding of justice as another Christian misapprehension: "In their innermost structure, Jewish concepts are not border concepts, not *limites*. Justice, life, the end of days, sacredness, etc. are not mechanically, infinitely approximable regulative ideas, they are distinguished by the fundamentally new stance toward time. That which is *limes* can be anticipated: this is Christianity's secret" (*T II*, 361).

Rather than a perpetually pending better law or new covenant, justice is the substance of law by which it is fulfilled. Not an infinite task, justice is conceived as "the indifference of the Last Judgment" and at the same time as the condition of possibility of the messianic: "Were justice not present, then the messianic realm too would not only not be present but would be altogether impossible."[13] Thus, the temporality of deferral is not to be understood as strictly future oriented. More than just the difference between the present state and coming justice, it is what makes justice possible in the first place.

Jonah's misunderstanding consists in his "mechanical" understanding of the future. As noted above, Jonah misunderstands the sentence "Forty days more and Nineveh is overturned." The grammatical tense is indeed somewhat unspecific in Hebrew, as we will see.[14] This mistake is of central importance to Scholem: "The deep conflict of the Book of Jonah resides in Jonah's desire to see an identity between prophecy, which from an empirical point of view is a prediction of the future, and historiography, which is a prediction of the past.

---

12. Scholem, "On Jonah," 358.

13. "On Jonah," 357, 359. Scholem cites Maimonides here: "'The reason for what the wise men call the world to come is not that this coming world is not already present, and that only after the demise of this world the other one would come. This is not how things are; rather, that world is continually present'" (ibid., 359). See also Benjamin's reflections on the difference between gentile and Jewish notions of the Day of Judgment ("The Meaning of Time in the Moral Universe, in *Selected Writings*, vol. 1, 286–287), along with Bettine Menke's commentary ("Benjamin vor dem Gesetz," 249ff.).

14. Remarkably, Scholem does not address the dual meaning of *haphak*, which can mean "to destroy" as well as "to change." Furthermore, the preposition *'od* (more) stresses the length of time until the event more than the event itself. See Wolff, *Dodekapropheten*, vol. 3, 123–124.

The prediction about the future should not be any different from one about the past: Nineveh *is* annihilated *in* the prophecy (precisely from a historian's standpoint)."[15] It is because Jonah has a one-dimensional understanding of time that he understands the future as completed through God's proclaimed (lawful) vengeance: "For why does Jonah want to identify prophetism with historiography? It is clear that he is confusing the eternal and the noneternal present. In Nineveh he is supposed to make a prediction about the eternal present, but he himself considers this prediction as bearing on the noneternal one. The times that *transform* themselves within the eternal present are supposed to be identical."[16] Jonah's misunderstanding consists in a schematic understanding of time that situates justice in a determinable future, whereas it actually exists in coming, and at once it has always already come: "In the same way that the world to come already exists, the justice to come also exists. This coming is its unfolding; *zedakah* does not become but reveals, unfolds itself (Isaiah 56:1). Its coming is only the breaking through of the shining medium through a darkening."[17]

In his commentary, Scholem expands on the basic principles of this prophetic misunderstanding and the difference between linear time and the eternal present. Drawing on considerations previously developed elsewhere, he explores four additional factors: the Hebrew language, specifically its organization of grammatical tenses; the normative content of Jewish tradition, especially the significance of the commandments; the relationship between the different parts of Jewish tradition, especially Torah, prophecy, and oral tradition; and finally, the theory of revelation itself. Once again, Scholem uses a particular text—the commentary on Jonah—as an occasion to summarize different considerations and bring them into relation with one another.

The Hebrew language plays a role here insofar as Jonah's misunderstanding of time is also a concrete misunderstanding of the Hebrew tenses. The connection between language and time in Hebrew is something that Scholem was already grappling with before writing the Jonah essay, as demonstrated by his diaries: "All of this is intimately tied to the metaphysics of Hebrew, whose designation of Time is able to offer us the deepest possible clues" (*LY*, 246). He focuses mainly on three grammatical properties of Hebrew. The first point relates to the jussive, which in Hebrew can express an imperative but usually cannot be distinguished from the imperfect, which serves to convey posteriority as well

---

15. Scholem, "On Jonah," 356–357.
16. Scholem, "On Jonah," 360.
17. Scholem, "On Jonah," 359–360.

as general facts and circumstances. The Decalogue, for example, is formulated in the jussive and should be translated as: "Thou shalt not . . ." Scholem speaks here of "the general presentation of the present through the future." He interprets this as ethical—"The future is a *command*, just as is the command in the present, *to be*"—and substantiates this ethics in connection to divine speech by taking Lev. 19.2 as his example: "*Kedoshim thuju*, 'you should be holy,' that is to say, you should be, meaning both that you will be and that you are. You *are* holy because I am holy. *Only* this is the meaning of the command to spread holiness into the present moment" (*LY*, 246). As in the case of prophetic irony, we see a connection between different speech acts (divine and human) constituting transformation.

The second point developed by Scholem has to do with the wav-form in the biblical tense system. In Hebrew, the addition of the prefix "wav," which on its own means "and," transforms a verb form from the past to the present and vice versa. This form is also called wav consecutive, or narrative, because it is used primarily to convey a continuous action in the past, as in this example: "Ezra opened (perfect) the book and read (wav imperfect: 'and will read') from it, and the people listened (wav imperfect: 'and will listen') all day long." Scholem interprets this form explicitly as a transformation of time: "What happens here? *Time is transformed through fusion*: the past is in the future and the future is in the past. How does this happen? Through the vehicle of the present. The conception of Time as the Wav ha-Hippuch is the messianic Time. Only the name of God guarantees the metaphysical possibilities of this grammatical construction. Only what can happen again has happened" (*LY*, 246).

Thus, the structure of the Hebrew tenses serves as a paradigm for the dialectics of deferral.[18] Linguistics, theology, and metaphysics are related in the name of God. Once again, we are not dealing with a purely linguistic-theoretical construction. The assertion is "guaranteed" in God's name, for, as Scholem notes on another occasion, this name also has a temporal structure in Exodus 3:14: the famous *ehyeh asher ehyeh* (I will be who I will be): "The God who 'will be' demands from Time that it 'will be.' But just as God *is*, so *is* Time" (*LY*, 246). Third and finally, Scholem interprets a combination of the two other cases, when a command is expressed in the future through the wav imperfect: "a

---

18. In the Jonah essay, Scholem goes into detail regarding the *va-yehi* (and it was so), which opens the book and constitutes the wav imperfect of "to be, to happen": "Although the episodic 'and' is entirely customary in the usage of historical narrative, perhaps it may be permitted here to take it in its original meaning as a symbol of the infinitude of the event in which God's word goes out to Jonah" ("On Jonah," 360).

command in Wav ha-Hippuch may be spoken out in the *past*, as an obligatory past. *'Ve 'ahavta'*—You shall love, which is a command that can only be made because you have already loved. The most overpowering thing of all is when the messianic realm makes an appearance in language because messianic beams of light elevate the past. Only a *Jewish* language is capable of such construction" (*LY*, 247). The wav tense constitutes a space in which justice can be presented, as already formulated in "95 Theses": "The time of the Wav ha-Hippuch [wav consecutive] is messianic time" (*T II*, 305).

Along with the Hebrew language, Jewish tradition and the relation of its different parts also factor into Scholem's reflections. Prophecy connects both to the written Torah, the Mosaic books, on the one hand and the oral Torah, rabbinic commentary, on the other: "Torah, prophetism, and tradition are the three parts . . . of the Jewish system. None can be thought through to the end without the other" (*T II*, 359). These three parts help to determine what justice is, according to preliminary notes for the Jonah essay: "The written Torah cannot be executed. It is revelation. Understood ethically, revelation is the *limes* of all implementability, *limes* not in the sense of the convergence of the whole series on revelation, but that it is the *immediate limes* of *every* individual act altogether" (*T II*, 355). If justice is the content of revelation, conceived as distinct from execution and law, then the written Torah cannot be thought of simply as a law book.

Retrospectively, Scholem highlights the question of how to implement the Torah as the context of the Jonah text. As he recounts in *Story of a Friendship*, he read the text to Walter and Dora Benjamin, who had asked him why he did not take on the Orthodox way of life given his strong emphasis on Jewishness: "At that time I formulated my explanation something like this: for me that manner of life was connected with the concretization of the Torah in a false, premature sphere—as evidenced by the paradoxes of the tricks that become manifest in the process. . . . Something is wrong with the application; the orders clash. I said I had to maintain the anarchic suspension."[19] "Trick" (*Dreh*) is the common designation for regulations effectively overriding commandments that are recognized in principle. For example, the commandment of the Jubilee year can be circumvented in a manner that is legal in the halachic sense by

---

19. Scholem, *Story of a Friendship*, 89. See also *T II*, 401, and a precursor to the text in *T II*, 335–336. The notion of "concretization in a false sphere" can be found in Scholem's diaries as early as February 1918: see *T II*, 140. Scholem's retrospective commentary that this question had been "disposed of" (*Story of a Friendship*, 89) conceals the significance that it continued to hold for him.

transferring land to non-Jews or non-Orthodox Jews. For Scholem, this shows that the Torah cannot be understood simply as a collection of commandments. The justice that reveals itself only indirectly in the Torah is made possible via prophetic irony and the deferral of justice—via "anarchic suspension"—and the Torah is not sublated or superseded as a result.

The practical consequences that Scholem draws from this conclusion are also formulated in a letter to Erich Breuer from 1919:

> I have always, unambiguously, declared myself to be a skeptic in terms of the concrete manifestation of the Torah today (and I have very specific reasons for this, chief among them being the "unavoidable bending of the rules"). Though I don't know if it's of any use, I am always prepared to be convinced one way or the other. And this *concretization* of the Torah (and not what one can call the Torah itself, which is a spiritual power; this sounds silly, and I won't bind myself to the expression—the Torah is an agent, a mediator between realms, an agent through which something breaks and appears: in particular, the idea of the just life and of history). (*LL*, 100)

Scholem "confesses" his point of view—namely, that of the skeptic and anarchist who nevertheless considers himself bound to "the Torah itself"—a point of view that corresponds to the anarchistic confession of pure Zionism from within Zion. This not only gives Scholem a certain freedom and independence with respect to the halachic way of life but also makes it possible for him to acknowledge these requirements in principle without implementing them in practice. As in the case of the ideology of "Zion," this confession is effective because Scholem adds to his own idiom, in this case by articulating the idea of deferral.

Based on the idea of deferral, Scholem can also formulate the relationship of tradition to the canonical in the Jonah essay, taking up the question of the "fulfillment" of tradition:

> In Judaism it is the idea of justice that designates the relationship of the canonical to tradition. Without this idea, tradition and the canonical remain strangers without any actual connection to each other. But precisely in the justice that arises from the canonical, tradition is attained and founded at the deepest level. For the idea of tradition means just this: the (written) Torah cannot be applied. It is the Law of God, the right that is not yet justice but rather transforms into it in the unending deferral of tradition. In it, revelation and messianic time are bound together inseparably.[20]

---

20. Scholem, "On Jonah," 359.

Justice manifests via the detour of prophetic irony, mediated through tradition. Scholem understands "the canonical" neither as an applicable law nor as something entirely different from the law; the function of the canonical is rather to establish tradition as an unapplied, deferred law. Insofar as revelation is meant to reveal God's justice, it already implies tradition, for justice can only show itself as a transformation in the eternal present that finds expression in tradition. Correspondingly, Scholem also characterizes the "unending deferral" through tradition using the previously developed dialectics of question and answer:

> The question is an unending cycle; the symbol of this infinitude ... is the rhetorical question. This ("Jewish") question can be justly characterized as medial; it knows no answer, which means its answer must in essence be another question; in the innermost basis of Judaism the concept of an answer does not exist. In the Torah there are neither questions nor answers. The Hebrew word for answer is *teshuvah*, which, correctly translated, means: response, reversal—reversal of the question, that is, which is assigned a new value and thus returns, as it were. Viewed in this way the principle of Talmudic dialectics is easily comprehensible.[21]

The "infinitude" of the medium of tradition can always also be understood as deferral in the unending continuum of questions. In addition to the relationship between tradition and the canonical, Scholem addresses the canonical itself. In the Jonah essay, he briefly mentions the Book of Job, viewed in parallel with the Book of Jonah: "Both books are themselves questions; both offer no answer, rather the question itself is the solution"; yet in spite of this structure, they differ radically: "Its object—God's justice—seems the same yet nevertheless totally different, for in the very last instance Job questions what cannot be questioned about this justice, what eludes all prophecy and is incommensurable with it. But Jonah presents precisely what can be questioned about justice (*not* the answerable, for that does not exist at all), and this is the root of prophetism."[22]

Scholem thus introduces a further element into his theory of question and answer—"what cannot be questioned" (*das Nichterfragbare*)—and radicalizes it: Jonah asks about God's law, a question that proves to have no object, since

---

21. Scholem, "On Jonah," 356. See the very similar formulation in "On Talmudic Style": "The Hebrew word for answer is *teshuva*, that is, correctly translated, rejoinder. Reversal, namely of the question that gains a new inflection and returns, so to speak. The only possible concept of the answer is the religious concept in the meaning of answering a prayer (*ana*)" (*T II*, 311).

22. Scholem, "On Jonah," 355–356, 356.

"the boundary of the 'good' versus the 'real'" that would constitute the law is only "a metaphysical semblance."[23] The question finds no answer, only indirect instruction, demonstrating the difference between law and justice, which in Scholem's words is "what can be questioned" about God's justice.

For Job, in contrast, the "boundary of the 'good' versus the 'real'" is not metaphysical semblance "but only because a question is raised that is not fitting for us—that is the irony of Job."[24] The meaning of Scholem's statement is clarified in a series of notes from the same period. The Book of Job is also ironic: "by wanting to teach a certain attitude but not expressing that attitude, it takes the opposing stance" (*T II*, 376). The book ironically raises the question of theodicy while teaching that it is not a meaningful question: "That which is not a demand to justice is not to be inquired about; in principle, it has no object in human areas. God's justice is no problem. Prophetism cannot be pushed too far, or raised to a higher power" (*T II*, 376–377). What can be questioned of God's justice is only that which is portrayed in the Book of Jonah—namely, the boundary separating justice from law and thus from what is human. Justice appears only in prophetic proclamation, which—when the task is understood correctly—criticizes human law through God's justice; beyond this no question is possible. Job's inquiry goes beyond the medium, so to speak, and therein lies his relationship to lament as language of the boundary or limit: "In its first part, the Book of Job is a lament, and the—naturally—futile attempt to respond to lament. For if someone has seen the boundaries that extend all around his life, he is right to lament.... His friends do not understand this, they do not want to comfort, but to respond. Yet only God can respond to lament, and this principle is confirmed by the second part" (*T II*, 378).

The structure of the Book of Job itself contributes to indirect instruction. Job inquires into God's justice, and in the course of the following discussion, "it is shown that, once raised, the question is not answerable or refutable. *Job is in the right*" (*T II*, 377). Herein lies the decisive difference between Job and Jonah, according to Scholem: unlike Jonah, Job's irrefutability is not based on mistaking law and justice—that is, on a "metaphysical semblance." Job also does not "mechanically" ask for retribution; he only asks to return to a just relationship with his God. Nevertheless, the question has no object, as demonstrated by the middle section of the book: "In the endlessness of the circling discussions,

---

23. Scholem, "On Jonah," 356.
24. Scholem, "On Jonah," 356.

it is made symbolically visible that there is no legitimate question here" (*T II*, 377). The book does not end there, however. Job increases his complaints in the course of the dialogue, ultimately challenging God to a legal battle. God appears to answer Job's complaints: "Who is this that obscures my plans with words without knowledge? Brace yourself like a man; I will question you, and you shall answer me. Where were you when I laid the earth's foundation? Tell me, if you understand" (Job 38:2–4). For Scholem, the key to the book lies in God's counterposition: "But he does not *answer*, he does not *decide*, he does not *teach*. Instead, he *asks* in return, but—and this is the most tremendous symbol of what this book has to say—whereas Job had asked on an (apparently) *ethical* level, indicting God on *history*, God asks and answers with a question about *nature*, cosmogony. This is irony. God is speaking about something that the argument seemingly was not about" (*T II*, 377).

There is no discussion, no encounter between man and God, but God "ironically reflects the question [and thus] he shows Job that his own question is no good" (*T II*, 377). In spite of this, God does not judge Job, but he does judge the friends who had attempted to answer Job's question. Scholem seems to assume that the legal battle that does not take place has a salubrious effect nevertheless, since here, too, the law is annihilated: "The orders of the court are overthrown, and at the bottom of this overthrow dwells the great insight that God cannot be defended—just as God judges, gives evidence for, and indicts others, but never defends *himself*, always only others" (*T II*, 377). It appears that the question of God's justice is real, but not to be asked. Prior to writing the Jonah text, Scholem notes: "It is neither possible nor obligatory to refute the consistent doubter" (*T II*, 276). His skepticism regarding dialogue and his preference for silence thus also have a theological dimension: "Naturally the atheist may have a right to ask me about God, but I have an infinitely greater right not to answer him. A discussion lacking in resonance is a priori forbidden" (*LY*, 264).

The Book of Job and the notion of what cannot be questioned continue to play a role in Scholem's later writings. Much later, for example, he characterizes the Kabbalah as "a body of thought that cannot be constructed from question and answer" (*KS*, 87) and paraphrases the epistemology of the Zohar accordingly: "There are certain spheres of Divinity where questions can be asked and answers obtained. . . . In the end, however, meditation reaches a point where it is still possible to question 'who', but no longer possible to get an answer; rather does the question itself constitute an answer" (*MT*, 220–221). In another late essay, he also continues to stress the irony of Job, whose claim to justice "is recognized by God in an ironic manner, because no response that God gives to Job is at the level on which the question had been posed."[25] Here, Scholem even describes this as absurdity rather than irony: "I would say that it is scandalous to give a response like this one [from God]. It does not make sense."[26] The "questions of the Book of Job, unanswered and echoing through the millennia to this day" represent the decisive moment in the history of religion, the moment in which "questioning thought" ventures to approach God, who is "no product of thought"; it is also in this context that God proves to be "a truly Jewish God, answering unanswerable questions with questions that are even more unanswerable."[27] Once again, it is Job's reaction that is remarkable to Scholem: "And yet, the obvious inadequacy of the answer to an all-too reasonable question does not provoke skepticism in its partner, it overwhelms him, if one may take this as a form of persuasion. The God who speaks to Job from the storm is so real that he can shout down the questions of a stirring conscience, and this shout calms his critic. In his unity, this God—from Moses to Job—is at the same time entirely a personality, and because he is a personality, there is revelation."[28]

Scholem no longer presents the Book of Job as a book of indirect instruction that could be comprehended by a theory of Judaism. Instead, he characterizes it through a revelation that is real to the point of violence, nearly demonstrating demonic epiphany, and in any event showing itself to be overpowering. It seems that the element of "what cannot be questioned" (*das Nichterfragbare*) represents a boundary of the theory of Judaism itself, at least to the extent that it is conceived as a theory of question and answer. The epiphany that manifests itself in the answer to an inappropriate question points beyond this theory, on the one hand to a theory of revelation already sketched in the margins of the Jonah essay and on the other hand to ideas of religious history that will

---

25. Scholem, "Quelques remarques sur le mythe de la peine," 141. The text also exists in English: "On Sin and Punishment." The French version is cited here for the sake of the discussion that follows.

26. Scholem, "Quelques remarques sur le mythe de la peine," 159. The course of the subsequent discussion is revealing: Scholem offers fierce resistance to the hermeneutically oriented attempts of his fellow discussants to "understand" the Bible (for instance, by calling on the frame story of the Book of Job, God's bet with the devil; see ibid., 149). To Castelli's objection: "You are making a fundamental distinction between texts and hermeneutics, correct? Here, we are hermeneuticists," Scholem answers that hermeneutics is "precisely what the author has forbidden. In effect, you are saying: I refuse this choice" (ibid., 155; see also 160).

27. Scholem, *Über einige Grundbegriffe*, 10, 10–11.

28. Scholem, *Über einige Grundbegriffe*, 11.

become important for Scholem only much later. As Scholem writes in preliminary notes for the Jonah essay: "Religious concepts are those in which an area of 'what cannot be questioned' can be substantiated. If this is not a definition, it is a statement. The history of religion—which naturally does not exist as such—comes about in making this limit precise on the one hand, and transgressing it on the other" (*T II*, 373). Before Scholem develops this process historically, however, he aims at more clearly grasping what revelation could mean in theological terms.

TWELVE

REVELATION

Problematic Foundations

AS WE HAVE SEEN, SCHOLEM later links the category of "what cannot be questioned" (*das Nichterfragbare*) to the notion of revelation, at least in the Book of Job, where indeed a moment of theophany can be related to a sort of dialogue in which God reveals himself after a series of questions, albeit not really answering these questions. Revelation is figured here as something on the border between the human and the divine as well as between discursive thinking and pure presence. To a large extent, this corresponds to the way Scholem relates to the notion of revelation as situated between philosophy and theology. As tradition, revelation can have a broad, ambiguous meaning. It can be conceived in terms of the Kantian project, where real experience reveals reality in contrast to mere speculative semblance, and it can also be related to language, as in Benjamin's early speculation on language revealing the essence of things. But it can also be related to more straightforward theological reflections that see revelation as the cornerstone and foundation of theological knowledge as something different from philosophy. Scholem's scattered indirect reflections on Jewish theology are among the most important forms in which his insights into Judaism live on. Thus, in what follows, I consider these reflections before turning to the other forms in which Scholem's insights live on—namely, his work as a philologist and as a historian of the Kabbalah.

In Scholem's early texts, it is hardly possible to distinguish between philosophical and theological statements. This boundary only became distinct in the 1930s, above all in the context of his engagement with the renaissance of Jewish theology, particularly Franz Rosenzweig's 1921 book *The Star of Redemption*. Having read the book shortly after it appeared, Scholem delivered a speech on it in Hebrew in 1930 and devoted a short text to it in German in

1931. Rosenzweig broke new ground for Jewish theology, according to Scholem. While his *Star* is "a philosophical system, as can be seen from its form," it is theology that covertly "appears here at the heart of concepts familiar to all of us" (*PM*, 206). Scholem does not entirely agree with the form that Rosenzweig gives this theology, however. Rosenzweig's critique of Zionism initially spoiled the book for him, according to a letter to Edith Rosenzweig (*Br I*, 246ff.). In addition, Scholem views Rosenzweig's thought as shaped by "Kabbalah-phobia" (*MI*, 321) as well as a "deep-seated tendency to remove the apocalyptic thorn from the organism of Judaism" and to deny the "recognition of the catastrophic potential of all historical order in an unredeemed world" (*MI*, 323). Yet Scholem does seem to accept Rosenzweig's distinction between philosophy and theology, along with the associated critique of Judaism's older theologies, stressing "that hardly ever had there been a Jewish theology of such vacuity and insignificance as existed in the decades before World War I" (*MI*, 321). In particular, it was the theology of liberalism that led to this evacuation of Judaism: "The seductive illusion of man's moral autonomy determined the theology of Jewish liberalism, which had its origins essentially in idealism. From here no path lay open . . . back toward the mysteries of revelation" (*MI*, 322). This theology is distinguished by the "inability to penetrate religious reality with rigorous concepts" and the "lack of readiness to perceive the religious world of Judaism in its totality" (*MI*, 321). The theology of liberalism "became impoverished when in the last century it consented, equally among Jews and Christians, to position itself at philosophy's furthest boundary, a kind of ornament bedecking the roofs of philosophy's vast structures, rather than insisting on its own; so theology suffered the same dismal fate as philosophy" (*PM*, 202–203). What remained was only an illusion of theology, and "even problems no one could doubt belong to it have fled and have ensconced themselves in arts and literature" (*PM*, 203).

More than anything else, Scholem pays attention to the diagnosis of the crisis of the past that he finds not only in Rosenzweig's work but also "equally among Jews and Christians" who give up on the old idea of an autonomous subjectivity, placing new emphasis on the givenness of reality as well as the reality of theology. Such formulations point beyond Rosenzweig to the epochal impact of "dialectical theology," which countered the interpretation of religion as a subregion of culture by stressing religion's originality and its difference from culture. In the radical case of Karl Barth, even the concept of "religion" was rejected based on the view that faith's originality does not represent a human relationship to God but rather a gift of God that always remains incommensurable when it comes to man. The dialectical theologians are all the more interesting to Scholem because they wanted to restore the discussion of God as a discussion in its own right, employing figures of paradox and the dialectics of radical distinctions with explicit recourse to Kierkegaard. Theology thus becomes a discourse of crisis, and at the same time once again a discourse of experience, as Scholem highlights in his speech on Rosenzweig: "The autonomy of thought has broken down, and henceforth it, thought, will not create its subjects but will find them" (*PM*, 202).

For the dialectical theologians, the primal object that cannot be easily grasped by rational, human, or cultural categories is "the Word of God," or revelation. Scholem came across this idea much earlier than in the above-quoted remarks from the 1930s. For Scholem, the idea that revelation must be understood as a fact—and that therefore it must be "found"—also relates to thinkers other than Rosenzweig. In 1921 he writes that revelation is "the central foundational fact of religion," not as an "amorphous experience playing out on an inscrutable blurred sphere of interiority, just like its emanations" but rather as "audition in the strict sense of the term" (*T II*, 667). The actual givenness of revelation lies precisely in its clarity, not in diffuse experience. Scholem frequently invokes Salomon Ludwig Steinheim (1789–1866), whose book *The Revelation According to the Doctrine of the Synagogue* he read with great appreciation shortly after engaging with Hirsch. Scholem refers to Steinheim's work as, "to my mind, a highly significant and absolutely unknown, very rare book, considering" (*Br I*, 205). Steinheim offers another "conservative" interpretation, criticizing the liberal theology of the nineteenth century based on the tendency to modernize revelation: "The real concept was discarded by those who no longer believed in the thing itself. But they could not very well dare to dispose of the word, since it had so ancient a tradition, extending far back into prehistory. Therefore, in keeping with the system of a progressive religious development of feeling and human consciousness, the term was skinned."[1]

For Steinheim, religion must be founded not in feeling or consciousness but through revelation, which is opposed to natural reason rather than supplementing or preceding it. He refers to Kant's dialectics of reason, according to which reason constantly raises questions that it cannot resolve; this dilemma can only be confronted in the decision to accept revelation, in "*the capture of reason*

---

1. Steinheim, *The Revelation According to the Doctrine of Judaism*, 100–101. See the respective chapters on Steinheim in Guttmann, *Philosophies of Judaism*, and Rotenstreich, *Jewish Philosophy*.

by faith."² Take, for example, the doctrine of "creation out of nothing" that Steinheim views as a bulwark against materialism: contradicting the rational principle *ex nihilo nihil fit*, this doctrine cannot emerge from reason. However, once accepted, it resolves the Kantian antinomy of the beginning of the world. It is the search for a new methodological foundation for theology that compels Steinheim to draw on the traditional supranaturalistic concept of revelation: "This teaching of revelation should not be accessible either by way of reflection or experience or by any other means by which the human mind develops other truths within and out of itself. But it should be of a kind that can reach man *only through a perceptible word from an external source*, through the ear."³

Revelation is something given, according to Steinheim, something that approaches human beings from the outside, as *"communication of an unknown fact"* or as a "message" that goes back to a specific moment: "the strict sense of the word *revelation* implies a historical event.... A proclamation, a communication, is an act that occurs at a definite or definable moment in time. In contrast to pure cognition by means of innate mental capacity, that proclamation or communication is an actual learning *experience*, conveyed through external senses."⁴ This objectivism of revelation as articulated by Steinheim contributes to Scholem's early project of a theory of Judaism while also consistently serving as a counterweight to his engagement with tradition.

This tension between the concrete message of revelation and its interpretive tradition is at the center of Scholem's confrontation with Hans Joachim Schoeps's book *Jewish Faith in These Times* in an open letter published in 1937. Scholem presents his text as a sketch of a *"correctly* understood theology" in a letter to Benjamin that David Biale has interpreted as an "antiexistentialist manifesto."⁵ It contains essential formulations developed in Scholem's diaries—formulations that are already familiar to us—transforming them into a contribution to a theological argument not only with Schoeps but with the entire theological renaissance of the time. In his book, Schoeps refers to Barth and Steinheim explicitly, polemicizing against liberalism, along with "ethical

---

2. Steinheim, *The Revelation*, 87. Steinheim repeatedly emphasizes the negative character of reason: "reason's main strength is in tearing down and criticizing, but not in building up and consolidating" (ibid., 88).

3. Steinheim, *The Revelation*, 102.

4. Steinheim, *The Revelation*, 137, 98. This also distinguishes natural religion from revealed religion, which is always historical: *"We do not develop it, but it develops us"* (ibid., 65).

5. Scholem, *Correspondence of Benjamin and Scholem*, 126; Biale, *Kabbalah and Counter-History*, 130.

nomism" in Jewish theology and its "immanently founded" interpretation of life, in which revelation is equated with timeless, generally valid truths, and revelation's "claim to validity for its own life [is] *neutralized*."[6] For Jewish faith, long interpreted as purely rational, everything depends on whether "it can prove itself as a religion of *revelation*, in the face of which the person who is compelled to make a decision only has the alternative to believe or not to believe."[7] Schoeps thus attempts to transfer the turn to a theology of revelation onto Judaism, calling for "reflection that will reach the truth of the fact of revelation" as the groundwork for theology "*before* any proclamation in the living space of the synagogue."[8] Only when one goes back to the "understanding of existence of Old Testament man . . . , which speaks to us from the Holy Scriptures as *faith in revelation*," is it possible to avoid the liberal reduction of religion to universally human morality on the one hand, and on the other hand to overcome the "unhistoricalness of the Orthodox claim that our concrete emergency of general faithlessness could somehow be helped through 'learning' in the Talmud and serious sinking into the disputes of halachic commentary on laws."[9] Similarly to Steinheim, Schoeps then attempts to establish a series of biblical "dogmas" as cornerstones of a biblical faith, including the dogma of creation out of nothing.

Scholem's critique of Schoeps is characteristically sharp, although the two are in agreement when it comes to the rejection of liberalism. Scholem finds it "very commendable" that Schoeps draws on Steinheim to polemicize against the "perversion of the concepts of revelation and redemption under the rule of thought that has deteriorated from illusions of autonomy" (*Br I*, 466). However, he criticizes Schoeps's tendency to make Judaism into an object of faith, attributing this tendency to Schoeps's "explicit rejection of tradition as the essential category of the religious way of life in Judaism—a rejection that amounts to a leap to nowhere, or what you call biblical theology" (*Br I*, 468). Scholem remains highly skeptical of Schoeps's "abrogation of the inquiry into the religious meaning of the oral Torah and its basic concepts (transmission, commentary, questions, and what can be questioned)" (*Br I*, 469). In Scholem's view, the proclaimed leap to a biblical understanding of existence is impossible, as this understanding is entirely foreign to modern man, and such a leap would represent a "neutralization of Jewish historical consciousness" (*Br I*, 468). Furthermore,

---

6. Schoeps, *Jüdischer Glaube in dieser Zeit*, 1.
7. Schoeps, *Jüdischer Glaube in dieser Zeit*, 2.
8. Schoeps, *Jüdischer Glaube in dieser Zeit*, 3.
9. Schoeps, *Jüdischer Glaube in dieser Zeit*, 4.

recourse to the "existential problematic of modern Judaism" could all too easily slip into "a very unexistential subjectivism that we all know quite well" (*Br I*, 469). This leads Scholem to an explicitly theological formulation of the problem of revelation:

> Revelation—an old and deep truth that comes up short in your writing, just as it did in Steinheim's writing—for all of its uniqueness, revelation is a *medium*. As the absolute, that which gives meaning but is in itself meaningless, it is the *interpretable*, which only lays itself out in the continuous relationship to time, in tradition. The word of God in its absolute symbolic fullness would be destructive, even if it were immediately (undialectically) significant at the same time. In relation to historical time, nothing... is more in need of concretization than the "absolute concreteness" (to use your words) of the word of revelation. Yet the absolutely concrete is the unexecutable [*das Unvollziehbare*] as such, the absoluteness of which determines its infinite reflection in the contingencies of execution. It is only here, equipped with the index of applicability that the absolute lacks, that the human act becomes graspable as something concrete. (*Br I*, 469–470)

These formulations are crucial for Scholem. Clearly drawn from formulations regarding the concretization of the Torah in the Jonah essay, Scholem later prominently employs them again in "Revelation and Tradition as Religious Categories in Judaism" (*MI*, 296). Scholem wants to define revelation dialectically, not as a call to decision. The absolute is only "graspable" in its unfolding; in its immediacy it cannot be "executed" by human beings. Several arguments are linked here. The nonapplicability of revelation represents a *hermeneutic* problem: beyond the reference to "the contingencies of execution" and to time, the word does not *mean* anything that a human being could decide on at all. Scholem illustrates this point based on the dogma of "creation out of nothing" as emphasized by Steinheim and Schoeps: "For what this nothing actually 'is,' or 'is not,' if you will—a determination of God (a 'nothingness of God') or not—this decisive question that instantly exposes the ambiguity of the formula is the only thing that can precipitate a decision as to whether this principle in fact has the fundamental meaning that it claims" (*Br I*, 467–468). However, this question cannot be decided without interpretations of tradition, or without the history of the impact of revelation that tradition represents. Scholem describes this with the metaphor of "voice" employed frequently in his work: "The *voice* we hear, that is the medium in which we live, and where it is not that, the voice is hollow, taking on the character of the ghostly, in which the word of God no longer takes effect, but rather—even if it is in dogmas—circumvents" (*Br I*, 470).

Scholem simultaneously evokes another problem here, related less to the meaning of revelation than to what he characterizes as "what cannot be questioned" of revelation, or as the "blinding glare ... that emanates from revelation" (*Br I*, 470). Obscure and meaningless in itself, revelation has a *force*, "that which gives meaning" (*Br I*, 469). Scholem offers the comparison of a "voice" that is the condition of possibility for utterance but not yet utterance itself. This force can no longer be understood simply on the level of hermeneutics, as the above-cited passage on the immediate word of God shows: "The word of God in its absolute symbolic fullness would be destructive, even if it were immediately (undialectically) significant at the same time" (*Br I*, 469). This sentence, typical of Scholem's writing, evinces a dialectical rhetoric. Scholem does not rest with the hermeneutic assertion that there is no immediate meaning of revelation; he goes on to speak of this immediacy as a destructive force, albeit in the brackets of the subjunctive. The figure of force serves as a means of conceiving the fulfillment of tradition and the dialectics of deferral. Tradition cannot be detached from revelation, yet it never reaches revelation, and neither revelation nor tradition can determine life directly and simply.[10]

The significance of this dialectics of deferral can be demonstrated by comparing Scholem's critique of Schoeps to that of Alexander Altmann. Like Scholem, Altmann resists Schoeps's Protestant hypostatization of the moment of decision and the "leap" into faith. Altmann does not begin with the problem of revelation, however, instead directing his argument against the "gnostic" impact of dialectical theology that is also apparent in Schoeps's work: "The Jewish 'decision' will not be able to turn its back on the world as can that of Barth.... There the motive of decision is grounded in a specific presupposition that we cannot accept on the basis of Jewish consciousness: in the doctrine of the opposition of history and primal history, of the temporal and the eternal."[11] However, according to Altmann, the Jewish way of life, determined by Jewish law, "cannot be given to us in the instability of decision. Decision is like a dot,

---

10. See also Schoeps's response: "The fact that you designate the absolutely concrete in the word of revelation as the 'unexecutable as such' fills me with concern for you as a person and for your 'salvation'—pardon the pietistic word. I am beginning to sense who it is that is speaking to me." In a later remark, Schoeps adds: "I fully understood that a nihilist wanted to teach me about revelation" (Schoeps, *Ja—Nein—und Trotzdem*, 49–50).

11. Altmann, "A Discussion with Dialectical Theology," in *The Meaning of Jewish Existence*, 78. In an excursus not included in the English translation, Altmann works out how Schoeps "simply adopts the conceptual framework of dialectical theology for Judaism in an entirely naive way" ("Zur Auseinandersetzung mit der 'Dialektischen Theologie,'" in *Lust an der Erkenntnis*, 268–269).

action means extending into time; it is a path."[12] Whereas Schoeps, like Barth, claims "that the unbelieving world, falling away from revelation, is full of *demonic* potency and threatens to destroy itself in its demonic possession—that is, to lose its *quality of creation*," Altmann sees this as "apocalyptic through and through," with "a false tone for Jewish ears."[13]

It is revealing that Scholem's critique is almost the opposite. Whereas Altmann sees in Schoeps's work more apocalypticism than is good for Judaism, Scholem describes the apocalyptic in itself as entirely legitimate: "It seems to me that the relationship of a historical present to an eternal present can only be realized in two ways (which by no means exclude one another): in the medium of apocalypticism or of tradition. The 'biblical' standpoint beyond both is a chimera" (*Br I*, 470). Indeed, Scholem strikes apocalyptic tones in his discussion of the blinding or destructive force of revelation, yet in his view, this is precisely what rules out Schoeps's existential appropriation (or "biblical standpoint"). For Scholem, the apocalyptic moment maintains a tension that fully corresponds to the paradoxical relatedness of revelation, tradition, and life. When it comes to apocalypticism, "precisely understood, there is nothing concrete which can be accomplished by the unredeemed," and thus Scholem refers to it as "the real anti-existentialist idea" (*MI*, 35). The unexecutability of the concrete is consequently realized in the idea of tradition as well as in apocalypticism. Both are deeply dialectical ideas in the sense that, through them, the divine and human are related, but related in such a way that they can never encounter one another.

These ideas also shape the correspondence with Benjamin regarding Kafka, which contains some of Scholem's most-discussed theological reflections. In 1928 Scholem writes to Werner Kraft that Kafka's *The Trial* constitutes "the first retelling of the book of Job that a human being—naturally a Jew—has managed to produce" (*LL*, 163). Three years later, he advises Benjamin "to begin any inquiry into Kafka with the Book of Job, or at least with a discussion of the possibility of divine judgment.... The ideas I expressed many years ago in my theses on justice (which you know) would in their relationship to language serve me as a guide in my reflections on Kafka."[14] The discussion with Benjamin thus revolves around the difference between the unexecutability of revelation and its absence. Scholem criticizes Benjamin's Kafka essay for presenting Kafka from

---

12. Altmann, "A Discussion with Dialectical Theology," 86.
13. Schoeps, *Jüdischer Glaube in dieser Zeit*, 3; Altmann, "Zur Auseinandersetzung mit der 'Dialektischen Theologie,'" 269.
14. Scholem, *Story of a Friendship*, 216; *Correspondence of Benjamin and Scholem*, 126.

the perspective of the absence of revelation, arguing that revelation is present everywhere in Kafka's world: "Its problem is not, dear Walter, its *absence* in a preanimistic world, but [its *unexecutability* (*Unvollziehbarkeit*)].... Those pupils of whom you speak at the end are not so much those who have lost the Scripture... but rather those students who cannot decipher it."[15] Responding to Benjamin's objection that "without the key that belongs to it, the Scripture is not Scripture, but life," Scholem emphasizes: "When I speak of the nothingness of revelation, I do so precisely to characterize the difference between these two positions."[16]

The "nothingness of revelation" appears already in Scholem's first letter to Benjamin on the subject: "Kafka's world is the world of revelation, but of revelation seen of course from that perspective in which it is returned to its own nothingness."[17] This formula offers an alternate description of the problem of the paradoxical givenness of revelation that we have already encountered. At Benjamin's request, Scholem clarifies his meaning:

> I understand by it a state in which revelation appears to be without meaning, in which it still asserts itself, in which it has *validity* but *no significance*. A state in which the wealth of meaning is lost and what is in the process of appearing (for revelation is such a process) still does not disappear, even though it is reduced to the zero point of its own content, so to speak. This is obviously a borderline case in the religious sense, and whether it can really come to pass is a very dubious point.[18]

Here, too, Scholem is thinking of a revelation beyond meaning. However, in this context revelation is not characterized by destructive force but by phenomenality on the one hand and validity on the other: it appears, it becomes perceptible, and it has a certain binding force. Moreover, Scholem no longer describes the nothingness of revelation as immediate but as the *residuum* of a revelation that was originally richer. In another essay, this remainder prompts the question of the "value and worth of language ... the language from which God will have withdrawn."[19] A similar figure also seems to shape the poem that Scholem sends to Benjamin:

> Only so does revelation
> Shine in the time that rejected you.

---

15. Scholem, *Correspondence of Benjamin and Scholem*, 126–127.
16. Scholem, *Correspondence of Benjamin and Scholem*, 135, 142.
17. Scholem, *Correspondence of Benjamin and Scholem*, 126.
18. Scholem, *Correspondence of Benjamin and Scholem*, 142.
19. Scholem, "The Name of God and the Linguistic Theory of the Kabbala," 194.

> Only your nothingness is the experience
> It is entitled to have of you.[20]

How are we to conceive of God's nothingness, which will become an essential figure in Scholem's theological reflections? He sometimes relates it to the Lurianic notion of *zimzum*, which is a form of self-contraction.[21] For Luria, the notion of a God "who concentrated Himself into Himself" (*MT*, 261) is meant to solve the problem of creation: Why is there a world independent of God at all, when God was originally everything? The world is determined negatively by the active absence or withdrawal of God. At the same time, the *zimzum* can also be read as the "deepest symbol of Exile" (*MT*, 261). Moreover, if self-contraction is an essential act of God, a God-forsaken world can always also be seen as a world that was forsaken *by* God, and this view can extend into agency, as Scholem argues in his speech on Rosenzweig: "The divinity, banished from man by psychology and from the world by sociology, no longer wanting to reside in the heavens, has handed over the throne of justice to dialectical materialism and the seat of mercy to psychoanalysis and has withdrawn to some hidden place and does not disclose Himself" (*PM*, 203). The figure of self-contraction thus makes it possible for Scholem to figure the disenchanted present in theological terms of a hidden God: "Is He truly undisclosed? Perhaps this last withdrawal is His revelation. Perhaps God's removal to the point of nothingness was a higher need, and He will reveal His kingship only to a world that has been emptied" (*PM*, 203). For Scholem, the notion of self-contraction represents a historical-theological surpassing of skepticism and doubt, a theology of the absent God that includes the messianic expectation of his return.

Even more specifically, self-contraction can be thought of as a property of revelation rather than an act of God. In the context of Scholem's correspondence with Benjamin, it is not the "nothingness of God" that is up for discussion, nor faith in the concealed God, but the "nothingness of revelation." Scholem also alludes to this in his letter to Schoeps, in the barely developed figure of the "*voice* . . . that is the medium in which we live" (*Br I*, 470). In the

---

20. Scholem, *Correspondence of Benjamin and Scholem*, 124. On this poem, see Mosès, *The Angel of History*, chapter 2, and Liska, *German-Jewish Thought and Its Afterlife*, chapter 2.

21. On the motif of *zimzum*, see also Schulte, "Die Buchstaben haben . . . ihre Wurzeln oben," and Wohlfahrt, "Haarscharf auf der Grenze." Idel has emphasized that Scholem's interpretation of Lurianic *zimzum* as a symbol of exile is not evident in the sources and that Scholem himself always presents this interpretation with great caution. See Idel, "Zur Funktion von Symbolen," 72ff.

logic of this image, the reduction of revelation corresponds to the shift from the fixed, distinct word of revelation to the infinitely plastic voice. Immediate revelation thus dissolves into the medium of its conveyance, to be understood as the pure possibility of its potential realizations. As Scholem later writes, this notion of the "unlimited mystical plasticity of the divine word" is "perhaps the only way in which the idea of a revealed word of God can be taken seriously" (KS, 76).

At first glance, it seems that the dialectics of "unexecutability" that is central to the letter to Schoeps also dissolves, as the permanent interpretation and reinterpretation of tradition follows naturally from the infinite plasticity of the revelatory voice. Yet the connotations of revelation in the strict sense, including its potential destructiveness, do not disappear completely. Scholem calls the mystical dissolution of revelation "a borderline case in the religious sense, and whether it can really come to pass is a very dubious point."[22] This borderline status is already evident in the way that Scholem thinks of the reduction of God and the reduction of revelation not only as the exposure of essence but also as a loss of fullness. Scholem further associates God's self-concealment with the historical crisis of Judaism in the modern period. In his poem on Kafka, this is expressed in reference to the "time that rejected you" as well as in the "we" that permanently addresses an absent God, most notably in a series of questions and an open ending:[23]

> Who is the accused here?
> The creature or yourself?
> If anyone should ask you,
> You would sink into silence.
>
> Can such a question be raised?
> Is the answer indefinite?
> Oh, we must all live the same
> Until your court examines us.[24]

As in the case of Job, questions are not answered so much as they are quashed. The poem itself dissolves in this open end, eluding any clear theological

---

22. Scholem, *Correspondence of Benjamin and Scholem*, 142.
23. Mosès stresses "the paradoxical discursive status of that poem that deals with the absence of God yet incessantly invokes him" (*The Angel of History*, 155). The poem highlights its status as an utterance through the strong use of deictic pronouns and adverbs (such as "here") and personal pronouns ("you" and "we" function as shifters).
24. Scholem, *Correspondence of Benjamin and Scholem*, 125.

interpretation. The direction of history can no longer be discerned. This lack of direction also comes to the fore in a letter from Scholem to Benjamin, returning to Benjamin's image of the flow of tradition and its waves (see chap. 9). According to Scholem, the illegibility of the law in Kafka's work by no means entails distance from that which is Jewish: "I would say such an enfeebling is rooted in the nature of the mystical tradition itself: it is only natural that the *capacity* of tradition to be transmitted remains as its sole living feature when it decays, when it is on the crest of a wave [later corrected by Scholem to 'trough of the wave']."[25] Again and again, the image suggests, tradition in the state of reduction reaches the point of nothingness, and again and again it unfolds from there. Scholem thus makes it clear that the mystical interpretation of tradition is not the truth of the unmystical interpretation of revelation but rather its complement. For the flow of tradition cannot consist solely of the troughs of waves or else it would lose its momentum.

These considerations are not limited to Scholem's discussion of Kafka. In 1939, not long after his correspondence with Benjamin regarding Kafka, Scholem incisively presented his position and the theological implications of his views in a discussion of the so-called Ha'ol group, a range of liberal to left-wing religious intellectuals.[26] According to Scholem in this discussion, in order to know what the Torah should mean today, one must start with a strict interpretation: "There is no Torah without revelation (*maton Torah*), and there is no Torah without heteronomy (*hetronomiah*), and there is no Torah without an authoritative tradition."[27] For written as well as oral revelation, it is essential that there be authority with respect to which the individual is heteronomous: "The Torah is the sounding of a supernal voice that obliges one in an absolute manner. It does not acknowledge the autonomy (*autonomiah*) of the individual."[28] It might be true that the totality of oral and written Torah changes in the course of time, but "in spite of this development, there is nothing arbitrary about it whatsoever. [Although] every generation wishes 'its' Torah to be the divine voice of revelation, there is no place here for the individual's freedom of decision. In principle, therefore, Orthodoxy is correct."[29]

---

25. Scholem, *Correspondence of Benjamin and Scholem*, 236–237.
26. English translation in Mendes-Flohr, *Divided Passions*, 344–346. See also Zadoff, *Gershom Scholem*, chapter 3.
27. Mendes-Flohr, *Divided Passions*, 345.
28. Mendes-Flohr, *Divided Passions*, 344.
29. Mendes-Flohr, *Divided Passions*, 345.

Scholem once again orients himself based on the position of Orthodoxy as an internally consistent form of engagement with the Torah, but he does not take up this position. To gain distance, he makes an important distinction between the interrelated elements of oral and written Torah: "We are unable to accept the Oral Torah of Orthodoxy."[30] For him, however, it does not follow from this that the written Torah has authority while the oral Torah does not (this would be the fictional standpoint of "biblical theology"). More radically, with the loss of the oral Torah, the written Torah becomes incomprehensible for us as well: "The Torah is understandable only as Oral Torah, only through its relativization."[31] The hermeneutic problem that Scholem had articulated in his polemic against Schoeps thus affects "us" as well—that is, those who can no longer simply share the supernaturalism of Orthodoxy, who no longer believe in the divinity of the Bible and tradition.

Scholem attempts to make this position positively comprehensible via two different thoughts. On the one hand, he evokes a *coming* tradition: "We must therefore wait for *our* own Oral Torah, which will have to be binding for us, leaving no room for free, nonauthoritative decision."[32] Released from the bonds of the oral Torah yet still waiting for a new one, "we" live in an interim state that Scholem also designates as anarchism: "To a known degree we are all anarchists. But our anarchism is *transitional*, for we are the living example that this [our anarchism] does not remove us from Judaism."[33] Living on the consciousness of its weakness and provisionality, this passive anarchism is nevertheless necessary: "I do not have a feeling of inferiority with respect to those who observe [the Law]. We are not less legitimate than our forefathers; they merely had a clearer text."[34] According to this assertion, "transitional anarchism" is more than an empty interim period of waiting for a new bond; it describes a Jewish position that should be just as legitimate as that of Orthodox traditionalism. This position clearly corresponds to the "nothingness of revelation," the state in which every particular meaning falls away and all that remains is formal validity, no longer executable as law.

With the figure of the illegible text, the question of revelation shifts once again. In its limit state as pure inscription beyond meaning, revelation is now

---

30. Mendes-Flohr, *Divided Passions*, 345.
31. Mendes-Flohr, *Divided Passions*, 345. "There is no Written Torah without the Oral Torah. Were we to desire to restrict the Torah to the Torah transmitted in writing, we would not be able to read even the Pentateuch, only the ten commandments" (ibid.).
32. Mendes-Flohr, *Divided Passions*, 345.
33. Mendes-Flohr, *Divided Passions*, 346.
34. Mendes-Flohr, *Divided Passions*, 346.

less "voice" than "script." This is connected to the distinction between written and oral Torah and its rabbinic and kabbalistic interpretation. As Scholem continues to stress, the rabbis already conceived of the oral Torah both as original revelation and as somehow implied in the written Torah; the kabbalists radicalized this view to include the idea of an ur-Torah, of which the written Torah is only an interpretation. According to another view, the Torah in its transmitted form is only one of the possible combinations of its letters; in another epoch of the world, the same letters will be differently combined, and they will mean something different. According to Scholem, these ideas combine the "strict traditionalist view that not one letter of the Torah as given on Mount Sinai may be changed, with the conception that in other aeons this same Torah, without modifying its essence, will show another face" (*KS*, 80).[35]

As in the letter to Schoeps, Scholem describes revelation as something that "gives meaning but is in itself meaningless," yet here this is figured not as changeable voice but as a script in the sense of a material code that is realized in its interpretations. Definite, formally delimited communication (revelation as "Word" or message) is thus replaced by the revelation of medium—namely, that of "script"—which simultaneously designates the fixing of revelation in biblical books and the medium of this fixing. This double meaning underlies Scholem's integration of positive and mystical understandings of revelation. For a time, he seems to have found this notion to be theologically fruitful, although he hardly ever articulated it explicitly.

In his 1974 essay "Reflections on Jewish Theology," Scholem takes up the same set of problems, albeit from a far more skeptical position. With some irony, he concedes that he is not among the "fortunate ones" who could build a systematic theology from an "Archimedean point": "for I have no positive theology of an inflexible Judaism" (*JJC*, 261). He therefore only wants to consider "the position and possibilities of Jewish theology today" (*JJC*, 261), taking a "methodological perspective" (*JJC*, 277). He takes neither a philosophical approach nor a purely historical approach (as in the history of theology), instead inquiring into possible sources and foundations: "Before one can speak about theology, one must necessarily speak about the sources on which such theology can draw"

---

35. In an earlier passage, Scholem clarifies: "These ideas represent a most illuminating combination of the *absolute* and the *relative*. In line with orthodox belief, the Torah remains an essentially unchanging and absolute entity. But at the same time, seen in historical perspective, it takes on specific meaning only in relation to the changing state of man in the universe, so that the meaning itself is subject to change" (*KS*, 73). See also the passages on rabbinic and kabbalistic understandings of tradition in "Revelation and Tradition."

(*JJC*, 263). Theology cannot develop freely as a philosophical construction but only in relation to something given. Above all, the question to be posed is that of the authority and legitimacy of theological discourse: "The question of the authoritative sources on which such a theology can draw; in other words, the question of the legitimacy of Revelation and Tradition as religious categories which can constitute the foundation of a Jewish theology" (*JJC*, 261).

For Scholem, *only* revelation and tradition can provide a foundation for theology: "I did not start out from the faith in God. The reason is obvious. The conviction of the existence of God . . . can be regarded as entirely independent of Revelation. No theology flows from it" (*JJC*, 275–276). Pure faith in God might constitute an anthropology of religion or a vague religiosity, but it is theologically fruitless, as demonstrated by the fate of nineteenth-century liberal theology. Theology has to go back to sources, and thus Scholem subsequently discusses the possible sources of a Jewish theology—namely, the Bible, rabbinic tradition, and the Kabbalah. He stresses their inconsistency, particularly with respect to views on revelation: "the most important of these contradictions, and precisely for the contemporary observer, surely does not concern the conviction of the existence of God. . . . It concerns the interpretation to which the concept of Revelation has been subjected" (*JJC*, 265). Revelation (and, derivatively, tradition), and the question of how it should be understood, is essential; revelation and tradition are never purely descriptive terms; they always already imply a theology themselves. Scholem proceeds to cite Steinheim—"a genuine antimystic" (*JJC*, 273)—in order to criticize "new thinking" in Jewish theology and its attempts to develop a new understanding of revelation. According to Scholem, such attempts blur the distinction between "divine communication establishing an authority" and mere theophany, resulting in an "attenuating and subjectivist talk of Revelation which was bound to destroy Revelation's authoritative character" (*JJC*, 272). For example, Buber's notion of revelation is purely mystical, "with, however, the big difference that for the mystics historical revelation implies mystical revelation, in that the former is articulated and developed by the latter. There is, to be sure, no longer any talk of that in Buber. He knows only one revelation, and that is the mystical one" (*JJC*, 157). Where Buber writes, "revelation does not pour into the world by using its recipient like a funnel," Scholem comments, "*it is, to be sure, precisely this that historical revelations do!*" (*JJC*, 159).[36] It is this notion of revelation that has been

---

36. Similarly, he writes in "Revelation and Tradition" that revelation was originally understood "naturally," as a "concrete communication of a positive, substantive, and expressible content" (*MI*, 284).

called into question, particularly through historical biblical criticism: "one of its most important victims, if not *the* most important one" (*JJC*, 274). With this crisis in the understanding of revelation, the possibility of *any* theology is also called into question.

Scholem's doubts become particularly clear in the 1963 essay "Reflections on the Possibility of Mysticism in Our Time." First delivered as a lecture, Scholem's argument was anticipated with high expectations and received with great disappointment.[37] In the essay, Scholem is once again focused on the fundamental requirements for a mystical theology, and thus, indirectly, for his own theological considerations. He explicitly distinguishes between the Kabbalah and present forms of mysticism. The kabbalists may have had a free relationship with what was handed down, but this freedom was always tied to revelation in the strict sense: "What is the basic assumption upon which all traditional Jewish mysticism in Kabbalah and Hasidism is based? The acceptance of the Torah, in the strictest and most precise understanding of the concept of the word of God" (*PM*, 14). Revelation is not considered from the point of view of mysticism; conversely, Scholem stresses that mysticism is only possible through ties to prior revelation: "Thus, once a person has accepted . . . this strict, exact concept of Torah from heaven, without any whitewashing—from then on, he enjoys an extraordinary measure of freedom. . . . He becomes so to speak a member of the family" (*PM*, 14).

Scholem clarifies the meaning of this statement *ex negativo*: "We do not believe in Torah from heaven in the specific sense of a fixed body of revelation having infinite significance. And without this basic assumption one cannot move" (*PM*, 15). While we as moderns may be able to comprehend and share the view of revelation as an indefinite and infinitely changeable medium, this does not hold for the view of revelation as a "fixed body of revelation," but it is this second view that now appears to be a requirement of mysticism for Scholem: "The moment this assumption falls, the entire structure upon which mysticism was built, and by means of which it was to be accepted among the people as legitimate, likewise falls" (*PM*, 15).

Scholem thus acknowledges that the kabbalistic theory of revelation itself has an implicit presupposition that can no longer be taken for granted: the rigid sense of revelation as "Word" or message, or, in Steinheim's terms, the "historical revelation" (*PM*, 16). A mystical understanding can only be established *alongside* an unmystical concept of revelation—it *supplements* the traditional

---

37. See Weiner's account in *9 ½ Mystics*, 84ff.

understanding, yet it becomes unsubstantial when the rigid concept ceases to exist. While he does not want to rule out the possibility that there is still mystical experience (as in the case of Rav Kook, for example), such experience will hardly have collective meaning, and it cannot establish the authority necessary for a theology proper: "If there is to be a mysticism that reflects the experience of an individual or individuals, it will not easily, if at all, assume the simultaneously free and obligatory expression that derives from its being bound to an historical revelation" (*PM*, 16). As highlighted in "Reflections on Jewish Theology," the legitimizing force of revelation is called into question along with its rigid meaning: "The binding character of Revelation for a collective has disappeared. The word of God no longer serves as a source for the definition of possible contents of a religious Tradition and thus of a possible theology. Even where a mystical conception of Revelation is positively admitted, it necessarily lacks authoritative character" (*JJC*, 274).

Whereas Scholem still pointed to the religious anarchist as the legitimate successor to the mystic in the Ha'ol discussion, this figure is only an epigone and outsider in the context of these later texts. No longer a member of the family, no longer able to move, the religious anarchist is hardly the one to challenge the definite form of the oral Torah for the sake of a Torah to come. Indeed, he has lost the basic assumption of Jewish tradition, including mysticism—that is, the assumption of the Torah from Mount Sinai. This almost becomes part of Scholem's definition of anarchism: "Anyone attempting today to bring matters of inspiration and mystical cognition within the range of public understanding, without seeing himself, with a clear conscience, as being connected in an unqualified way with the great principle of Torah from heaven, of that selfsame Torah with those selfsame letters as it is, is a religious anarchist" (*PM*, 15–16). Elsewhere, Scholem makes it clear that this description also applies to him: "I myself believe in God, but I am a religious anarchist. I do not believe in the Torah of Moses from Sinai. If [!] God really exists, then there is something sublime in the very wrestling over belief in Him" (*PM*, 85).[38] What remains of tradition is a doubtful faith that Scholem himself has declared theologically unfruitful.

This version of anarchism is now the ineluctable condition of the modern, not merely a rebellion against form or against dogmas. Thus, Scholem's theological reflections are necessarily "weak," as they do not rest on stable foundations.

---

38. Similarly, Scholem states in conclusion to the Ha'ol discussion: "I believe in God, this is the basis of my life and faith. All the rest [of Judaism] is in doubt and open to debate" (Mendes-Flohr, *Divided Passions*, 346).

When he speaks of the "nothingness of revelation," or tradition or language as the medium of revelation, by no means is this backed by an unshakeable faith in revelation even where it is invisible, or where only tradition remains. Scholem is critical enough to imagine the end of tradition—or at least tradition that is "fulfilled" in the sense of granting meaning and authority. The result is in fact paradoxical. On one side, the side on which "we" stand, we cannot imagine any revelation other than mystical revelation; on the other side, this mystical revelation is only executable when it is conceived as dependent on historical revelation. While Scholem recognizes the "historical" meaning of revelation as a concrete message, he cannot accept it due to historical skepticism. However, he does suggest repeatedly that other forms of relating to Jewish tradition are still possible, if perhaps weaker and less productive. Philology is one of these.

THIRTEEN

PHILOLOGY
Poetically Spoken

IN AN ENTHUSIASTIC LETTER TO his future wife, Escha Burchhardt, from the summer of 1918, Scholem reports on his many recent philological realizations. Studying the Book of Isaiah, he has many insights into history, lament, the philosophy of the Hebrew language, and "philology, of which I have in fact developed an extraordinary conception and which should be discussed only with the greatest reverence. Philology is truly a secret science and the only legitimate form of historical science that has existed until now. It is the greatest confirmation of my view of the central importance of Tradition, though of course in a new sense of the word" (*LL*, 78). Inversely, "philology" is a new term that he uses to speak about tradition, a term that finally opens up a transition from his attempt at a theory or system of Judaism to historical engagement. This transition came at a time when Scholem was devoting himself to historical study—in 1920 he began his dissertation on the *Book Bahir*—and ultimately became central to his self-description; he referred to himself as a philologist just as often as he referred to himself as a historian.

In his diaries and letters, the term first appears in the summer of 1918. During his "philological studies of Isaiah," Scholem begins "to understand the meaning of philology in a deep and historical sense" (*LY*, 262). Scholem is now less focused on the traditional commentaries than on the "critical" philology of his day, as in the commentaries of Protestant Old Testament scholars such as Bernhard Duhm, Wilhelm Gesenius, and Adalbert Merx. He finds Merx "*methodologically* highly exemplary" (*Br I*, 177), probably because of Merx's focus on the history of exegesis. As we will see in part 3, Scholem's engagement with these scholars is decisive for the development of his historical method. At the same time, he also develops a more general idea of philology, especially in discussions with Benjamin and inspired by the early Romantics, specifically Friedrich Schlegel's rudimentary theory of philology.[1]

Scholem's idea of philology combines different moments. First and foremost, he sees in philology itself a kind of tradition: "philology is among the most precise examples of the proper conception of *Tradition*. The labor of an entire generation is condensed into a handful of sentences, which then form the basis for the next generation of work. Seemingly forgotten, previous labors vanish into this new foundation, where they remain vital" (*LY*, 262). Second, philology is related to *religious* tradition, often standing in contrast: "Philology in the empty, technical sense emerges where commentary is no longer recognized as a historical-religious category. Commentary is the legitimate form of philological literature. Herein is revealed the relationship of philology to mysticism, which is tradition" (*T II*, 329). The form of commentary, already designated by Scholem as essential for Judaism in his readings of Molitor and Hirsch, is also essential for philology. Thus, third, Scholem can think of philology as the continuation of tradition, or at least as its defense: "The apology for mysticism has mostly been supplied from the negative side only. In reality, it has had its positive apology since time immemorial (outside of mathematics, which it is no accomplishment to misunderstand mystically): philology. The philologist is the mystic *kat exochen*" (*T II*, 329). This link is emphatically formulated in Scholem's first publication on the Kabbalah, a review of a Kabbalah anthology that appeared in 1921, in which he explicitly protests against the scolding of philologists: "It seems . . . to be a generally modern sport to let it rip against these ossified, traditionless scoundrels, who are also calcified in their 'lexical' traditions. . . . They are inclined to the seemingly unmystical view that it is sometimes more difficult, and in any case a farther-reaching duty, to understand a text than to experience it" (*T II*, 678). However, it is in fact possible for "deep philology to have a truly mystical function"; it is close to the Kabbalah because "a worthy transmission . . . , perhaps involves a deeper relationship to a Kabbalah that is called 'transmission' for a reason, deeper than that achieved by the arbitrariness of those who stumble" (*T II*, 684).

Thus, fourth, the concept of philology gains a systematic function within Scholem's reflections. Above, we saw that the key function of tradition lies in

---

1. Scholem was not aware of the decisive role that philology played for Schlegel, as Schlegel's fragments "Philosophie der Philologie" (Philosophy of Philology) were only published in 1928. Thus, Scholem notes that a "philosophy of philology has not been seriously attempted by anyone" (*T II*, 329) while recognizing that Schlegel already knew philology as a "secret science" (*LY*, 262).

its relation to the systematic, critical problem of the communicability of truth. Tradition was supposed to solve the problem of truth in history; now philology slips into this systematic position, becoming the paradigm for historiography. Asserting that philology has not been properly understood thus far due to the "inability to philosophically develop the concept of history and its foundation" (*T II*, 329), Scholem tries to develop a systematic understanding, as in a long note from the fall of 1918:

> That which can be represented of history is not its course, but a sequence of highly unreal constellations: in every historical moment, the sequence of events, historical movement, stands still in time, and this system sustains peculiar virtual shifts. *This* state is the designated object of a scientific history. Immanent changes in relations without temporal variation take place in the transition of history into literature, into sources or even oral tradition, both of which have highly peculiar laws of historical mechanics.... Thus, the teaching itself is never representable, but always only its (unreal yet exact) rigidification in infinitely small shifts of its reality. (*T II*, 387–388)

It is not historical change as such that can be understood but rather a sequence of constellations, each of which is to be reconstructed individually; the construction of such a sequence from sources is the task of history. A few years later, Benjamin develops this thought further in a discussion with Scholem. In his view, philology presents

> one side of history, or better, one layer of what is historical, for which a person may indeed be able to gain regulative and systematic, as well as constitutive, elementary logical concepts; but the connection between them must remain hidden. I define philology, not as the science or history of language, but as the *history of terminology* at its deepest level. In doing this, a most puzzling concept of time and very puzzling phenomena must surely be taken into consideration. If I am not mistaken, I have an idea of what you are getting at, without being able to elaborate on it, when you suggest that philology is close to history viewed as a chronicle. The chronicle is fundamentally interpolated history. Philological interpolation in chronicles simply reveals in its form the intention of the content, since its content interpolates history.[2]

This discussion of philology resonates with the discussion of the paradox of written tradition, which Scholem had already addressed in the context of early Romanticism. When it comes to philology, Scholem shifts the development

---

2. Letter to Scholem from 1921 in Benjamin, *Correspondence*, 176. The letter clearly responds to ideas developed by Scholem that have been lost.

of a theory firmly into the territory of history: "The system of mysticism is its history, there cannot be another.... The attempt to present the mystical idea of tradition otherwise than in its system" is doomed to failure (*T II*, 382).

As a result, Scholem's discussion of philology can also be taken as a description of his emerging position as a historian. In 1916 he still experienced it as a "paradox" that as a "foe of Europe and a follower of the New Orient" he should go to Palestine as a "teacher of a very European science" (*LY*, 93). He subsequently found a way to make this paradox productive, allowing him to better understand Jewish tradition and also enabling him to say something: "If I could write like the philologists—and if I were truly *permitted* to write thus (granted, there are frontiers where this seems to be the case)—I could create a forbidden library out of the few things I hope to know someday" (*LY*, 287). Yet how does one gain permission to write like the philologists, and, above all, how can one justify the gesture? This theoretical displacement calls for another form of writing and inscription in European research as well as Jewish tradition. As in the case of earlier shifts, this one requires rhetorical and poetic operations, and we can observe these in a series of texts written at the beginning of the 1920s around the notion of philology. Among them is a short note from 1921 that I will quote in its entirety and then analyze in depth:

"On the Kabbalah, Viewed from Beyond"
The philology of the Kabbalah is merely a projection onto a plane [*Fläche*]. In this projection, many relations are ultimately transformed into a punctuality that is only intensively perceptible, and naturally it is precisely these relations that are fundamental for the mystical-corporeal dimension of the Kabbalah, that which constitutes its space. Philology is a symbol, albeit an extraordinary one, a strangely constructed concave mirror in which a totality of the Kabbalah that is somehow still present can become visible for the people of today in a primary and pure way.

The critical history of the Kabbalah is its final goal: to roll up the symbolic carpet that is illuminated from within. The philology of mystical disciplines has to have the precise infinity of a Gobelin tapestry. This critical history is the appearance without which there can be no insight into the essence during an unmessianic time. In this history, the existence of the system—the basic fact of mysticism—is ironically challenged; indeed, the multidimensional-substantial-spatial element of the system necessarily disappears in the projection onto the plane, and is transformed into the great illusion of the line of development.

Yet whoever passes through and is able to stand in the middle, at the almost utopian yet infinitely near point from which the living source addresses him as a simultaneous manifestation, is redeemed and is himself a redeemer. For here, the situation is simple: it is simply a question of passing through the plane; nothing more is needed than virtual displacement and transformation into substantiality, the border of which was the very symbol that always belongs to its object. (*T II*, 685)[3]

Compared to other texts, such as "95 Theses," this text is more homogenous and coherent, with explicit syntax and strong, seemingly consistent vocabulary and imagery including philosophical concepts such as appearance, essence, system, and substance, as well as geometrical metaphors such as point, line, plane, space, projection, and virtual displacement. The text has an order and direction, with the final paragraph's transgression of the situation described in the first and second paragraphs.

Thus, the text suggests a reading according to which philological research would only perceive the Kabbalah from the outside, while the true aim is to transgress this outside in order to get at the thing itself, the Kabbalah proper. This argument is familiar from contemporary discussions on historicism: history only comprises reflections of something essentially unhistorical. We could add a biographical layer to this interpretation by noting that at this point in his life, Scholem was still vacillating between a metaphysical understanding of the Kabbalah and a historical understanding. Valid as it may be, however, several features of the text do not entirely fit into this interpretation. First, the strange metaphors of projection, the carpet, and the redeemer seem superfluous from this view, like personal arabesques on a common, simple argument. Moreover, upon closer inspection, these metaphors do not seem quite so coherent after all. While the historicism interpretation relies primarily on the Platonic philosophical terminology of essence and appearance, the geometrical figures operate differently. In them, the Platonic essence—the Kabbalah proper—is not figured as a dimensionless entity but something with extension, a corpus. Most importantly, this spatial metaphor implies a model of experience entirely different from the Platonic model—a phenomenological model. In the realm of spatial experience, to stay with the logic of the image, it is no longer possible to have a direct, immediate perception of the thing itself in its integrity, just as it is not possible to perceive a three-dimensional cube in its integrity unless one moves around it. If the thing itself is a corpus, there is no immediate experience of it, at least not in this model.

---

3. On this text and its variants, see Schäfer, "'Die Philologie der Kabbalah ist nur eine Projektion auf eine Fläche.'" See also Hamacher, *Gershom Scholem und die allgemeine Religionsgeschichte*, 63ff.

The text seems to be conflictual or paradoxical. Whereas the philosophical terminology suggests a Platonic model of passive vision and contemplative knowledge of an intelligible substance, the geometrical terminology points instead to a phenomenological model of a process of active yet always partial experience. Accordingly, the philologist is modeled in a twofold manner. In the Platonic model, he is naïve, perceiving only a secondary image of reality, while in the geometrical model, he is the one who *produces* images via projection, an activity that is even more explicit in the most elaborate image of the text—namely, the concave mirror. For a concave mirror does not show objects in their normal two-dimensional appearance but rather visualizes their depth, albeit in a distorted manner. As a concave mirror, philology can only produce a virtual image of the Kabbalah, yet this image does somehow represent the unrepresentable. As these two models of experience—the Platonic and the phenomenological—are hardly compatible, it becomes difficult to resolve the text's metaphors into a single interpretation. On second look, not even the third paragraph is as clear as it initially seemed. While the first sentence of this paragraph describes a crossing into the unhistorical essence of the Kabbalah itself, the second sentence proclaims the same transgression yet again. Is transgression already accomplished or yet to be achieved? Where is the "here" from which the second sentence speaks? Is it located before or beyond transgression?

Thus, if one takes the metaphors and structure of the text seriously, our first reading leads to an impasse. On closer inspection, we can make out what Michel Riffaterre calls "ungrammaticalities," details that cannot simply be interpreted "mimetically" as representations of the world, instead pointing to the text and its specific structure.[4] Thus, we realize that this is not just another realization of the common ideological discourse of historicism but a specific and unique utterance that has to be understood on its own terms. Far from being the message of Scholem's text, historicism is what Riffaterre calls a "hypogram," a prefabricated system of meaning, a cultural cliché that the text reworks and transposes to give it a more complex meaning. In this text, this happens with a double reference, with the main elements no longer referring to one code

---

4. See Riffaterre, *The Semiotics of Poetry*. According to Riffaterre, seemingly irrelevant details appear to be realizations of a common "matrix," the central but implicit structure of the poem. This matrix may be epitomized by a word that is not present in the poem but that is nevertheless transformed by the poem according to a certain "model." In Scholem's case, this matrix is probably "tradition," transformed according to the model of "geometry."

but (at least) two. The Kabbalah is characterized by oxymorons like "mystical-corporeal" or "multidimensional-substantial-spatial," which refer to both the historicist hypotext and the geometrical model. Similarly, the "concave mirror" of philological criticism is passive and reflective as well as active and operative. Finally, the "plane" (*Fläche*) onto which the Kabbalah is projected stands for its historical appearance, which is at the same time a delusion; while we are able to see the Kabbalah on this plane, we are also urged to transgress it.

The significance of the plane is even more obvious in an earlier version of the above-cited text, "Observations on the Meaning and Appearance of the Kabbalah." Scholem refers to the "plane" as "the ironic paper of historiography" as well as "a wall—history," "history's veil," or "history's veil of fog" (*T II*, 687). Here, the paradoxical image of the plane is distributed between two images—paper and veil—that are implicitly connected. "On the Kabbalah" condenses these images into the singular "dual sign," to use Riffattere's terminology once again: an equivocal expression belonging to two different and mutually exclusive codes, which therefore cannot be completely paraphrased in either of these codes.[5]

Significantly, in this earlier version, Scholem also comments on the text's status and intention—"The following observations do not have a philological goal" (*T II*, 686)—and his use of terms like "we" and "today" points to a specific situation. In contrast, "On the Kabbalah, Viewed from Beyond" omits such references and does not directly speak about itself. Even the title contributes to its ambivalence, for the viewpoint "from beyond" seems to designate the position of the redeemer articulated in the third paragraph, yet this position is ultimately not so clear, as we have already seen: Is the transgression already achieved, or is it yet to come? Moreover, the last line relating the object and its symbol seems to deconstruct the opposition of Kabbalah and philology that is constitutive for the text. Does this imply that we have come to an end or that the text negates itself? Does the last line complete the text, or does it invite another reading informed by this end? This technique of compositional irony—common in literary discourse and typical of Scholem's writing at the time, as in "The Teaching of Zion," dedicated to "the students I do not have" (see chap. 4)—further disturbs direct reading. The reader cannot determine whether the text itself already constitutes observation of the Kabbalah from beyond or whether it refers to such observation as something yet to come.

---

5. On dual signs, see Riffaterre, *The Semiotics of Poetry*, 86–109.

Double reference, openness to different readings, ambiguity, and undecidability are all essential features of poetic texts. Indeed, Scholem's texts from the early 1920s are poetic in a technical sense: what is expressed in them cannot be easily said in direct language; they cannot be paraphrased, for their meaning consists less in a specific message than in a structure that makes them into unique utterances.[6] We have seen similar mechanisms of condensation and isolation from context at work already in earlier texts of Scholem, most notably in his fragmentary writing from 1918 and 1919. These fragments are now worked out in texts like "On the Kabbalah" as well as "Politics of Zionism" or "The Teaching of Zion," which I discussed in part 1. In their imagery and structure, these texts perform a semantic closure by which the meaning of words is determined less by the general codes of language than by the internal structure of the text and its displacement of such codes. Therefore, rather than trying to say what they say, we need to understand how they say it. The question is not so much how they position themselves in a common field of philosophical positions, for example, but how they create *new* meaning and a *new* idiom that Scholem can use to handle difficulties and paradoxes that he cannot really resolve.

Scholem continues to use the figures, procedures, and formulations of "On the Kabbalah" in several other texts that deal with the relationship between Kabbalah and philology—and, by extension, his own self-understanding. In 1937 he writes an open letter to Salman Schocken entitled "A Candid Word Regarding the True Intentions of My Study of the Kabbalah," which integrates the imagery of "On the Kabbalah" into an autobiographical narrative. Scholem stresses that he turned to the philology of the Kabbalah not by accident but out of metaphysical longing. In his youth, he sought a key to the Kabbalah:

> For the mountain, the corpus of things, requires no key at all; only the misty wall of history hanging around it must be penetrated. To penetrate this wall was the task I set for myself. Will I get stuck in the mist, will I suffer a "professorial death," so to speak? But the necessity of historical criticism and critical history cannot be satisfied by anything else, even where it demands sacrifice.
>
> Certainly, history may be fundamentally an illusion [*Schein*], but an illusion without which, in time, no insight into the essence of things is possible. In the peculiar concave mirror of philological critique, that mystical totality of the system whose existence disappears precisely in its projection

---

6. See Jakobson, "Closing Statement: *Linguistics and Poetics*," in *Style and Language*, 352–377.

onto historical time can become visible for the people of today in the purest way, in the legitimate orders of commentary.

Today, as on the first day, my work lives in this paradox, in the hope of being properly addressed from within the mountain, and of that most invisible, smallest shift of history that causes truth to break forth from the illusion of "development." (*Br I*, 472)

Juxtaposed with "On the Kabbalah," this text clearly refers to similar problems and employs similar images and figures of thought, but here they are framed autobiographically, and the paradoxes seem less pressing as a result. An existential code of courage and desperation—already alluded to in the figure of the redeemer in "On the Kabbalah"—is much more present here, while at the same time there is less compositional irony, and the images of the concave mirror and of projection are somewhat isolated; indeed, the second sentence of the second paragraph appears rather opaque without the geometric imagery of the earlier text. The reader of both texts is left with the impression that Scholem's older formulation no longer fits its new context in this letter. Yet, despite this sentence, and despite some other open questions—Is Scholem striving to reach the mountain, or is he already sitting upon it, hearing? Is courage or hope the central virtue here?—the text is "readerly" and relatively easy to interpret, for example, as a kind of personal compromise between science and metaphysics.

Nevertheless, this text also contains dual signs, albeit of a different type. The "mountain" is particularly rich in associations. It refers not only to the corporeality of the Kabbalah as in the earlier text but also to Mount Sinai, the site of revelation, as well as the proverbial mountain to which the prophet must go if the mountain does not come to the prophet. The misty mountain has a certain air of early Romanticism, as in Ludwig Tieck's "Runenberg" (in which Ernst Bloch and Walter Benjamin saw an allegory for memory); the philologist facing the mountain is strongly suggestive of Kafka's parable "Before the Law," and so on.[7] The mountain remains ambiguous but not paradoxical, since the different codes do not annul each other in the way the more abstract figures in the earlier text do—here, it is this abundance that fascinates. In a sense, Scholem recasts his earlier thoughts in the later text through a kind of secondary mimesis: he transforms abstract speculations into a clear image that blurs contradictions by its very materiality. However, precisely because the image of the mountain

---

7. See Bloch, "Bilder des Déjà vu," in *Gesamtausgabe*, 232–242.

appears to be simple and natural (compared to the imagery of projection, plane, etc.), the difficulties of deciphering it are all the more astonishing. The reader faces an intriguing tension between the image and its content, a tension that is typical of allegory, revealing the unbridgeable distance between signs and their reference.

Finally, Scholem rewrites—and overwrites—this text once more in his "Ten Unhistorical Aphorisms on Kabbalah," published in 1958 in a relatively obscure festschrift. This text, too, has often been read as a key to Scholem's work that unlocks the mysteries of his historical writings.[8] The first of these aphorisms reads as follows:

> The philology of a mystical discipline like the Kabbalah has something ironic to it. It is engaged with a veil of fog that hangs as the history of mystical tradition around the corpus, the space of the thing itself, a fog, however, that comes from that very thing.
>
> Is there something of the law of the thing itself remaining in this fog, visible to the philologist, or does the essential disappear in this projection of the historical? The uncertainty in answering this question belongs to the nature of the philological enterprise itself, and thus the hope on which this work lives retains something ironic that cannot be detached from it. But is it not so that this element of irony lies in the object of the Kabbalah itself, and not only in its history?
>
> The kabbalist asserts that there is a tradition regarding truth that is transmissible [*tradierbar*]. An ironic assertion, for the truth in question here is anything but transmissible. It can be recognized, but not handed down, and that within it which can be handed down does not contain it any longer. True tradition remains hidden; only fallen [*verfallende*] tradition falls [*verfällt*] upon an object, and only in falling [*Verfall*] does it become visible in its greatness.[9]

Again, there are obvious similarities between this text and "On the Kabbalah" in both content and form. The aphorism addresses the relationship between the Kabbalah and philology as an ironic one; it has the form of a general, impersonal statement articulated in a closed text, with three paragraphs running roughly parallel to those of the earlier text. However, the tone of the aphorism

---

8. The aphorisms are central to David Biale's general reading of Scholem as well as Nathan Rotenstreich's reading in "Symbolism and Transcendence: On Some Philosophical Aspects of Gershom Scholem's Opus," among others.

9. "Zehn unhistorische Sätze über Kabbala," in *Judaica*, vol. 3, 264. See also Biale, "Gershom Scholem's Ten Unhistorical Aphorisms on Kabbalah."

is smoother, the sentences are shorter and less complex, and there are neither abrupt turns nor disturbing repetitions. The later text only alludes to the imagery that was central to its precursor, and the geometrical code is only hinted at: Scholem refers to "corpus," "space," and "projection" but not "dimensions" or "the mountain." The Platonic code is present in "the essential" and "the thing itself," but its opposite, appearance, is lacking. Most significantly, the deconstruction of the Platonic code takes place already in the second sentence rather than at the end of the text as in "On the Kabbalah." Thus, irony is implicit throughout the entire aphorism. Framed by two questions, the second paragraph in particular demonstrates the double irony that the philologist claims for the thing itself, thereby losing it—but perhaps finding it precisely by losing it.

The most obvious change between the two texts involves the third paragraph. While the earlier text speaks about the Kabbalah "from beyond," addressing the relation between the philological subject, the Kabbalah, and its messianic end, the aphorism speaks about the Kabbalah itself, paraphrasing what the kabbalist would say. Significantly, the concluding sentence of the aphorism does not deal with the vanishing subject of the philologist but with the object, vanishing tradition. This one shift also entails another: only implicit in the earlier text, tradition becomes an explicit focus in the aphorism. Accordingly, the opposition of essence and appearance is replaced by an opposition that is *internal* to tradition—namely, the opposition between "true" and "fallen" tradition. Now explicit, the earlier text's matrix of "tradition" is most likely no longer the organizing center of the aphorism, instead functioning in another structure that we will have to seek.

At the same time, however, the explicitness of the matrix does not dissolve the aphorism's poeticity into bare mimetic description. The status of "tradition" is still equivocal in the last paragraph, as the kabbalist's assertion of tradition could refer to a certain content passed down through time (*traditum*) as well as the process of passing down (*traditio*); in turn, tradition can be understood (secularly) as a process of cultural transmission, or (religiously) as an authentic, authoritative, even sacred realm of authority. Moreover, tradition implies a broad range of internal semiotic oppositions such as living-dead, esoteric-exoteric, or written-spoken, allowing Scholem to formulate apparent paradoxes such as the silent or invisible tradition that we already encountered in "95 Theses." For Scholem, and even more generally in the context of Jewish discourse, tradition is never a simple descriptive term of a neutral metalanguage but always a highly overdetermined, even controversial category.

Thus, rather than leading to semantic stability, the presence of "tradition" prompts a series of semiotic shifts that serve to further destabilize the text.

To give an example, "the thing itself" representing the Kabbalah in the first paragraph becomes the "object" that the declining Kabbalah "falls upon" (*verfällt auf*) in the third. This blurs clear-cut divisions while enforcing the cohesion of the text through repetition, most obviously in the last sentence with "tradition" and "falling." The German verb *verfallen* means to fall upon, to decay, and to become addicted to something, and the last sentence is a play on this polysemy. Again, the repetition of words—as in rhyme or parallelism—is one of the essential traits of poetry, strongly contributing to semantic closure, as the meanings of "fallen" are contracted into this one sentence.[10] Simultaneously, repetition suggests a necessary relation between the different iterations of "fall," and even paradoxes such as "fallen tradition" seem natural, almost coming across as a truism when phrased as elegantly as in Scholem's last sentence.

Scholem's aphorisms combine formal closure with another strategy: reference to other texts. The condensed last sentence of the first aphorism refers to itself, thereby creating a figure of thought that is as suggestive as it is rich in meaning with "fallen tradition." It also points beyond itself to the "historical" texts of the same author, in which the reader may expect to hear more about this fascinating yet enigmatic idea; as any reader of Scholem's account of the Kabbalah can see, the third paragraph alludes to his version of the history of the Kabbalah, specifically the Sabbatian crisis that constitutes the precise moment of the falling (*Verfall*) of tradition, or in the words of a later essay, the very moment when "all concepts of Jewish mysticism seem to converge, only to explode in their own dialectics—or, said more sadly, to fizzle out."[11] In the aphorism, the ambiguity of *verfallen* denotes the moment in which the inner structure of the Kabbalah (its "greatness") becomes visible, the very moment when it "falls upon" messianic activity and simultaneously "falls into" pieces. In order to understand the mysterious figure of fallen tradition, we must refer to Scholem's other texts on the Kabbalah.

This reference also allows us to understand the function of the "Unhistorical Aphorisms." Whereas earlier texts such as "95 Theses" were programmatic in proclaiming what has to be done, the aphorisms are "paragrammatic" in the

---

10. See Jakobson's famous formulation: "any sequence of semantic units strives to build an equation. Similarity superimposed on contiguity imparts to poetry its throughgoing symbolic, multiplex, polysemantic essence" ("Closing Statement: Linguistics and Poetics," 370).

11. "Die Theologie des Sabbatianismus im Lichte Abraham Cardosos," in *Judaica*, vol. 1, 131–132.

sense that they refer to what has already been written. They are "paratexts," with the title already revealing that they are (negatively) related to Scholem's historical texts. As forewords, authorial comments or blurbs, paratexts are thresholds rather than foundations: they point to other texts and must be understood based on their function, be it to clarify what has already been written, to ensure an accurate reading, or to arouse the reader's interest.[12] More often than not, paratexts have an authorial function—namely, to direct the reader to other works by the same author, affirming the author's authority regarding what he or she has said or, in this case, demonstrating that Scholem can only be understood by Scholem.[13] In order for this gesture to be effective, it is essential not to use literal expression. It is precisely through their at once cryptic and seemingly evident form that the aphorisms evoke the reader's desire to seek more of this deep but easily accessible knowledge by turning to Scholem's historiographic work, where what is hinted at here will be developed more fully. Thus it is only logical that Scholem would refuse any request to comment on his own aphorisms, such as the request by Adorno. They must remain isolated, brilliant in their auratic solitariness, pointing to the authority of their author, as Scholem answers in a 1963 letter to Adorno:

> I decidedly sinned against myself when I agreed to publish the unhistorical aphorisms on the Kabbalah, assuming, however, according to what is said in one of those aphorisms, that no one would take notice of it, and that the safest way to hide it would be to place it in print in such a festschrift. Now you want a commentary. Well, what do you think? Such a thing only existed in former times, when authors wrote the commentaries themselves, directly, and if they were smart, those commentaries mostly contained the opposite of what was in the text. I shall take care not to step into the nettles here. On my aphorisms: save yourself if you can. (*Br II*, 91)

---

12. See Genette, *Paratext*. Scholem himself did not think of his aphorisms as fundamental. In his view, Biale referred to the aphorisms too much; Scholem wrote to Biale: "To quote remarks which I myself called unhistorical as proof of my anachronistic concepts in 'counterhistory' is no way to judge my historical *researches*. They were written consciously in *contrast* to these and every reader I know has read them as such" (quoted in Schäfer, "Die Philologie der Kabbala," 24). Even here, Scholem does not offer a clarification of what he "really meant" by the aphorisms, instead sending another text that is not any clearer: the open letter to Schocken.

13. "The correctness of the authorial . . . point of view is the implicit creed and spontaneous ideology of the paratext" (Genette, *Paratexts*, 408).

The aphorisms no longer seek to establish a new code ("tradition") or distort an older one ("historicism"). Instead, they aim to establish a particular reading of existing texts—namely, Scholem's own texts on the Kabbalah. Relating Scholem to Scholem, the ultimate function of the aphorisms is to constitute the totality of an œuvre. The aphorisms do not do so explicitly but by poetic means of allusion, condensation, and semiotic displacement.

PART 3

PRODUCING HISTORY: SCHOLEM'S SCHOLARSHIP

> Having given up philosophy in despair, I have turned to the writing of history, and I can only speak as a historian, with a certain philosophical memory. ("Discussion," 13)

Readers of Scholem's work often ask whether he was "only" a historian or something "more," be it a secret philosopher, a cryptotheologian, or an artist. However, this question overstates the contrast between history and philosophy, theology, or art while further ignoring the fact that the writing of history has its own logic and its own weight. A major part of Scholem's work is historiographical: beginning with his dissertation, he studied the Kabbalah with great consistency and methodological tenacity. As we have already seen, it is no coincidence that he became a historian, for this is where he ultimately found the project that allowed him to realize his intellectual identity as well as a distinct way to make Jewish tradition his own.

First and foremost, we must therefore understand Scholem the historian *as* a historian. This is not a matter of arriving at a presentation or critique of Scholem's results—both must be left to Kabbalah specialists—but rather understanding his approach, his perspective on the Kabbalah, and the means by which he presents its history. This approach has its own logic, and it cannot be reduced to an underlying (Zionist or anarchistic) "worldview" that determines his writing of history, nor to a "philosophy of history" understood as the ultimate intellectual unity of that writing.

Scholem's project of writing the history of the Kabbalah is connected to modern Jewish historiography, which played a particular role in the constitution of modern Judaism in the post-emancipation era. A reaction to the crisis of traditional Jewish memory, Jewish historiography became "the faith of fallen Jews," in the words of Yerushalmi, though it could never fully compensate that crisis and thus perpetuated a tense relationship to living memory.[1] Scholem formulates this ambivalence as a dialectics between construction and destruction:

> Historical criticism as a scientific method is by its very nature unable to avoid this dialectic. Its destructive function—and there is no doubt that its natural and most striking feature is its destructive one—can be completely turned about: to free all of those bodies of data or values which in one moment change the entire perspective, a liberation which may unintentionally transform all of the remnants of the past into marvelous symbols of life. The historical critic must at every moment consider the possibility that he will turn out to be a conservative at the next turn of the road. (PM, 55–56)

The historian is portrayed here as someone who revives "dead" facts of the past so that they can gain new significance, in turn vitally determining the present. However, this is not merely a process of empathy or re-creation as the passage suggests. Like any historian, Scholem brings the past back to life not directly but via the detour of destruction, through scholarly criticism and polemics. The polemical element in this writing of history can be described with David Biale as "counterhistory," based on "the belief that the true history lies in a subterranean tradition that must be brought into light, much as the apocalyptic thinker decoded an ancient prophecy or as Walter Benjamin spoke of, 'brushing history against the grain.'"[2] Counterhistories are essentially polemical: "Their method consists of the systematic exploitation of the adversary's most trusted sources against their grain—'die Geschichte gegen den Strich kämmen.' Their aim is the distortion of the adversary's self-image, of his identity, through the

---

1. Yerushalmi, *Zakhor*, 86. Modern Jewish historiography "must at least functionally repudiate premises that were basic to all Jewish conceptions of history in the past. In effect, it must stand in sharp opposition to its own subject matter" (ibid., 89).

2. Biale, *Kabbalah and Counter-History*, 7. See also Weidner, "'Geschichte gegen den Strich bürsten,'" and Krochmalnik, "Neue Tafeln."

deconstruction of his memory."[3] For Scholem, this primarily means writing against liberal historical Jewish scholarship; it also entails reading religious kabbalistic texts as historical sources even as they present themselves as timeless wisdom. Counterhistory does not exhaust itself in the reversal of values. Instead, it presupposes a different way of forming narrative meaning and a different kind of reading.

Scholem wants to understand the Kabbalah historically rather than adapting it. This implies a twofold temporality. On the one hand, it brings past time into the present. On the other hand, it yields this past time as a sequence of successive events in the past, as the comprehensible, necessary development of a "story."[4] This concentration on the story is specific to modern historiography, whereas religious memory and also exemplary historiography ascribe meaning directly to the past. Later in this part, I will examine the "story" element in Scholem's history of the Kabbalah, its step-by-step emergence, its inner structure and dramatics, and its implications and consequences.

Modern historiography does not emerge through narrative plotting alone, however. The critical treatment of sources is no less decisive. Far from a neutral, auxiliary scholarly condition, the decision about *how* to read sources in the first place is an essential preliminary decision about the nature of history. Criticism that is philological and historical does not follow a strict methodology. It is oriented by the disciplinary standards specific to respective fields and schools, a largely diffuse mixture of leading questions, basic concepts, accepted methodological means, and so on, which can be designated as "paradigms" of historiography. Taking a look at such paradigms also reveals an essential shift that originated in the nineteenth century on the margins of historiographical research, in political economy, classics, and religious studies. This is where the methodological prerequisites for counterhistory emerged in a hermeneutics of suspicion that destroys the logic of its object in order to reconstruct it.[5] As we will see in biblical criticism especially, this constitutes a new way of reading tradition and a different way of writing history as confrontation with the other.[6] The next chapters will deal with these procedures and the paradigm of the history of religion, which helps Scholem to gain access to the Kabbalah.

---

3. Funkenstein, *Perceptions of Jewish History*, 36.
4. On the concept of the story, see the introduction in White, *Metahistory*, as well as Veyne, *Writing History*, chapter 3.
5. See Ricoeur, *Freud and Philosophy*, chapter 2; Cassirer, *The Problem of Knowledge*, chapter 18.
6. See also de Certeau, *The Writing of History*, esp. chapter 2.

These two elements of historical writing—scholarly paradigm and historical narrative—come together in Scholem's exploration of the Kabbalah. For him, the sources are already "dead," illegible, and remote. Characteristically, he often speaks of "ruins." They cannot simply be brought back to their own life, and thus they must be reconstructed in an entirely *different* rationality. A straightforward historical narrative of the Kabbalah would tell the story of the great mystics and comprehend their work; it would bring the past close to us just as if we could live it. By contrast, Scholem's portrayal offers a split representation of the past. On the one hand, the aim is not only to revive the object intuitively but also to make it comprehensible in its inner logic. On the other hand, *within* this logic, the object itself appears in its radical foreignness, all the more impressive because we cannot easily familiarize ourselves with it.

To understand Scholem's writing of history, the following chapters will develop its different elements, roughly following the chronology in which they emerged while representing their different systematic roles. Thus we begin with the paradigm that Scholem adopted early in his career, the history of religion as practiced by Protestant critics, which determined his approach to the Kabbalah as well as his conceptualization of terms such as "myth" and "mysticism" much more strongly than philosophical speculation. We will see how this paradigm operates through attention to Gnosticism and its symbolism on the one hand and a history of apocalyptic thought on the other. Finally, in the later twentieth century, he discovered that the Sabbatian crisis could provide a plot for a historical narrative of the Kabbalah and its effect on Judaism, including the transformation of that crisis into a specifically Jewish modernity via thinkers of a clandestine Enlightenment. It is this plot, the largest plot that connects the most extreme positions—mystical nihilism and merely rational religiosity—that increasingly fascinated Scholem in his old age.

FOURTEEN

HISTORY OF RELIGION
A Paradigm

FOR SCHOLEM, THE KABBALAH IS a phenomenon of the history of religion. In his dissertation, he criticizes Jewish historians who "in principle seek the development of the Kabbalah in the context of history of philosophy rather than in the history of religion";[1] in 1921 he stresses that the Kabbalah seems "to need to be once again proven as a legitimate object of research by historians of religion" (*T II*, 659). In the first outline of his research program from 1925, he writes that the goal of Kabbalah research must be "the knowledge and record of the *history of the Kabbalah's development.*"[2] While this historical knowledge still seems to be a means to the end of metaphysical knowledge for Scholem here, he takes it as self-evident that scholarly exploration of the Kabbalah must be based in the history of religion.

In 1928 Scholem published the essay "On the Question of the Origin of the Kabbalah," which represents an important step in his development as a scholar. While leaving open the question of the authenticity of the *Zohar*, in this essay Scholem already explicitly rejects the direct derivation of the Kabbalah from late antique tradition. At the same time, he criticizes older research that attempted to "prove a speculative system [in the *Zohar*], a definite, consistent view of the world that is philosophical and mystical in nature, only artificially veiled in mythological and homiletic form."[3] Such an interpretation overlooks the particularity of the text, in which "not a few rudiments of older stages of

---

1. Scholem, *Das Buch Bahir*, 20n1.
2. Scholem, letter to C. N. Bialik, in *Judaica*, vol. 6, 55.
3. Scholem, "Zur Frage der Entstehung der Kabbala," 13.

development and sources of the Kabbalah remain preserved."[4] Essentially hybrid, multilayered, and inconsistent, the *Zohar* cannot be understood through conceptual construction but only through a "history of mystical terminology."[5] Scholem deduces fundamental consequences for the study of the Kabbalah: "The simple and yet very successfully operating methodological prerequisite of the approaches represented here is that the kabbalistic movement cannot be adequately portrayed in the categories of the history of philosophy, but rather only in those of the history of religion. . . . The attempt to express a more or less immediately experienced religious reality in language . . . rightfully belongs only to the realm of the history of religion and should be described using its methods."[6] Whatever interests him about the Kabbalah at this point—its metaphysical value, its political potential, the expression it gives to the spirit of the Jewish people—he decides that *scholarly* exploration of the Kabbalah must operate within the framework of history of religion.

In the interwar period, history of religion was less a discipline than a specific approach. Designated by contemporaries as the "Religionsgeschichtliche Schule" (history of religions school), a group of young exegetes at the end of the nineteenth century devoted themselves to "late Judaism" and the early history of Christianity as well as comparison of the biblical religions with neighboring religions. Among others, this group included Hermann Gunkel, Wilhelm Bousset, Hugo Gressmann, Siegfried Mowinckel, and Ernst Troeltsch.[7] Methodologically, their research primarily emerged from the development of Old Testament criticism, in particular from the link between historical and philological criticism in the work of Julius Wellhausen.

Unlike older source criticism, Wellhausen does not stop at the "mechanical dissection" of texts; instead, criticism "must aim at bringing the different writings when thus arranged into relation with each other, must seek to render them intelligible as phases of a living process, and thus to make it possible to trace a graduated development of the tradition."[8] Wellhausen pursues criticism beyond the negative result of the text's inconsistency to arrive at a conception of its inner development. To do so, he decisively breaks with the explicit account

---

4. Scholem, "Zur Frage der Entstehung," 13.
5. Scholem, "Zur Frage der Entstehung," 7.
6. Scholem, "Zur Frage der Entstehung," 6–7.
7. See Gressmann, *Albert Eichhorn und die Religionsgeschichtliche Schule*; Murrmann-Kahl, *Die entzauberte Heilsgeschichte*.
8. Wellhausen, *Prolegomena to the History of Israel*, 295. On Wellhausen, see Perlitt, *Vatke und Wellhausen*, and above all the very lucid study by Boschwitz, *Julius Wellhausen* (praised by Scholem, see *Br II*, 24). See also Weidner, "The Political Theology of Ethical Monotheism."

of the biblical text, which although "strictly uniform" he considers "only made and applied retrospectively. Recent research has burst this unity. Under the uniform surface, there are disparate remnants of lower layers, which one must bring out in order to arrive at historical reality."[9] Intentionally and methodologically, Wellhausen reads his sources "against the grain," attending to what they show to the critical reader rather than just what they say.

Methodologically, the work of the history of religions school proceeds in similar ways, but whereas Wellhausen operated largely within the realm of biblical history, the history of religions school also explores the relation of this history to extrabiblical mythology, such as the Babylonian creation myth. It is characteristic of this school that it does not limit itself "to maintaining the Babylonian origin of biblical material, but rather, throughout, [it explains] the particular ways by which these materials were taken into Israel and reformed."[10] The historical critic does not aim at a proof of origin; interpretation begins precisely with the late phase and works through the entire development in order "to reconstruct the original context and to indicate the basis of its alteration, i.e., to write the history of the tradition."[11] Moreover, the history of religions school no longer focuses on the larger literary units but rather on "materials" and "motifs"—that is, the conjunction of certain religious ideas with certain forms of expression that precede the actual texts. While Wellhausen, for example, still imagined individual authors behind the presumed sources, scholars from the history of religions school stress that the writers are bound to what is given, be it the material or the conventions of representation. "As a rule, literary critics do not consider that there has also been an unwritten history, and that one must go beyond the literary texts if one wants to capture the driving motifs. How often is the unwritten more important than the written!"[12] For to a certain extent, religious texts originate "in the unconscious, in the uncontrollable depths of the group psyche of a community,"[13] and they have a *Sitz im Leben* in the cultic praxis of this community. This is particularly important when it comes to generic forms related to recurrent

---

9. Wellhausen, *Grundrisse zum Alten Testament*, 68.
10. Gunkel, *Creation and Chaos*, xl. "I hold it to be methodologically objectionable to investigate only the beginning of a thing and to ignore the subsequent, often more important and more valuable, history of the same" (ibid., xxxix).
11. Gunkel, *Creation and Chaos*, 164.
12. Gressmann, *Albert Eichhorn und die Religionsgeschichtliche Schule*, 30. On the difference between history of religion and literary criticism, see also Koch, *The Growth of Biblical Tradition*, chapter 6.
13. Bousset, *Kyrios Christos: A History*, 146.

situations in the community that respond to constant needs. Hence, the history of transmission can also be an analytical tool for the development of "piety"—or in modern terms, "mentality": "the task of research is to clarify that part of a people's life to which the relevant genre belongs, and thus to understand one from the other."[14]

Scholem gained familiarity with works on the history of religion in his youth.[15] While studying the Bible, he read a lot of historical criticism, including works by among others Wellhausen, Bernhard Duhm, Kurt Marti, and Hermann Gunkel, whom he found "more congenial than Wellhausen in every respect" (*Br I*, 129).[16] In 1914 he writes in his diary, "Wellhausen's hypothesis is a product of scientific anti-Semitism and Christian insolence. On the one hand, Wellhausen wants to date the rise of Judaism as recently as possible, while on the other, he puts Judaism in as poor a light as he can vis-à-vis the New Testament" (*LY*, 39). A year later, however, Scholem wavers between Wellhausen and the Orthodox view (*T I*, 146), and in 1916 he is "amused" to note that an acquaintance is still "poisoned by Wellhausen" (*LY*, 157). At the end of 1917, he considers Wellhausen again in order to "finally come closer to confrontation" (*Br I*, 129) and criticizes the entire approach: "Without a historical-philosophical assumption on the development of Israel, the critic can't establish or prove a thing, *nothing*. This assumption is not the *result* of research, but *precedes* it. Like a shut door, the assumption even constrains research" (*LY*, 157). Subsequently, however, Scholem notes that Wellhausen could "nevertheless be right with this approach and it would not be a circle but an inverse method of approximation, through which he uses things that are probable from other places . . . for textual criticism, thereby once again grounding the theory more firmly" (*T II*, 83). Scholem thus recognizes the duality of Wellhausen's approach, but he remains skeptical regarding its positive result and the "whole 'historical' view of today,"

---

14. Gunkel, "Literaturgeschichte Israels," col. 1193.

15. Biale makes a comparison between Scholem and Hans Jonas as "heirs to and dissenters from the Religionswissenschaftschule" (*Kabbalah and Counter-History*, 66), but compared to Jonas, Scholem seems to me much closer to classical literary criticism. See further discussion below. Hamacher also stresses "that the later scholar of the Kabbalah found the way to his philological method primarily through Christian Bible scholarship" (*Gershom Scholem und die allgemeine Religionsgeschichte*, 82). In spite of her title, Hamacher concentrates primarily on later phenomenology of religion (ibid., esp. 73ff., 170ff., 296ff.).

16. Gunkel "does not defile the Bible, honestly attempting *evaluation*" (*Br I*, 129). Scholem also reads De Wette (*T I*, 325–326), Duhm (*Br I*, 29), Marti (*Br I*, 184), and Merx (*Br I*, 177), and Jewish Bible scholars, as well as scholars of the New Testament and church history, such as Marheineke (*T I*, 325).

which is hardly able to "historically explain the emergence of Judaism and not leave those mysteries that the old view inevitably brought with it. Yet what value would this ... view have if it *misses* the aim that alone gives it meaning? If Judaism is as mysterious afterwards as it was before" (*T II*, 83–84).

We have already seen that Scholem's theological reflections later move in a completely different direction, which should make this problem "irrelevant" in a certain sense (*Br I*, 183). Yet we have also seen that historical criticism is an essential catalyst for "religious anarchism," and Scholem thus remains ambivalent regarding the approaches and questions of biblical scholarship. In a lecture from 1952, he writes that for him, "the efforts of present-day biblical scholars" are not convincing, because too much is "based upon arduously constructed yet highly precarious hypotheses.... In the Kabbalistic writings of medieval Judaism, all those things that in the Bible must be forceably wrenched and twisted out are evident here for all to see. With regard to the survival or revival of mythical notions, which modern biblical researchers must strive so hard to clarify, the texts with which the scholar of the Kabbalah is concerned allow him to proceed with far greater methodological confidence" (*MS*, 140–141). As this passage shows, Scholem's skepticism regarding biblical criticism does not prevent him from adopting methods, tendencies, and questions for material that he sees as better suited to the approach—namely, the Kabbalah.

A scholarly paradigm such as the history of religion is more than a mere method but less than a worldview. It is contingent, for treating the Kabbalah as part of the history of religion is not self-evident. Rejecting the history of philosophy, Scholem could have drawn on other models as well. For example, it is possible to consider the Kabbalah as part of an esoteric school, as is the case in most French scholarship; it can also be linked more closely to Jewish history, as Heinrich Graetz does, considering it as a result of the crisis of Judaism in the Diaspora without taking the detour via religion. Once a paradigm has been chosen, however, it has certain consequences, directing interests and overshadowing other aspects. Considering the Kabbalah in terms of the history of religion not only prescribes a general approach of historicization but also brings into focus the mythical mode of expression, symbolism, and the way both myths and symbols are adopted and rewritten. This choice also distracts from other possible questions, such as the question of mystical experience or systematic consistency. For Scholem, the history of religion is central in giving his object its own coherence and, not least, its own dignity. Even though he is primarily interested in proving the Kabbalah to be a legitimate component of Jewish history, the scholarly justification for this argument remains determined by the history of religion.

In *Major Trends*, Scholem's recourse to general categories of the history of religion—such as myth and mysticism—contributes significantly to his understanding of the Kabbalah as a unified phenomenon, a "religious movement covering many centuries" (*MT*, 3). In his lectures in the Eranos circle, Scholem comes back again and again to concepts and phenomena that were also central to the older history of religions school: myth, tradition, and symbolism. In this respect, his own history of religion approach appears faintly antiquated in comparison to the newer paradigms of comparative religious studies, phenomenology of religion, and phenomenological hermeneutics that dominated postwar discussion. In the following chapters, I will explore Scholem's paradigm with respect to three central concepts of the history of religion—myth, mysticism, and Gnosticism—and then examine the category of productive misunderstanding in order to summarize the general hermeneutical consequences that he draws from this paradigm.

FIFTEEN

MYTH AND MYSTICISM
Fundamental Concepts

SCHOLEM'S USE OF THE CONCEPT of myth demonstrates a revealing shift from philosophical and dogmatic concepts of myth to a history of mythical ideas. As previously indicated, the young Scholem discussed the tension between myth and Judaism with an eye to Buber and Cohen. As he later explains in a letter to Schocken, his original interest in the Kabbalah was also anchored in this tension: he was disappointed by the "rationalist" philosophers of Judaism—Saadia, Maimonides, Cohen—because of "how they made it their main task to establish antitheses again myth and pantheism, to 'refute' them, while it should have been a matter of raising them to a higher order [sie zu einer höheren Ordnung aufzuheben].... I sensed such a higher order in the Kabbalah" (Br I, 471).[1]

At first sight, it appears that Scholem applies this notion of *Aufhebung* in his scholarly work via the schema of "myth," "religion," and "mysticism" invoked in the introduction to *Major Trends*. In this schema, the initial period of myth represents the stage of immediate religiosity: the "abyss between Man and God has not become a fact of the inner consciousness" (MT, 7). The stage of religion would be the antithesis: "Man becomes aware of a fundamental duality, of a vast gulf [between God and Man] which can be crossed by nothing but the *voice*" (MT, 7). Finally, the stage of mysticism would be the synthesis: mysticism "strives to piece together the fragments broken by the religious cataclysm,

---

1. See also: "It was nothing to show that myth and pantheism are 'false.' Much more important to me was the remark first made to me by a pious Jew, that there is indeed something to it" (Br I, 471). From Scholem's diaries, it is evident that this pious Jew was Benjamin (see T II, 322).

to bring back the old unity which religion has destroyed, but on a new plane, where the world of mythology and that of revelation meet in the soul of man" (*MT*, 8).

This schema is frequently taken as the key to interpreting Scholem's work, as his "dialectical philosophy of history," often with reference to Hegel or Graetz.[2] Such an understanding of the status of the schema may not be warranted, however. For one thing, it appears in Scholem's work only in this single passage, a passage that he was dissatisfied with throughout his life.[3] For another, by no means does it have the function of a philosophy of history here, serving instead to generate and delimit a definition of mysticism as the "totality of concrete historical phenomena" (*MT*, 6). The differentiation of the "stages" makes it clear that mysticism is a secondary, late phenomenon, different from prophetic experience.

In earlier texts, Scholem discusses similar issues in relation to the notion of "pantheism." In his 1932 article for the German-language *Encyclopaedia Judaica*, the connection between the Kabbalah and pantheism has its own section, and this problem is discussed repeatedly in *Major Trends*. In both cases, Scholem always emphasizes the specific difference between the Kabbalah and pantheism as such.[4] Later, Scholem seems to avoid this term; he speaks instead of Neoplatonism, and the problem generally plays a lesser role.[5] Scholem has a specific

---

2. Biale draws the parallel to Graetz's conception of Jewish history as steps, which is based on Hegel (*Kabbalah and Counter-History*, 42ff.). Weiner even speaks of an "evolutionary program" (9½ *Mystics*, 74), while Hamacher sees in this Scholem's "fundamental theory" (*Gershom Scholem und die allgemeine Religionsgeschichte*, 6), centrally determined by the differentiation between living and dead religion (ibid., 225ff.). Schweid points to the difficulty of classifying biblical religion in this schema (*Judaism and Mysticism*, 38ff., 61ff.).

3. See also: "Mrs. Fania Scholem repeatedly described Scholem's attitude to this chapter as one of deep dissatisfaction. He refused to allow its translation in Hebrew, and there are very few references to it in later works" (Schäfer and Dan, "Introduction," 9n38). The schema is not yet present in *Mysticism and Philosophy* from 1937, nor does he use it in "Kabbala und Mythos" from 1949, which is even more conspicuous because he does repeat formulations of the gnostic "revolt of myth" from *Major Trends* (see *KS*, 98n1).

4. Scholem, art. "Kabbala," cols. 699ff.

5. In "Devekut" (1950), Scholem discusses the absence of an experience of *unio*, completely bypassing the term "pantheism." In "Das Ringen zwischen dem biblischen Gott und dem Gott Plotins in der alten Kabbala" (1964), Neoplatonism plays the role of pantheism; the opposition here is not between the proximity and distance of God but between a personal and impersonal God. "Pantheism" also does not appear in "Schöpfung aus Nichts und Selbstverschränkung Gottes" (1956). In *Kabbalah*, Scholem criticizes Franck and Joel for describing the Kabbalah as "pantheistic" (*Kabbalah*, 96ff.).

myth in mind when he speaks of the Kabbalah as "revenge of myth upon its conqueror," and this "myth" is not pantheistic but *gnostic*: "It was Gnosticism, one of the last great manifestations of mythology in religious thought, and definitely conceived in the struggle against Judaism as the conqueror of mythology, which lent figures of speech to the Jewish mystic. The importance of this paradox can hardly be exaggerated" (*MT*, 35). This is a paradox because Gnosticism is decidedly anti-Jewish—as Scholem reportedly once said, "The greatest case of metaphysical anti-Semitism!"[6]—and also because gnostic myths express the exact opposite of the mythical world of immediacy, or God's omnipresence: they are myths of radical difference between God and the world.

In Scholem's writing, "myth" usually does not refer to an original and immediate stage of religious consciousness so much as it refers to a mostly gnostic world of images. Moreover, mysticism and myth are related not because they both have the same (pantheistic) conception of God but because mysticism draws on mythical images in order to reinterpret them. The affinity of myth and mysticism thus has the form of *Aufhebung* only in the trivial sense of *conservare*: mysticism is an interpretation of tradition's mythical moments. No longer representing a contradiction on the level of dogmatic concepts of God and the world, myth and religion are categories for the description of religious processes of de- and remythologization that can be investigated historically in a history of motifs and themes.

The prohibition of images implies a particular conception of God, through "a renunciation, indeed a polemical rejection, of the images and symbols in which the mythical world finds its expression" (*KS*, 88). This applies not only to visual depictions but also to the figurative speech of God; if such a language was "preserved here and there," in traditional Judaism, it was "shorn of [its] original symbolic power and taken in a purely metaphorical sense" (*KS*, 88).[7] Again, Scholem is not concerned with the predicative problem that God must necessarily be described with human attributes—as he once put it, the "sterile" problem of anthropomorphism[8]—but rather with the historical tendency

---

6. See Jonas, *Gnosis und Spätantiker Geist*, vol. 2, 354, English in original.

7. Scholem is referring to the "students of Biblical literature" (*KS*, 88), who worked on this topic. Elsewhere, with some irony, he plays Gunkel and Benno Jacob against one another on this question: "Both authors are to a large extent correct, yet both distort their basic thesis through misleading generalizations" (*MS*, 19); see also Scholem's juxtaposition of Jacob and von Rad in "The Name of God and the Linguistic Theory of the Kabbala," 64–66.

8. See also: "The paradox necessarily engendered by investing God with human attributes is sterile" (*JJC*, 281).

of biblical religion—namely, the "tendency of the classical Jewish tradition to liquidate myth as a central spiritual power," which "is not diminished by such quasi-mythical vestiges transformed into metaphors" (*KS*, 88). For though rabbinic accounts of God are often strikingly anthropomorphic, the effect of this is neutralized by the framework of rabbinic exegesis and religious law. Here, too, there is no a priori contradiction between religion and myth, and an un- or antimythical religion such as Judaism can very well draw on mythical expressions without losing its character. Scholem first identifies a change within medieval theology, which abandons this mode of expression in favor of a systematic conceptualization: "The price of God's purity is the loss of His living reality. For the living God can never be subsumed under a pure concept" (*KS*, 88). Thus, only within medieval Judaism does it make sense to speak of mythical ideas, for "our knowledge of this historical process, which I would like to refer to as the 'Rebellion of Images,' should not induce us to rashly date it to an earlier period, in which it could not have really taken place" (*MS*, 147). For Scholem, the critical methods that lead to dubious results at best when applied to biblical and rabbinic history only work when applied to later phenomena—namely, the Kabbalah, which can (indeed, must) be understood from processes of demythologization and remythologization.

Scholem mostly keeps his distance from mainstream religious studies and history of religion in his later essays, except when it comes to the relationship between the Kabbalah and mysticism. Here, he draws on insights from religious phenomenology and history, although not without some reservations. Initially reluctant to interpret the Kabbalah as mysticism at all, he later repeatedly stresses the particularity of the Kabbalah compared to mysticism in general. This has often been explained biographically, with reference to Scholem's vehement departure from Buber's mysticism of *Erlebnis*, or ideologically, in terms of his concern for the right image of God.[9] As justified as such explanations may be in biographical terms, it is also important to understand these positions with respect to the particular scholarly paradigm that Scholem adopts.

Mysticism was a central theme in religious studies and philosophy of religion at the turn of the twentieth century. The work of Ernst Troeltsch—whom Scholem encountered early on—may be taken as an example, for he depicts the

---

9. For example, Biale primarily emphasizes the rejection of Buber and of existentialism (*Kabbalah and Counter-History*, 112ff.), while Hamacher evokes "discretion" (*Gershom Scholem und die allgemeine Religionsgeschichte*, 267), and Dan refers to a rejection of pantheism ("Gershom Scholem: Mystiker oder Geschichtsschreiber des Mystischen?," 43).

very ambivalent role that mysticism plays in contemporary discourse.[10] Mysticism has two distinct, even contradictory functions in Troeltsch's work. In his texts on philosophy of religion, he emphasizes "that the primal phenomenon of *all* religions is mysticism, that is, faith in presence and effect of superhuman powers with the possibility of inner connection with them."[11] Against historicism and relativism, he argues that the same primal phenomenon ultimately underlies a disturbing variety of religious phenomena. Moreover, this notion of mysticism allows him to construe the history of development as leading toward a mystical religion that would leave behind all constrictions—a kind of Buberian religiosity that would be acceptable for skeptical moderns. On the other hand, in his more historical writings, Troeltsch stresses that mysticism is "always something secondary," presupposing "the objective forms of religious life in worship, ritual, myth, and dogma," whereas "the primitive religious fact itself" is never mystical.[12] Mysticism naturally has a subjective and psychological element, yet mystical visions are "rarely creative in the sense of imparting fresh knowledge; they are almost always expansions and interpretations of the common faith."[13] Moreover, despite being founded on personal experience, mysticism unfolds in social context, for the mystic remains "human, and he feels the need for the give-and-take of intimate fellowship with other souls. In the mystic, too, this is no mere human weakness but a Christian duty."[14] The historically concrete effect of mysticism thus appears entirely ambivalent. Unlike church or sect, mysticism only has a weak power to form a community, while at the same time, "it lives in and on communities which have been brought into existence by other ruder energies."[15] If mysticism today is the "secret religion of the educated classes," this implies not only a deepening of religious experience but also a danger for the very future of religion.[16]

As in other areas of his thought, Scholem's own conception of mysticism develops step by step. Early on, he polemicizes against Buber's view of mysticism,

---

10. In the late essay "Mysticisme et société," Scholem describes Troeltsch's *Soziallehren* as "extremely interesting and fertile" (4). In the winter semester of 1915/1916, he heard Troeltsch's lecture "Religionsphilosophie auf religionsgeschichtlicher Grundlage," which struck him as *"very* easy . . . but not worth anything deep down" (*Br I*, 104).
11. Troeltsch, "Wesen der Religion und der Religionswissenschaft," in *Gesammelte Schriften*, vol. 2, 493.
12. Troeltsch, *Social Teaching*, vol. 2, 730–731.
13. Troeltsch, *Social Teaching*, vol. 2, 731.
14. Troeltsch, *Social Teaching*, vol. 2, 745.
15. Troeltsch, *Social Teaching*, vol. 2, 796.
16. Troeltsch, *Social Teaching*, vol. 2, 794.

since "Jewish mysticism does not establish itself on an experience [*Erlebnis*] but . . . on tradition" (*Br I*, 50). His first publications are also directed against Meir Wiener's "presumptuous mysticism" (*T II*, 666), and here, Scholem even claims generally that the "point of view of religious psychology ultimately does not possess the density and dignity that would make it appear applicable for an investigation that seeks to probe the systematic connections of religious phenomena" (*T II*, 667). This is only an assertion, however. In a manner that is typical of the young Scholem, the argument consists of a mix of vague insinuations, apodictic statements, and sharp criticism that would have been barely comprehensible to his reader.

Scholem develops a more substantial account of the relationship between the Kabbalah and mysticism in his 1932 article for the *Encyclopaedia Judaica*:

> The K[abbalah] absorbed all mystical movements in Judaism into itself; however, if one accepts mysticism only where there is an immediate unification of man and God with the renunciation of human individuality, only a very limited part of the K[abbalah] would be mystical, as few of its representatives aspired to such a goal, or even explicitly formulated such a goal as worth striving for. Yet K[abbalah] is mysticism to the extent that it aims at a knowledge of the world with foundations that are won on the path to contemplation and enlightenment, going beyond the rational, although it rarely rejected the rational directly.[17]

The problem of pantheism is still in the foreground here, along with Scholem's need to dissociate himself from it. The notion of mysticism has become virulent, because by this point Scholem has distanced himself from the self-image of the Kabbalah as ancient tradition. Thus, the experimental moment—the individual contribution of kabbalists—comes into stronger focus, albeit without recourse to the categories of religious psychology on Scholem's part. In the introduction to *Major Trends*, Scholem finally emphasizes that "we should not dwell too much upon such abstractions" as the mystical experience (*MT*, 6) and "that there is no such thing as mysticism in the abstract, that is to say, a phenomenon or experience which has no particular relation to other religious phenomena. There is no mysticism as such, there is only the mysticism of a particular religious system" (*MT*, 5–6).

The crux of Scholem's access to mysticism lies neither in the definition of the essence of mysticism nor in its historical-philosophical determination by a three-stage law but rather in his insight into the dynamic between mysticism

---

17. Scholem, art. "Kabbala," cols. 630–631.

and that *of which* it is mysticism. In the case of the Kabbalah, this pertains to its relationship with rabbinic Judaism. Scholem first expresses his thoughts on this matter in 1937 in *Philosophy and Jewish Mysticism* and then transfers the essence of these thoughts to the introduction of *Major Trends*. They are part of his reflection on the "secret of the success of the Kabbalah" (*MT*, 23), in contrast to the minor impact that rational philosophy had on Jewish life, as he sees it. This success is ultimately based on the relationship of the Kabbalah to the "spiritual heritage of rabbinical Judaism. This relationship differs from that of rationalist philosophy, in that it is more deeply and in a more vital sense connected with the main forces active in Judaism" (*MT*, 23). Precisely this relatedness to the "primal production" of religion is what makes the Kabbalah effective in a traditional society, but it also means that the Kabbalah cannot be viewed in isolation from traditional, official religion.

On the one hand, the mystic is dependent on his context. He draws on the religious language of tradition in order to give expression to his experiences. On the other hand, the mystic can also become socially effective in various ways. He can reinterpret or enrich tradition, embody and assert new values, or form a sect. Thus, by no means does the tension in which the mystic lives exist only generally between ephemeral experience and verbal expression—this tension is much more evident between the mystic and his particular historical milieu. Scholem frequently stresses that kabbalists hardly ever complain about the principal limitation of language, unlike other mystics; as a rule, they also do not compose autobiographical reports of ecstatic experiences, which by necessity reach the limits of language.[18] Instead, they write commentaries that remain rather traditional in formal terms. The "creative paradox" of Jewish mysticism lies not in the relationship between language and religious content but in the relationship to the *particular* language and tradition in which it lives.[19]

This paradox is all the more significant for being essentially unconscious. For Scholem, the kabbalist is not an individual who only seems to express himself by traditional means or who does so for tactical reasons, as Graetz and Franck assumed. Instead, the kabbalist is someone who actually wants to speak within tradition and who believes that he does so: "Actually the thought processes of mystics are largely unconscious, and they may be quite unaware of the clash between old and new which is of such passionate interest to the historian" (*KS*, 33). As a result, this paradox only becomes legible from a different

---

18. See *MT*, 4, 14–18; *KS*, 8.
19. Scholem, "Mysticisme et société," 7.

perspective—namely, that of the historian. Later, Scholem often emphasizes that the significance of the Kabbalah does not lie in the personal religiosity of kabbalists but in "the light it throws on the 'historical psychology' of the Jews" (KS, 2). For if the problem of the Kabbalah is not how one can speak of God at all but rather how to speak of Him *legitimately*, this question immediately has a political aspect: "by the paradox alone that he proclaims, the mystic has always stirred society in its depths."[20] For the historian, this means shifting focus from individual Kabbalists to all of Judaism and reading kabbalistic texts as "symbols . . . in which the spiritual experience of the mystics was almost inextricably intertwined with the historical experience of the Jewish people. It is this interweaving of two realms, which in most other religious mysticisms have remained separate, that gave the Kabbalah its specific imprint" (KS, 2). This dimension of the Kabbalah can be better grasped by the history of religion than by religious psychology or religious phenomenology, for only the critical separation of old and new makes the difference visible, thus revealing the paradox blurred by concepts of *Einfühlung* and *Erlebnis*. Philological criticism does not simply work on the surface of the form of expression, and neither does it merely prepare for engagement with mystical experience; instead, it is precisely the work of critical philology on this layer of expression that enables the historian to decipher these tensions and paradoxes.

The example of mysticism clearly shows how useful it can be to pay attention to the underlying paradigm of Scholem's research. First, the systematic refutation of the question of mystical experience by no means implies that Scholem does not "believe" in the existence of immediate experience in the Kabbalah. Tellingly, as soon as he finds his approach, he becomes much more relaxed and no longer vehemently denies that there is also an experience of *unio*, or ahistorical experience, in the Kabbalah: "I consider it mainly a matter of interpretation whether it is seen as an immediate or a mediated experience" (Br III, 35, English in original). Second, it turns out that the reasons for Scholem's reserve when it comes to mystical experience are not just personal or based on his worldview but linked to a specific paradigm. Third, it is also misleading to simply chalk Scholem's reserve up to scholarly distance. This reserve is not present in the same way in other paradigms, such as religious phenomenology. The alternative is not primarily between religious and scholarly access

---

20. Scholem, "Mysticisme et société," 28. In 1940 Scholem wrote that the "unique nature" and "specific character" of Jewish mysticism could be recognized from a "historical viewpoint"—namely, "the fact that these were mystical movements which strove increasingly for influence in the social and national realms" (PM, 122).

but between different scholarly perspectives. Again, we can see the irony of exploring the Kabbalah: it is only recognizable from an outsider perspective, for only by bracketing its claim to truth as well as the question of what the mystic "actually" experiences can one begin to recognize something of the Kabbalah's inner dynamics.

SIXTEEN

GNOSTICISM, MISUNDERSTANDING, AND SYMBOLISM

More Operative Terms?

LINKED TO THE PARADIGM OF history of religion, Scholem's interest in the development of the Kabbalah is particularly focused on its origin, as emphasized already in 1925: "Only when we succeed in finding a *solid point of reference* for the origin of the Kabbalah ... will we be in a position to explain the course of its development more exactly and reliably; otherwise the whole thing would be a castle in the air."[1] Scholem initially thought he had found this point of reference in the *Zohar*, which he first viewed as a collection of old traditions. As he became more and more skeptical of the authenticity of the *Zohar*, the question of origin grew more and more complex. The 1928 essay "On the Question of the Origin of the Kabbalah" is central to this shift, and the baselines sketched here extend in large part to later works. While the issue of the age of the *Zohar* remains open in the essay, the objective of Scholem's explanation and questions changes.[2] The undifferentiated question of the provenance of the Kabbalah as a whole gives way to the specific problem of the emergence of the Kabbalah in the narrower sense—that is, the medieval Jewish mysticism that suddenly appeared in the thirteenth century in Provence and Spain. Previous currents of Jewish mysticism—the mysticism of the *Merkabah* and *Hekhalot* as well as Ashkenazi Hasidism—are only thematized as prehistory.

---

1. Scholem, letter to C. N. Bialik, in *Judaica*, vol. 6, 57.
2. If the age of the *Zohar* could be proven, "it would naturally make our task much easier. As things stand, however, we must do without this 'royal road' and content ourselves with the thornier path of historical analysis of the texts closer to the beginnings of the Kabbalah" (Scholem, "Zur Frage der Entstehung," 4).

Scholem clarifies what he means with an analysis of the oldest sources of the actual Kabbalah, the *Sefer ha-Bahir*, first printed in the thirteenth century. Older scholarship often tried to identify in this book "a speculative system, a definite, consistent view of the world that is philosophical and mystical in nature, only artificially veiled in mythological and homiletic form."[3] However, this interpretation was based on a complete misunderstanding of the kind of literature at hand. In reality, the *Bahir* is a compilation of different layers, in which "not a few rudiments of older stages of development and sources of the Kabbalah remain preserved."[4] In this context as well, Scholem is trying to understand the Kabbalah in its particularity by means of the history of religion and criticism of form. While vague about the manner in which old ideas have survived, he highlights the "whispers" or "fragmentary leaves" of older traditions in the book.[5] For the oldest texts testify "irreproachably to a Gnosticism that—here on the soil of Judaism—has been divested of its otherwise so prominent dualistic and heretical character."[6] Scholem thereby links the exploration of the Kabbalah to the exploration of Gnosticism, a prominent topic of contemporary discussions, differently conceived within different paradigms.[7]

Older research on the history of dogmas, represented, for example, by the work of Adolf von Harnack, saw in Gnosticism the Hellenization of Christianity. According to this thinking, the Gnostics were Christianity's first theologians and philosophers of religion, the ones who spiritualized Christian teachings. Particular to the Gnostics is their emphatic concept of knowledge, or *gnosis*, derived from Greek and Neoplatonic sources for this concept. Actual dualism and mythological elements do not play a large role in this account, and Gnosticism is by definition post-Christian.

---

3. Scholem, "Zur Frage der Entstehung," 13.
4. Scholem, "Zur Frage der Entstehung," 13. "The literary form of midrash was not artificially given to the book by an 'author' who wanted to conceal in it his speculations of a theoretical nature"; it is actually a matter of mystical dicta and "ancient mythologems" (ibid., 13).
5. "In many cases, whispers, and that in esoteric hints, were the only medium of transmission" (*MT*, 119–120). Elsewhere Scholem speaks of "the vestiges of an unarticulated tradition that survived in the form of old notebooks and fragmentary leaves; and these came from distant lands or from subterranean levels of the Jewish societies in which they emerged into the light of day" (*Origins of the Kabbalah*, 45).
6. Scholem, "Zur Frage der Entstehung," 8.
7. See Haardt, "Bemerkungen zu den Methoden"; Puech, "Das Problem des Gnostizismus"; and especially Colpe's warnings regarding the schematism of a gnostic "worldview" in *Die religionsgeschichtliche Schule*.

By contrast, the exegetes of the history of religions school conceived of Gnosticism as a mythical tradition from the "Orient" that adopted Iranian, Babylonian, or Egyptian conceptions. Bousset, the classical representative of this approach, emphasizes "that 'Gnosis' does not signify knowledge in our sense of the word, and that the Gnostics were no theoreticians of knowledge and philosophers of religion. Gnosis is rather mysterious wisdom which rests upon secret revelation; one might better call the Gnostics Theosophists."[8] Gnosticism is no longer philosophy but religion; indeed, it is "religion of redemption in the sharpest and most one-sided sense of that term," which did "not grow on the genuine ground of Christianity."[9] For Bousset, its fundamental feature is not spiritualization but a specific form of dualism, which he explains through a "mixture of the genuinely Persian assumption of two adversarial deities (principles) fighting against one another, and the Greek view of the superiority of the spiritually ideal over the sensually material world. . . . Only through the confluence of two pessimistic worldviews did the heightened, absolutely desolate dualism of Gnosticism emerge."[10] Because the history of religions school conceived of Gnosticism as pre-Christian, it could also serve as a background for the understanding of Christianity, particularly Pauline and Johannine anthropology and soteriology. Other scholars continued in this direction, above all Richard Reitzenstein and Rudolf Bultmann. Turning Harnack's solution on its head, they no longer cast Gnosticism as spiritualized Christianity, instead casting Christianity as demythologized Gnosticism.

Hans Jonas's hermeneutic approach to Gnosticism developed out of the history of religion approach, but Jonas criticizes the methods and conceptions of his predecessors as objectivist and reductive. In his view, what is specifically new in Gnosticism cannot be comprehended with metaphors of "mixture" or "merger." "Somehow it seems that this deduction, like similar deductions, involves the idea that an ideal process could 'unexpectedly' overshoot its goal and generate something quite different than what was logically within its own reach. Alchemy of ideas!"[11] Jonas insists that Gnosticism is not a composite but "recognizably and comprehensibly one thing, namely a certain experience of world and self—the experience of the world as an undefined coercive system,

---

8. Bousset, *Kyrios Christos: A History*, 252.

9. Bousset, *Kyrios Christos: A History*, 249; Art. "Gnosis, Gnostiker," 49.

10. Bousset, Art. "Gnosis, Gnostiker," 53. Bousset also emphasizes the "Gnostic's basic feeling of 'foreignness'" (*Hauptprobleme der Gnosis*, 188).

11. Jonas, *Gnosis und spätantiker Geist*, vol. 1, 32. To avoid quasi-mechanical "mixing," Jonas stresses the "productive role of misunderstanding in history" (Jonas, *Gnosis und spätantiker Geist*, vol. 1, 45).

inimical to God, and of the self as a being belonging not to the cosmos, but rather to an acosmic context."[12]

Scholem's interpretation of Gnosticism fluctuates between these different approaches.[13] In his 1928 essay, he generally strives for religious-historical understanding, yet rather than drawing on Bousset's definitions of Gnosticism, he has recourse to older concepts. Gnosticism is characterized by "the possession of insight that cannot be gained by ordinary intellectual means, but only via the path of revelation and mystical epiphany, the possession of secret teaching on the order of higher worlds, and knowledge of the magical and liturgical means that open access to them."[14] Thus, he is also able to designate the *Hekhalot* and *Merkabah* traditions as gnostic, although they contain neither dualism nor gnostic epistemology. Scholem seems to represent a very wide definition of Gnosticism, but in his research practice, evidence of Gnosticism is based primarily on evidence of individual gnostic motifs and terminology, such as the doctrine of the transmigration of souls or Aeon terminology. He develops his thoughts further in *Jewish Gnosticism, Merkabah Mysticism and Talmudic Tradition* from 1960. Here, he argues for the existence of an Orthodox Jewish Gnosticism that actually influenced extra-Jewish Gnosticism—a thesis that has been sharply criticized by various scholars, among them Hans Jonas.[15]

Clearly polemical, Scholem's construction of an originally Jewish Gnosticism is aimed against previous research, such as that of Heinrich Graetz, according to whom the Kabbalah shares "a decisive physiognomic similarity and common ancestry with Gnosticism," a physiognomy that makes both Kabbalah and Gnosticism necessarily foreign to normative Judaism.[16] Moreover, linking the Kabbalah to Gnosticism means underlining its difference from philosophy.

---

12. Jonas, *Gnosis und spätantiker Geist*, vol. 1, 47.
13. Biale emphasizes proximity to Jonas (*Kabbalah and Counter-History*, 66–67), while Hamacher stresses the context of older research, above all that of Leisegang (*Gershom Scholem und die allgemeine Religionsgeschichte*, 184ff.). For a general critique of the application of the notion of "Gnosis" to the Kabbalah, see Idel, "Subversive Katalysatoren," 83ff.
14. Scholem, "Zur Frage der Entstehung," 8. See the very similar definition in *Jewish Gnosticism*, 1.
15. Again, Jonas polemicizes against the idea of a smooth transition: "Jewish-Orthodox 'Gnosis' of itself just cannot lead to something basically different from itself. *Somebody* must have taken it and *made* it into something new, *turned* it upside down. *Who* did so? Gnostics ('properly speaking') to be sure" (*Gnosis und spätantiker Geist*, vol. 2, 356–357, English in original). See also Deutsch, *The Gnostic Imagination*, esp. 25ff., and Gruenwald, *From Apocalypticism to Gnosticism*, 190ff.
16. Graetz, *Gnosticismus und Judentum*, 5.

Especially in his earlier texts, Scholem repeatedly emphasizes the untheoretical, mythical character of the Kabbalah. Its images are, "as the religious history of syncretism teaches us, not a later addition, or 'signs of decline,' as the rationalistic observer could easy assume; they belong to the original domain of this movement."[17] However, the reference to Gnosticism also allows him to understand the late phase of the Kabbalah in Sabbatianism and Frankism, which moves to the center of his historical plot in "Redemption through Sin": "Indeed, to anyone familiar with the history of religion it might seem far more likely that he was dealing here with an antinomian myth from the second century composed by such nihilistic Gnostics as Carpocrates and his followers" (*MI*, 132). The term "Gnosticism" thus ties together the beginning and end of the story. The Sabbatian movement with its severe Gnosticism does not appear out of nowhere; on the contrary, tendencies inherent in the origins reveal themselves in continued development. Conversely, the Kabbalah's gnostic nature only becomes comprehensible against the background of its entire history. The manifold transformations of Gnosticism during this development facilitate the rich formation of the Kabbalah, and the unity of the object is not lost in the process. Yet the dynamics proper to this history of development only arise when Gnosticism mixes with entirely different traditions and when it engenders moments of crisis, as in Sabbatianism.

Even in his 1928 essay, Scholem does not simply trace the Kabbalah of the thirteenth century back to the prehistorical gnostic Kabbalah in his search for its "origin," also stressing the differences between them. He finds that the more recent texts have an "entirely different physiognomy," since one can "prove with certainty that Neoplatonic thought breached the older, prehistorical Kabbalah"; the decisive "second stage" in the emergence of the Kabbalah is thus the "transition" "from the world of Gnosticism into the world of Neoplatonism."[18] For Scholem, Kabbalah in the proper sense only emerges through an encounter of opposing tendencies.

The interpretation of the Kabbalah as a Neoplatonic system of emanation is by no means new. Adolphe Franck, for example, argued that dualism and mythological realism are overcome in the Kabbalah—for example, in the

---

17. Scholem, "Zur Frage der Entstehung," 9. In his essay on Cardozo, also published in 1928, Scholem writes about the *"construction of a virtual gnostic antinomianism within the world of Judaism"* ("Die Theologie des Sabbatianismus im Lichte Abraham Cardosos," in *Judaica*, vol. 1, 122), and the "primal gnostic central thought" of antinomianism (ibid., 129).

18. Scholem, "Zur Frage der Entstehung," 18. See a similar formulation in *MT*, 175; see also: "Kabbalah, in its historical significance, can be *defined* as the product of the interpenetration of Jewish Gnosticism and neoplatonism" (*Kabbalah*, 45, emphasis added).

Sefer Yetzirah: "The final word of this system is the substitution of absolute unity for every form of dualism; the dualism of Pagan philosophy which would find in matter an eternal substance . . . , as well as the dualism of the Bible, which . . . regards these two things, the universe and God, as two substances, absolutely distinct and separate."[19] Scholem, on the other hand, makes a sharp distinction between Gnosticism, Neoplatonism, and Kabbalah. For him, Neoplatonism is Jewish philosophy or theology of the Jewish Middle Ages, and its development is entirely independent from that of Gnosticism. By no means simply abstract, Neoplatonism as he sees it has an affinity with mysticism and represents an important source of negative theology for the Kabbalah. It differs from Gnosticism primarily in the interpretation of divine properties as only "emanations" of God, whereas the Gnostics conceive of them as actual beings. For Scholem, the Kabbalah in the proper sense arises from the encounter between these two tendencies: "as the mythological Kabbalah is platonized and Neoplatonism is kabbalized, a new structure of kabbalistic theology emerges."[20]

Thus, the Kabbalah has no unified, independent principle or worldview, nor a constant, authentic undercurrent. Instead, it is a hybrid structure of heterogeneous elements that Scholem figures in different ways. In 1928 he writes that Neoplatonism's "invasion" into the "prehistorical" Kabbalah had been executed "not without some intellectual violence," also emphasizing that there was "resistance" against it; here, he still seems to be operating under the assumption of an authentic gnostic movement that defended itself against transformation through philosophy.[21] In a later essay, by contrast, he stresses that the merger took place "unpolemically":

> The instrument of the reinterpretation that thereby appears, in which an entirely new view prevails, is what I like to call a productive misunderstanding. That which for the mystic is a deep intuition or a great symbol appears under the sober gaze of the historian of concepts—or even the philosopher—as a misunderstanding of philosophic conceptions. But it is precisely in misunderstandings that such conceptions in the history

---

19. Franck, *The Kabbalah*, 137.
20. Scholem, "Zur Frage der Entstehung," 20–21. Scholem vacillates regarding active and passive roles: sometimes Neoplatonism breaks into the world of gnostic mysticism, while sometimes, conversely, it is myth that breaks in; statements regarding "breaches of Neoplatonic thought" (ibid.) and "the reappearance . . . of a frankly mythical statement" (*KS*, 91) seem to be interchangeable.
21. Scholem, "Zur Frage der Entstehung," 20, 19.

of religion prove their productive essence, ensuring the continuity of the religious world of language, albeit at the price of their questionability.[22]

"Productive misunderstanding," a notion likely adapted from or inspired by Jonas, is a decisive category in Scholem's historical logic. It is meant to explain not only the formation of innovation but the *latency* of such innovation, without which innovation could not have any historical effect in traditionalist societies such as Judaism. Productive misunderstanding plays out in the unconscious insofar as it is not registered as misunderstanding, and thus it cannot simply be "resolved" or denounced, instead requiring a specific kind of reading. If misunderstanding is often the "paradoxical abbreviation of an original line of thought" (*MT*, 24), understanding must reconstruct this (unthought) line. This is a discursive task, or a reading that is necessarily directed against the intention of authors who do not recognize any such misunderstanding.

The category of productive misunderstanding further enables Scholem to construe a long developmental arc for historical dynamics. The tension inherent in the "compromise" between Gnosticism and Neoplatonism determines his narrative, in which the Kabbalah never appears as a real synthesis between Gnosticism and Neoplatonism or between theology and mythology but as a compromise that can be comprehended only by following its development. Historically, this tension continually increases. With respect to the *Zohar*, Scholem still speaks of a "colorful though not unproblematic whole" (*MT*, 243), whereas in the Lurianic Kabbalah of the sixteenth century, "intrinsic conflict between the theistic and the pantheistic tendencies in the mystical theology of Kabbalism is nowhere brought out more clearly" (*MT*, 252). In Frankism, the latent Gnosticism of the Kabbalah resurfaces precisely through vulgarization, and an undisguised mythical Gnosticism lies at the end just as it did at the beginning.

Scholem sometimes refers to the concept of the symbol to model these processes of misunderstanding. In the introduction to *Major Trends*, he distinguishes between philosophical and kabbalistic exegesis: philosophers view biblical representations as allegories for other philosophical conceptions, whereas mystics see in them symbols of theosophical secrets. Unlike "allegorical immanence," the symbol shows something else: "If the symbol is thus also a sign or representation it is nevertheless more than that" (*MT*, 27). Further, "in the mystical symbol a reality which in itself has, for us, no form or shape becomes

---

22. Scholem, *Über einige Grundbegriffe*, 21, 67–68. See also similar formulations in *KS*, 102, and *MT*, 24–25, as well as Jonas's formulations (above).

transparent and, as it were, visible through the medium of another reality" (*MT*, 27). Decisive in Scholem's definition of the symbol is not so much *what* is designated as *how* this happens. The distinction between allegory and symbol goes back to the idea of the artistic symbol usually attributed to Goethe, yet it is misleading to a certain extent.[23] According to Scholem, kabbalistic concepts do not become transparent in the harmony of what they express—the relation between the finite and the infinite—so much as they reveal inherent tension. They are fundamentally broken symbols, and even as signifiers, they present themselves not as individual wholes but as parts of a complex of references to other texts and symbols: the tree of *sefirot* is more of a diagram than an image. As a result, no individual symbol can be understood on its own—they must always be *read* in relation to one another and in relation to an already existing tradition: "The Kabbalists created images and symbols; perhaps they revived an age-old heritage. But they seldom had the courage to commit themselves without reservation to these images" (*KS*, 96). This leads to "profound ambiguity . . . and it also explains the apparent self-contradiction inherent in a great many Kabbalist symbols and images" (*MT*, 34). Even the historian of religion does not simply consider the contents of symbols, instead interpreting them in relation to other symbols and to their specific prehistory in particular.

In Scholem's presentation, the Kabbalah appears not as a timeless world of symbols but as a movement under constant tension. The primary function of stressing the symbolic rather than the allegorical nature of the Kabbalah is to refuse a philosophical interpretation without suggesting that kabbalistic symbolism is in any way vague or metaphorical. As Scholem explains elsewhere, kabbalistic symbolism consists precisely "in a literalness written to the extreme, in radical seriousness with respect not to the 'meaning' that is somehow intended, but the word as left to itself. In this extreme literalness, words turn; they leave the context of the sober understanding of Scripture for a new context of holy names, in which they designate a reality of divine light that is enraptured and sealed off to us, and thus actually nameless and secret. In a word: they become symbols."[24]

---

23. Scholem refers to Georg Friedrich Creuzer, who describes the symbol as "'a beam of light which, from the dark and abysmal depths of existence and cognition, falls into our eye and penetrates our whole being.' It is a 'momentary totality' which is perceived intuitively in a mystical *now*—the dimension of time proper to the symbol" (*MT*, 27).

24. Scholem, *Die Geheimnisse der Schöpfung*, 28.

SEVENTEEN

HISTORY OF MESSIANISM
Continuity and Rupture?

AT THE END OF THE 1920s, in addition to the religious-historical schema of myth, mysticism, and Gnosticism, Scholem also laid out another fundamental element of his model of the Kabbalah: the plot organizing its development. In Oxford in 1927, before finally giving up on the idea that the *Zohar* could be an authentic origin, Scholem made the "very surprising discovery [of] Sabbatian theology" in a manuscript of Abraham Cardozo.[1] One year later, Scholem published an essay on this text as a key to Sabbatianism, arguing that the external development of Sabbatianism may be familiar, "but little is known about that which is actually decisive: the profound religious movement that took place within Judaism after his [Zevi's] conversion [to Islam].... Nowhere is it more visible than in Sabbatianism that the key to the understanding of a historical movement is provided less by its historical setting [*Schauplatz*], which can be described by historical dates, than by its metaphysical setting, which concerns its theological premises."[2] The emphatic description of a "metaphysical setting" is typical of this essay, in which Scholem argues relatively impartially on the level of ideas even as the notion of the "setting" (*Schauplatz*) with its theatrical associations points to a more dramatic conception. Over the next years, he developed a presentation of the second phase of the Kabbalah, making the contradictions latently contained in the classical Kabbalah manifest in this setting—and it is this conception of the crisis of the Kabbalah that first imparts drama to its history.

---

1. Scholem, *Story of a Friendship*, 164.
2. Scholem, "Die Theologie des Sabbatianismus," in *Judaica*, vol. 1, 119.

According to Scholem's account, the second phase of the Kabbalah began in 1492 with the expulsion of the Jews from Spain, a traumatic experience for Jews across the entire Diaspora. It continued with the emergence of the Lurianic Kabbalah of Isaac Luria, which Scholem reads as an interpretation of this event, a "myth of exile." The next step was the messianic movement of Sabbatianism in the seventeenth century, which took a tragic turn in 1666, when Zevi was forced by the sultan to convert to Islam, thus committing the worst imaginable sin for a Jew. Judaism has only recovered from this to a limited extent, in Scholem's view. On the one hand, great disappointment remains along with diverse antimessianic countermovements, among which he counts Hasidism. On the other hand, and of greater interest to him, there are groups that cling to the belief that Zevi was the Messiah; as Scholem later argues, this subsequent history "suggests that it expressed a dialectical process within Jewish history" (SS, 691).

Scholem sees a consistent development here, in which the demand for a developmental history of the Kabbalah is met, as he emphasizes in a later sketch: "A single continuous, clear, progressive movement leads from messianism, established in connection with the expulsion from Spain, to the Sabbatian movement . . . and from faith in Sabbatai Zevi to religious nihilism. . . . And from nihilism as a religious attitude . . . it leads to the new world of the Haskalah. This is nothing other than the dialectical movement of the messianic idea and the longing for redemption in the Jewish people."[3] In this movement, the Kabbalah becomes historical in a twofold sense: it gains historical significance insofar as it has an important influence on Jewish history in general, and it becomes historical insofar as it shows consistent development. The discovery of Sabbatianism gave Scholem the terminus ad quem for his plot at the very moment toward the end of the 1920s when he was beginning to dispense with the assumption on an authentic *Zohar*. Scholem thus found a new rationality for the Kabbalah's presentation. In the following decade, he developed the foundations of his understanding of Sabbatianism, largely retained in later writings.

In his studies on Sabbatianism, Scholem polemicizes sharply against previous research for missing the theological "setting." For Heinrich Graetz, Sabbatianism represents the downfall of medieval Judaism via the Kabbalah: after the suffering of the expulsion of 1492, the "secret doctrine with its reveries and gimmicks, which until then had only haunted the heads of a few adepts, generally spread among the Jews and afflicted healthy minds."[4] Graetz's prehistory

---

3. Scholem, "Ursprünge, Widersprüche und Auswirkungen des Sabbatianismus," in *Judaica*, vol. 5, 130.
4. Graetz, *Geschichte der Juden*, vol. 9, 203.

of Sabbatianism, entitled "Die Wühler" (The Hustlers), begins with a telling image. Covered with many layers, the noble core of Judaism was barely visible: "and these layers and strata were enclosed by an ugly crust, by a fungus-like structure, a coating of mold, by the Kabbalah, which little by little settled itself into cracks and gaps, growing rampant and branching out."[5] "Frenzy" (*Raserei*) and "dizziness" (*Schwindel*) are Graetz's key words in the account that follows, in which he repeatedly suggests that a fraud was taking place.

The treatment of Sabbatianism by some Zionist historians is entirely different. For example, Ben-Zion Dinur, Scholem's colleague from Berlin, sees in Sabbatianism one of the numerous attempts of the Jewish people to liberate themselves after the Maccabean revolt: in his view, it is a premature expression of national uprising, an embodiment of the eternal longing for Zion on the part of the Jewish people. Dinur even designates Sabbatianism as the beginning of Jewish modernity, because Jews have been continuously migrating to Palestine once again ever since.[6] In this interpretation, the folkloric element of Sabbatianism comes to the fore, while the theological development of the Kabbalah is of little interest, only relevant up to Zevi's conversion. Sabbatianism is tragic and heroic—not secret and subterranean. Scholem's revision of such interpretations does not consist simply in a shift of the framework but in a different historical logic, linked above all to a new understanding of apocalypticism.

The decisive impulse for this new understanding of apocalypticism probably came from arguments in New Testament scholarship and the turn to apocalypticism at the beginning of the twentieth century. Rejecting the ruling liberal interpretation, scholars such as William Wrede, Johannes Weiß, and Albert Schweitzer argued that Jesus's preaching of the kingdom of God does not refer to spiritual or moral facts but can only be understood in apocalyptic terms— that is, that it presupposes the idea of the world's imminent end.[7] No longer conceived as a process of spiritualization, by this account the development of Christianity is determined by the double disappointment of its founder's death and the delayed apocalypse, which is transformed into spiritual victory by Paul. This emphasis on apocalypticism goes hand in hand with the new approach of the history of religions school. First, so-called late Judaism of the intertestamental period is no longer characterized through "Pharisaic" torpor, as religious historians identify and clearly prioritize a folkloric apocalyptic current

---

5. Graetz, *Geschichte der Juden*, vol. 10, 114.
6. See Myers, *Re-inventing the Jewish Past*, 140ff.
7. See Schweitzer, *The Quest of the Historical Jesus*; Koch, *The Rediscovery of Apocalyptic*. On the probable link in Scholem's work, see Davies, "From Schweitzer to Scholem."

in this context.[8] Second, historians of religion describe the mythical character of apocalypticism, which no longer gives expression to concrete hopes, as in prophecy, but paints the end times with mythical images. Gunkel, for instance, tries to show how cosmogenic myths such as that of a dragon of chaos are transferred onto the end times, processed in the motif of eschatological dragon battle. Third, this implies a critique of the assumption that apocalypses are the literary sketches of individual "authors" who wanted to express their own views in disguise. Instead, as Gunkel stresses, it is necessary to understand the specific apocalyptic tradition from which these writings emerged.[9]

While studying very different material, Scholem draws from religious-historical research on essential points, such as the significance of imminent eschatological expectation, the dynamic of eschatological disappointment, and the emphasis on a mythical tradition of apocalypticism. He develops his general approach in the extraordinarily effective late essay "Toward an Understanding of the Messianic Idea in Judaism." In this essay, he seeks to work out "the special tensions in the Messianic idea," aiming at a "sharper analysis of what it is that makes up the specific vitality of this phenomenon in the history of the Jewish religion" (MI, 2). Thus, rather than posing the question of the essence, cause, or origin of messianism, Scholem inquires into its dynamic *in* history: "The object of these remarks is not the initial development of the Messianic idea but the varying perspectives by which it became an effective force after its crystallization in historical Judaism" (MI, 2). This dynamic is driven by messianism as an amalgam of different tendencies: the "restorative," directed at the restitution of primordial time, and the "utopian," aimed at the new as such, coming together in different ways. Elsewhere, Scholem points to the "mixture—the controversy, the living contradiction, the back and forth, I would almost say the living debate between utopia and restoration in messianism—[as] that which established the living history, the heart of Jewish messianism" (PM, 108). In "Toward an Understanding of the Messianic Idea," Scholem describes this blending as a process through which "ancient mythical images are filled with utopian content" (MI, 6), or "the terrors of the real historical experiences of the Jewish people are

---

8. For Bousset, Judaism shows itself in this "piety of hope ... from its finer and more inward side" (*Religion des Judentums*, 242); according to him, apocalypticism is "literature of the rising, uneducated class of people, a literature with a strongly amateur character" (*Die jüdische Apokalyptik*, 9); Gressmann speaks of "unofficial Judaism" (*Der Messias*, 363). For a history of research on apocalypticism, see Schmidt, *Die jüdische Apokalyptik*; for a more general, pointed, and more polemical account, see Koch, *The Rediscovery of Apocalyptic*.

9. See Gunkel's critique of the *zeitgeschichtliche* method in *Creation and Chaos*, part 2, chapter 2.

joined with images drawn from the heritage of myth or mythical fantasy" (*MI*, 10). It is this combination of past and present that constitutes the history of the messianic idea, which is never sheer expectation of the future but always the expectation of a specific future. If there is a dialectics of the messianic idea, it does not consist in constant antagonism of the forces of renewal against the forces of inertia but rather in an *inner* antagonism of the messianic idea itself.

The mythical character of apocalypticism is most explicit in Scholem's description of the horrors of messianic time, which according to him are particularly significant because "Jewish Messianism is in its origins and by its nature—this cannot be sufficiently emphasized—a theory of catastrophe" (*MI*, 7):

> The paradoxical nature of this conception exists in the fact that the redemption ... is in no causal sense a result of previous history. It is precisely the lack of transition between history and the redemption which is always stressed by the prophets and apocalyptists. The Bible and the apocalyptic writers know of no progress in history leading to the redemption. The redemption is not the product of immanent developments such as we find it in modern Western reinterpretations of Messianism since the Enlightenment where, secularized as the belief in progress, Messianism still displayed unbroken and immense vigor. (*MI*, 10)[10]

No pure principle of futurity, Scholem's messianism thus reckons with a *break* in the future. He designates this messianism of imminent eschatological expectation as "acute" messianism: "When the Messianic idea appears as a living force in the world of Judaism ... it always occurs in the closest connection with apocalypticism.... Apocalypticism appears as the form necessarily created by acute Messianism" (*MI*, 4). Yet this apocalypticism is not simply the subterranean, "revolutionary" side of Judaism; the real liveliness of messianism can only be understood through interaction with its counterposition. The conservative attitude of "official" Judaism, condensed in the warning not to hasten the end, is consequential in Scholem's account because it "corresponds to and originates from the above-mentioned conception of the essential lack of relation between human history and the redemption. But we can understand why such an attitude was again and again in danger of being overrun by the apocalyptic certainty

---

10. On the problematics of the description of the idea of progress as a "reinterpretation" of the messianic idea, see Hans Blumenberg: "It is a formal, but for that very reason a manifest, difference that an eschatology speaks of an event breaking into history, an event that transcends and is heterogeneous to it, while the idea of progress extrapolates from a structure present in every moment to a future that is immanent in history" (*The Legitimacy of the Modern Age*, 30).

that the End had begun and all that was still required was the call to ingathering" (*MI*, 15). In this formulation, the lack of relation is "essential," while at the same time "we can understand" why this lack was overlooked. Apocalypticism, too, takes effect through a (comprehensible) misunderstanding.[11]

For Scholem, it is only in imminent eschatological expectation—and only through a misunderstanding—that messianism becomes truly vital and effective. It does already contain the opposing elements of utopia and restoration within itself, but these opposites lack force "as long as Messianism appeared only as an abstract hope, as an element totally deferred to the future.... These things could be united in pure thought, or at least they could be preserved next to one another, but they could not be united in their execution" (*MI*, 21–22). The messianic idea that Scholem speaks of is not conceived of as a constant force—whether this be universal or particular—but as the "great catalyst in Judaism," which accelerates explosive chemical reactions without actually causing them.[12] These reactions are also dangerous, as Scholem emphasizes in a letter: "The funny thing about this entire story is that the messianic idea devalued every historical action in its concrete execution. When the idea went beyond being a mere idea by entering into a messianic execution, it exploded in the course of this very execution" (*LL*, 378). Devaluation or explosion: messianism, although a vital force and necessary, seems to lead to an aporia.

For Scholem, the messianic idea is an idea in execution, which he contextualizes historically and politically. From a historical-philosophical perspective, the idea appears as "aporetic" insofar as the completely new cannot appear in history.[13] Characteristically, however, Scholem always speaks of paradox, never of aporia. His horizon is not that of the history of salvation or philosophy of history but that of the *effect* of the messianic idea. Rather than relying on historical-philosophical considerations, Scholem accesses the messianic idea via history of religion on the one hand and political experience on the other. Both of these perspectives come together in the understanding of Sabbatianism that he developed in the 1920s and 1930s.

---

11. Scholem also speaks of the "enticement to action" inherent in messianism, acknowledging that, with respect to Zionism, it is "little wonder that overtones of Messianism have accompanied the modern Jewish readiness for irrevocable action in the concrete realm" (*MI*, 15, 35).

12. Scholem, "Die Metamorphose des häretischen Messianismus der Sabbatianer in religiösen Nihilismus im 18. Jahrhundert," in *Judaica*, vol. 3, 199.

13. For Mosès, Scholem's messianism is the *"aspiration for the impossible"* or the "always renewed aspiration for the emergence, in the very heart of time, of the brand-new," and it can only be described aporetically (*Angel of History*, 132).

EIGHTEEN

EXPLOSION AND HISTORICAL TEST

The Essential Plot

ALREADY IN THE 1928 ESSAY on Cardozo, Scholem asserts that Sabbatianism is more than an external crisis, revealing developments "in the heart of Judaism."[1] In his subsequent research, he sketches the theological prehistory of Sabbatianism in the Kabbalah. It is decisive for Scholem's plot that the actual crisis in Sabbatianism was prepared over a long period—for example, in the Lurianic doctrine of the *tikkun* as preparation for redemption. According to this doctrine, all of creation lost its completeness through an original catastrophe, thus calling for restitution: every execution of the commandments restores a piece of nature and liberates some of the "sparks" of the divine caught in evil creation. This doctrine paved the way for acceptance of Sabbatai Zevi as Messiah, for even the apostasy of the Messiah can be understood as an act—albeit extreme—of *tikkun* that liberates the divine even among pagans. According to Scholem, "The Jewish writers of history strangely underestimated the seductive force of this new doctrine: they saw the historical and current *occasion* alone, recognizing in it only the embarrassed excuse."[2]

In the 1928 essay, Scholem presents historical development as driven by theology, with explosion as the guiding metaphor. Scholem designates Luria's messianic Kabbalah as "historical dynamite," in which "all elements ... were already given when they were united by the galvanic spark of a historical act"; this act itself, along with Zevi's messianic claim as well as his conversion, thus appear to be only a "small push."[3] Sabbatianism is nothing more than the end of

---

1. Scholem, "Die Theologie des Sabbatianismus," in *Judaica*, vol. 1, 119.
2. Scholem, "Die Theologie des Sabbatianismus," in *Judaica*, vol. 1, 136.
3. Scholem, "Die Theologie des Sabbatianismus," in *Judaica*, vol. 1, 137, 138.

a movement immanent in the Kabbalah, "in which all concepts of Jewish mysticism seem to converge, only to explode in their own dialectics—or, said more sadly, to fizzle out."[4] Viewed in this light, Sabbatianism no longer appears as an isolated, irrational crisis. It has a prehistory in the Lurianic Kabbalah as well as a post-history following the apostasy and lasting into modernity, because the collapse of the Kabbalah also destroyed the Judaism of the Middle Ages: "In Sabbatianism, the crisis externally documented by reform had already been permanently set into the innermost heart of Judaism 150 years earlier."[5] In a nutshell, the plot of Scholem's history of the Kabbalah is condensed in this statement. He proceeds to unfold dimensions of this plot in the years to come while at the same time relativizing the theological explanation.

For Scholem, the theosophical speculations of the Kabbalah are always also expressions of a particular mentality or piety. In 1928 he initially characterizes Sabbatianism as "Marranism's reaction to the Kabbalah."[6] The Marranos—Spanish Jews forced to convert to Christianity in the fifteenth century—had already experienced a schism: "The religion which they professed was not that in which they believed. This dualism could not but endanger, if it did not indeed destroy the unity of Jewish feeling and thinking" (*MT*, 309). Thus, they were susceptible to antinomianism and leanings toward Sabbatianism, the "psychology" of which Scholem describes at one point as "utterly paradoxical and 'Marranic.' Essentially its guiding principle was: Whoever is as he appears to be cannot be a true 'believer'" (*MI*, 109). Scholem first develops this argument in the essay "After the Expulsion from Spain," published in 1933/1934, and later transfers it to *Major Trends*. This text is clearly a reaction to the Nazis' rise to power: already in April 1933 he writes to Benjamin, "although the extent of the catastrophe is of historic proportions, and it can teach us something about 1492, the stuff of which resistance is made has been reduced in German Jewry to a very small fraction of what existed in those days."[7] Scholem thus brings the history of the Kabbalah into sync with the present.

According to the argument in "After the Expulsion from Spain," the result of the expulsion of 1492 was that "Kabbalism established its claim to spiritual domination in Judaism. This fact became immediately obvious in its transformation from an esoteric into a popular doctrine" (*MT*, 244). Initially, however, the expulsion provoked a strong apocalyptic movement that had little to do

---

4. Scholem, "Die Theologie des Sabbatianismus," in *Judaica*, vol. 1, 131–132.
5. Scholem, "Die Theologie des Sabbatianismus," in *Judaica*, vol. 1, 132.
6. Scholem, "Die Theologie des Sabbatianismus," in *Judaica*, vol. 1, 122.
7. Scholem, *Correspondence of Benjamin and Scholem*, 39; see also *Br I*, 252–253. The essay's German title is "Nach der Vertreibung aus Spanien: Zur Geschichte der Kabbala."

with the Kabbalah, as "the very belief that redemption was near prevented the drastic experiences of the Expulsion, vividly as they were still remembered, from being transmuted into ultimate religious concepts" (*MT*, 247). It was only as this movement combined with the Kabbalah, which has an entirely different constitution, that something new emerged, a process that Scholem describes as a merger in the depths of Jewish consciousness: "Only gradually ... did the flames which had flared up from the apocalyptical abyss sweep over wide areas of the Jewish world until they finally seized upon and recast the mystical theology of Kabbalism" (*MT*, 247). Thus, messianism and the Kabbalah came together only indirectly, in the latency of unconsciousness. The extraordinary effect and explosive power of the mystical messianism that arose as a result can be explained precisely through this complicated genesis and formation from opposing forces; Jewish life was no longer determined by the intellectual values of a rational philosophy of religion but rather by purely religious values. In this way, the kabbalists, elitists though they were, became representatives of popular religion. Along with his colleague Yitzhak Fritz Baer, Scholem seems to assume a tension between the intellectual and assimilated elite and pious lower class as a determining factor in the history of the Jews in medieval Spain.[8]

Through its blending with popular messianism, the Kabbalah became "the authentic voice of the people in the crisis produced by the banishment from Spain" (*MT*, 250). Therefore, "nothing seems more natural than that there should have been the closest correspondence between the historical conditions ... and the inner development of Jewish religious thought, including all its new forms" (*MT*, 287).[9] The attitude of radical exile was at once expressed and fortified in the Kabbalah, for the "sufferings" of this attitude were "not soothed and tranquilized, but stimulated and whipped up" by the Kabbalah (*MT*, 249). In the following years, Scholem gives further consideration to this indirect and unconscious repercussion of the Kabbalah for historical development.

---

8. On Baer's construction, see Myers, *Re-Inventing the Jewish Past*, 122ff. In 1944 Scholem speaks of tension between the assimilated upper class, "the small class of wealthy court Jews" (*PM*, 139), and pious lower class, "poor talmudic scholars and pious householders" (ibid.); the kabbalists are thereby the "representatives of the religious forces and beliefs which were active among the masses of the people" (ibid., 123), "not only ... mystics and esoteric devotees, but also ... ideologists defending the folk religion" (ibid., 138). He later explains that "social stratification cannot account for the actual alignment of forces," as the "messianic awakening clearly transcended all classes, insofar as we are at all entitled to apply this term to Jewish society" (*Sabbatai Sevi*, 5, 6).

9. This synchronicity also plays an important role in Scholem's interpretation of Luria's Kabbalah as a "myth of exile." See *MT*, 260–264; *KS*, 111. For critical accounts, see, for example, Liebes, "Myth vs. Symbol"; Idel, "Zur Funktion von Symbolen," 72ff.

One decisive step for Scholem is his engagement with Frankism, articulated primarily in "Redemption through Sin" from 1937, probably his most controversial essay. Here, Scholem no longer speaks of Sabbatianism's "metaphysical setting"; instead, he focuses on its "ideology" or "theology," the effect of which must be understood. This effect is not simply equated with popular religion, as Scholem now emphasizes that there is a latent contradiction between kabbalistic formulations and the piety they convey. His guiding ideas include the notion of the "eruption" of contradiction in realization as well as "crisis" and historical "test," which continue to play a central role in his historical logic of ideas.[10] Scholem stresses that the kabbalists themselves did not notice the ambiguity of their concepts, which could refer to concrete action as well as intellectual redemption: "As long as the Messianic expectancies they encouraged were not put to the test in the actual crucible of history, the dangers inherent in this shift of emphasis went unnoticed, for the Kabbalists themselves never once imagined a conflict might arise between the symbol and the reality it was intended to represent" (MI, 87). It is precisely the latency of these processes that facilitates the Kabbalah's success in a Jewish society determined by tradition. As Scholem later explains more broadly in *Sabbatai Sevi*, this unnoticed ambiguity also facilitates the integration of Judaism as a whole. Apparently, the realistic expectations of the masses and the refined teachings of the spiritual elite mean the same thing: "The political messianism of the masses and the mystical messianism of the kabbalists appeared to form an integral complex of ideas" (SS, 60). The notion of a *seemingly* integral complex of ideas presupposes a perspective from the other side; to exaggerate, one could say that the theology of Sabbatianism as well as its prehistory would not be understandable at all if the Sabbatian catastrophe had not made this latent contradiction visible. For Scholem, the Kabbalah is not understandable as a spiritual phenomenon, at least as far as its second, historical phase after 1492 is concerned. Instead, the Kabbalah reveals itself in its public "side effect," in misunderstanding, which releases that which is bound together and dissolves the compromise of opposing forces that drove its development.

---

10. Allusions to this line of thinking can already be found earlier; Scholem writes in 1921 that the kabbalists "wanted to leave a province to the people, apparently as property but actually belonging to them, which has now rebelliously made itself independent, so to speak. For indeed, the truth is that the kabbalists were defeated by the people here" (*T II*, 672). Scholem alludes to this in the Cardozo essay as well: in the Kabbalah, "those high historical shifts were exhibited, for the redemption of which history no longer held the narrow conventicles of the mystics liable, but rather the Jewish people" ("Die Theologie des Sabbatianismus," in *Judaica*, vol. 1, 127).

From this point of view, the crisis itself also gains particular significance. While in 1928 Scholem still grasped the crisis as a mere catalyst for processes that can be comprehended in purely theological terms, it now appears as a historical test that revealed the hidden content of the Kabbalah. Only Zevi's appearance and the resulting mass movement "caused this inner sense of freedom, of 'a world made pure again,' to become an immediate reality for thousands. This did not of course mean that Sabbatai Zevi himself was no longer expected to fulfill the various Messianic tasks assigned him by Jewish tradition, but in the meantime an irreversible change had taken place in the souls of the faithful" (*MI*, 87–88).

This shift in messianic expectation was possible because the concept of redemption had already acquired an internalized dimension in the Lurianic Kabbalah, and this is the only reason why Zevi could be recognized as Messiah in the first place. Even before apostasy, he sharply contradicted the image of the expected redeemer, above all because he occasionally committed ritual transgressions of the law. Scholem later explains this based on Zevi's manic-depressive condition, granting this factor significant weight for the emergence of subsequent antinomianism (*MT*, 289–294). Yet in his earlier texts as well as "Redemption through Sin," he does not address Zevi's actions before conversion, instead emphasizing conversion itself: "'Heretical' Sabbatianism was born at the moment of Sabbatai Zevi's totally unexpected conversion, when for the first time a contradiction appeared between the two levels of the drama of redemption, that of the subjective experience of the individual on the one hand, and that of the objective historical facts on the other" (*MI*, 88). The conflict between esoteric and exoteric redemption, seemingly resolved earlier in the *tikkun* doctrine, broke out once again as a result. "One had to choose: either one heard the voice of God in the decree of history, or else one heard it in the newly revealed reality within" (*MI*, 88).

The historical "test," or major "crisis," in Scholem's account thus comprised messianic disappointment, which led to a complete transformation of tradition. In *Major Trends* and more extensively in *Sabbatai Sevi*, Scholem makes an extremely illuminating comparison to the development of early Christianity and the formation of Pauline theology, in a sense returning to the intellectual context from which the debate on apocalypticism in the history of religion emerged.[11] Both phenomena are based on disappointments that

---

11. This is one of Scholem's rare explicitly religious-historical comparisons, and he stresses that he is less concerned with influences than he is with "similarities in the historical situations . . . and the inner logic of their respective doctrinal notions," which "led to similar results" (*SS*, 797). See also Taubes, *The Political Theology of Paul*, 7ff.

had to be explained—Christ's death on the cross and the apostasy of Sabbatai Zevi—and both relate to the paradox of the suffering servant of God, "which, however, they stressed with such radicalism that they practically stood it on its head" (SS, 795). This paradox, that the one who suffers is the one who is just, endows the phenomena themselves with the paradox that defeat was only apparent and that it was actually the defeat of the world: "not faith in imminent redemption but faith in the paradox of the messiah's mission was declared to be the crucial issue. The basic paradox of the new faith inevitably led to further and no less audacious paradoxes" (SS, 796). However, Scholem also highlights the difference between the movements. First, the founding paradox of Christ's death on the cross differs from that of the apostasy, which was more radical but also more destructive. Second, early Christianity was not only based on the paradoxical value of faith but also that of love. Third, Paul abandoned Judaism quickly and decisively, while Sabbatianism remained *within* Judaism, attempting "to defend, within the ghetto, a spiritual world that had already broken out of the ghetto walls" (SS, 796).

Scholem's description of Paul is markedly ambivalent. On the one hand, he designates Paul as "the most outstanding example . . . of a revolutionary Jewish mystic," who read "the Old Testament 'against the grain'" (KS, 14). On the other hand, Scholem downplays this revolution as a mere "religious strategy," since it was only "in the interest of Christian propaganda" that Paul abrogated Jewish law: "This impulse from the outside did not arise out of any immanent logic.... However, ... it then received a far-reaching dialectical and downright antinomian justification" (MI, 57–58). The difference that is actually decisive for Scholem goes unmentioned in his comparison. Sabbatianism did not remain within Judaism by chance but because it was based on a prior shift in Jewish tradition itself, specifically the transformation of the concept of redemption in the Kabbalah. As long as redemption was still understood as an unmysterious process—and as long as the criterion for the true Messiah was visible success—messianic outbursts and disappointments ended either with resigned return to the traditional form of Judaism or with its total renunciation, be it through formation of a new religion, as in early Christianity, or conversion. "Only a mystical interpretation of the fundamental categories of the Law and the Redemption was capable of preparing the ground for antinomian tendencies which strove to maintain themselves within the general framework of Judaism" (MT, 314). Therefore, the developments following conversion—constituting that which is specific to Sabbatianism, in Scholem's view, and that which actually requires explanation—can only be understood through the prehistory of Sabbatianism in the Kabbalah.

These considerations once again clarify Scholem's explanatory approach. He no longer claims that the Kabbalah "caused" Sabbatianism, presenting it instead as the "key" or "central and unifying factor."[12] It is the thread that connects the different phases, making a history of development possible. Second, only consideration of the Kabbalah facilitates a consistent explanation of Sabbatianism, making all of its phases and variants comprehensible. Given the extreme economic and social diversity of the Diaspora, the "patent unity of the Sabbatian movement" can only be explained through an "essentially religious" factor that "as such obeyed its own autonomous laws" (SS, 7). Third, this viewpoint allows for a complex portrayal; since 1492 the Kabbalah has had a "double function as an interpretation *of* history and as a factor *in* Jewish history" (SS, 44). The Kabbalah and Sabbatianism can be interwoven into one explanation. Fourth and finally, this reciprocal reference makes the Kabbalah into a historical phenomenon as well. Because Sabbatianism was *the* historical hour of the Kabbalah, Scholem tells the story of the Kabbalah as an unrepeatable story: the Kabbalah was drowned out by Sabbatianism's demons and thus gained its historical seal, becoming legible as a distinct historical development with a clear dramatic outline instead of a manifestation of mystical piety only visible from time to time.

Scholem once described the history of Sabbatianism as "a prime example for the dialectics of historical development."[13] His "dialectics" is not a philosophy of the history of successive epochs that could be reduced to the triad of myth, religion, and mysticism, nor is it a question of a general law of the different layers of historical happenings (base and superstructure, or life and form). In Scholem's historiography, "dialectics" never governs the totality of an epoch, a subject area, or the like. Instead, it is the particular historical phenomenon that is dialectical, as Scholem describes in an early, long unpublished version of the introduction to *Sabbatai Sevi*. Among his texts, this one probably comes closest to a theory of historical developments. Scholem concisely links the two foundational metaphors that he uses to characterize historical objects—namely, "dialectics" and "life": "Nothing would be more erroneous than to think that the truth is simple. . . . Perhaps the truth is sometimes 'simple' when it has not yet asserted itself in the crucible of history and fought for its probation—abstract truth. The truth was simple at the

---

12. Scholem, "Ürsprunge, Widerspruche und Auswirkungen des Sabbatianismus," in *Judaica*, vol. 5, 129; *Kabbalah*, 244.
13. Scholem, "Die Metamorphose des häretischen Messianismus der Sabbatianer," in *Judaica*, vol. 3, 200.

hour of its first revelation, when it arose on the 'mountains of the heart.' And perhaps also at the hour of its descent into speech and expression of human language. The truth that becomes a slogan in order to shake up and excite the masses—is simple, as slogans are."[14] Simplicity is thus aligned with abstraction, while the "dialectics of truth" involves not only an idea's inner richness but also its effect. The idea does not independently transition into its opposite; it becomes dialectical in taking effect: "A contentious truth, a truth that is capable of awakening and stirring up that which slumbers in our depths . . . , in brief: a truth that lives and is ready to step out among the living—does not retain its genteel simplicity for long. Its inner vitality will detonate that which is simple."[15] Neither identical nor opposed to one another, "life" and "truth" are interwoven. Moreover, the "life" of truth does not consist in organic unfolding or development but in the destruction of original simplicity and in the outbreak of paradoxes: "*The hidden side of truth is the emergence of its inner contradictions*—in the language of the great philosophers, we call this great and fundamental 'mystery' the 'dialectics of truth.'"[16]

Scholem's is a dialectics of crisis. He often speaks of the dialectics of decay but never of dialectical construction.[17] Development is dialectical insofar as it is constantly a matter of crossing a limit or boundary: the boundary between esoteric and exoteric, surface and depth, consequence and misunderstanding, and so on. The strong paradox at the center of Scholem's texts also represents these boundaries, for to speak of paradox is to point to boundaries without being able to deactivate and cross them once and for all; it is to bring into relation that which is separate. Hugo Bergmann shares in his diaries that Scholem once broke the "silence about his view of history":

> He said: that which is true is in itself completely historically ineffective. This is not at all what matters in history. That which is true contains in itself no demand, yet the demand is what is effective. The demand is nowhere to be

---

14. Scholem, "Ursprünge, Widerspruche und Auswirkungen des Sabbatianismus," in *Judaica*, vol. 5, 119. This introduction was written in the 1940s.
15. Scholem, "Ursprünge, Widerspruche und Auswirkungen des Sabbatianismus," in *Judaica*, vol. 5, 119.
16. Scholem, "Ursprünge, Widerspruche und Auswirkungen des Sabbatianismus," in *Judaica*, vol. 5, 119–120.
17. See also in a note from Scholem's papers: "Hegel says, superbly: 'asserting *abstractions* in reality means destroying reality.' He means: *undeveloped* concepts that are not vitally unfolded in their dialectics as such, not as *concrete* structures of dialectical shaping, must have a historically destructive (*not*: transformative) function" ("Schwindel der Revolutionen," 1–2).

derived from that which is true, it arises from it only through a virtual shift, and this is what is actually historically effective. Whoever wants to have a historical effect must appeal to the baser instincts of the people. Those who do not want to do so have no effect.... That which is reasonable and rational is a self-contained system, it is at rest. Taoism has recognized this and hence renounces history and does not want to have an effect. That which is apocalyptic always has an effect. Christianity as a religion of love, etc. would never have had an effect, it was the expectation of Christ's return that had an effect. Likewise in Socialism it was the future state. Only problematics have an effect.[18]

This statement is only transmitted indirectly, and it is characteristic of Scholem's view of history for precisely this reason. As we saw in part 1, Scholem describes the relationship between canonical and political language, including the catchphrase, in similar terms. Here, too, Scholem's distinctive gesture (that which is true does not have an effect) is less interesting than the relation he establishes (the effect arises from that which is true). Truth and effectiveness are different yet related, and Scholem's historical dialectics consists in making the effect comprehensible, as was already the case in the dual reading of the "productive misunderstanding." Three elements are essential: the closed context of the truth, the vulgarized effect, and finally the leap that links the two. Thus, a history of Sabbatianism must be at once theological and political, as it "depends on success in the attempt to link the earthly realm—the territory of history—to the heavenly realm—the territory of the Kabbalah—and to interpret the one in light of the other."[19] The outer development can be understood through the Kabbalah, while conversely, it also reveals the content of the Kabbalah—its inner life.

---

18. Bergmann, *Tagebücher und Briefe*, vol. 1, 242.
19. Scholem, "Ursprünge, Widerspruche und Auswirkungen des Sabbatianismus," in *Judaica*, vol. 5, 130.

NINETEEN

JEWISH MODERNITY

A Test of the Present

THE KABBALAH CAME TO AN end in the Sabbatian movement, with its latent tensions discharged and the grand line of development returning to its origin: "the explosion of the Messianic element contained in Lurianic Kabbalism was a fact which could not well be denied" (*MT*, 328). After the crisis, the Kabbalah could become completely esoteric, as in the case of the Kabbalah of Beth-El, where it became "at the end of its way what it was at the beginning; a genuine esoterism, a kind of mystery-religion which tries to keep the *profanum vulgus* at arm's length" (*MT*, 329). Alternately, it took the path of Hasidism, which Scholem sees as neutralizing messianism; this, too, closes the circle insofar as the magical qualities of the Zaddik and mystical enthusiasm increasingly come to the fore: "At the end of the long history of Jewish mysticism these two tendencies are as closely interwoven as they were in the beginning" (*MT*, 349).

This is not the only end, however. As closed as Scholem's story is, it does point beyond itself, as the great crisis of Sabbatianism coincides with a new beginning: the history of Jewish emancipation and thus of modern Jewry. Although Scholem devoted himself to this connection in his final years, throughout his writings it remains suggested rather than spelled out in detail.[1]

---

1. Scholem was working on a book about Hirschfeld shortly before his death, and he announced a lecture for the 1981 *World Congress for Jewish Studies*, which was canceled for health reasons (see Dan, "Jewish Studies after Gershom Scholem," 142). For critique of Scholem's thesis, see, for instance, Biale, *Kabbalah and Counter-History*, 82ff. and Schweid, *Judaism and Mysticism*, 133ff. Schweid considers this the weakest part of Scholem's work; Taubes calls it a "strange thesis, striking but without any historical foundation" (*From Cult to Culture*, 47).

Among other reasons, this connection is significant because it concerns the position of the historian himself. If the history of the Kabbalah were to reach into the Enlightenment, the historian's own origin and the methodological position of an "enlightened" writing of history could be integrated into the plot of the Kabbalah and conceived as part of the tradition itself, as we have seen Scholem repeatedly suggest.

The suggested connection between Kabbalah and modernity has a polemical side to it. Already in "Redemption through Sin," Scholem criticizes the liberal historians of the nineteenth century: "Indeed, as long as Jewish historiography was dominated by a spirit of assimilation, no one so much as suspected that positivism and religious reform were the progeny not only of the rational mind, but of an entirely different sort of psychology as well, that of the Kabbalah and the Sabbatian crisis—in other words, of that very 'lawless heresy' which was so soundly excoriated in their name!" (*MI*, 90–91). Contrary to his habit, Scholem explicitly refers to positive models for his critique—namely, Protestant research into the connection "between Christian sectarianism in Europe and the growth of the Enlightenment and the ideal of toleration in the seventeenth and eighteenth centuries" (*MI*, 90).[2] Among others, Ernst Troeltsch draws a link between the "old liberal theory of the inviolability of the inner personal life by the State" and Reformation religion: "The idea is at first religious. Later, it becomes secularized, and overgrown by the rationalistic, sceptical, and utilitarian idea of toleration."[3] Troeltsch also emphasizes that religion is only one factor among many and that its effect consists "mainly in indirect and unconsciously produced effects, nay, even in accidental side-influences, or again in influences produced against its will."[4] Designating this as "secularization," Troeltsch highlights the ambivalence of a process that, while initiated by religious motives, outgrew those motives in the course of their continuous transformation. Indeed, at the beginning of the twentieth century, this process was threatened by mass society and industrialization: "Let us jealously preserve that principle of freedom which draws its strength from a religious metaphysic; otherwise the cause of freedom and personality may well be lost in the very moment when we are boasting most loudly of our allegiance

---

2. See reference in Biale, *Kabbalah and Counter-History*, 87, as well as Twardella, "Soziologische Überlegungen zur jüdischen Mystik." For an overview of research on this topic from Scholem's time, see Bornkamm, *Mystik, Spiritualismus und die Anfänge des Pietismus*.
3. Troeltsch, *Protestantism and Progress*, 125.
4. Troeltsch, *Protestantism and Progress*, 87.

to it, and of our progress in this direction."[5] Secularization thus connotes both continuity and difference, both historical depth and contemporary risk.

Scholem's investigation into the prehistory of the Jewish Enlightenment parallels Troeltsch's project to a certain extent: Scholem, too, is seeking a prehistory of the Enlightenment in which mystics and heretical sects play a decisive role. He presents two versions of the argument. In most cases, Scholem explains the resounding success of the Enlightenment negatively, based on the fact that Sabbatianism destroyed traditional Judaism. Through antinomianism, "the bedrock upon which the moral consciousness of Judaism is founded crumbled . . . into dust."[6] Scholem often emphasizes that this was an *inner* process, proceeding from the entire Jewish Kabbalah itself. "Unlike the criticism of the Enlightenment . . . which was inspired by ideas and circumstances impinging from the outside, the Sabbatian criticism of rabbinic Judaism was an internal phenomenon: it was the criticism of 'spirituals' whose paradoxical values no longer fitted into the traditional mold and who sought new modes of expression for their utopian Judaism" (SS, 794). Once again, Graetz's view is reversed in Scholem's argument. The Enlightenment was not Judaism becoming self-aware after liberation from its "external" transformation by the Kabbalah; instead, the Kabbalah provoked self-destruction that enabled the infiltration of the Enlightenment from the "outside."

There is an even stronger version of this argument, according to which the criticism of antinomians and spirituals represented a positive principle— namely, the spirit of freedom that actually prefigured the Enlightenment. The Sabbatians transitioned to "assimilation and the Haskalah, two forces that accomplished without paradoxes, indeed without religion at all, what they, the members of the 'accursed sect,' had earnestly striven for in a stormy contention with truth, carried on in the half-light of a faith pregnant with paradoxes" (MI, 141). This anarchist spirit of total freedom clearly contributes to Scholem's fascination with Frankism: "A hundred years before Bakunin, Frank placed the redeeming power of destruction at the center of his utopia."[7] This freedom, however, is merely abstract, and thus it transforms into its opposite: "The goal is unfettered freedom, yet the path demands the strongest discipline. Thus, paradoxically enough, Frank becomes the first advocate and panegyrist of soldierhood among the Jews."[8] The true warrior of faith no longer retains

---

5. Troeltsch, *Protestantism and Progress*, 207.
6. Scholem, "Die Theologie des Sabbatianismus," in *Judaica*, vol. 1, 144–145.
7. Scholem, "Der Nihilismus als religiöses Phänomen," in *Judaica*, vol. 4, 178–179.
8. Scholem, "Der Nihilismus als religiöses Phänomen," in *Judaica*, vol. 4, 180.

any religion or visible practice but only an entirely invisible faith and the practices that protect this faith in its concealment: "In a peculiar epigram, [Frank] says that soldiers are not allowed to have any religion. Their object is to follow the general."[9]

Scholem also calls this attitude nihilistic, and nihilism is surely a possible outcome of the secularization of initially religious values. This is the case for Troeltsch, who sees the freedom of the individual founded in a religious past and fundamentally endangered in the present. Again, Scholem seems to point to a similar dialectic when he assumes that the worship of freedom for its own sake necessarily turns into the worship of rule: "This almost sensuous love for power, which Frank possessed in the highest degree, is the stigma of nihilism. To Frank the grand gesture of the ruler is everything" (*MT*, 337). For Jews, power remains a gesture, an imaginary power that feeds on real powerlessness. Frank is left with only the virtual court of Offenbach and the dream of a cataclysm from the underground, following the example of the Russian revolutionaries. As Scholem highlights in other essays, this nihilism did not emerge in the modern era: "It has played a role in the history of religion all along."[10] In terms of history of religion, the paradigmatic representatives of nihilism are not atheists or negative theologians but rather Gnostics and pantheistic spiritual figures for whom there is a "religious nihilism": "Under this term I do not understand a nihilism that extends to religion, but rather a nihilism that appears in the name of religious claims and with a religious claim. It recognizes the religious sphere, but radically negates the authority that presumes to control this sphere. It does not aim at the stabilization of new structures in the place of the old ones, but rather at their dismantling. Often but not always, this happens in the name of mystical experience."[11]

Like "religious anarchism," and clearly related, Scholem's religious nihilism is an ambivalent concept. On the one hand, it can refer to cleansing religion of all kinds of authority, while on the other, a sphere without authority may undermine itself. Thus, freedom—the central "value" of religious nihilism—is only abstract, precisely because it is only inner, concealed freedom. For Scholem, the exemplary nihilist is not the free spirit or the cheerful creator but Jakob Frank, a demonic personality consumed by his contradictions and ressentiments, free

---

9. Scholem, "Die Metamorphose des häretischen Messianismus," in *Judaica*, vol. 3, 213.

10. Scholem, "Der Nihilismus als religiöses Phänomen," in *Judaica*, vol. 4, 133. Scholem is primarily referring to Jonas, who designated Gnosticism as "nihilism between the ages" (*Gnosis und spätantiker Geist*, vol. 1, 234).

11. Scholem, "Der Nihilismus als religiöses Phänomen," in *Judaica*, vol. 4, 134–135.

only in imagination. In Scholem's portrayal, Frank is painted as "a personality in every fiber of his being, [and] also the most hideous and uncanny figure in the whole history of Jewish Messianism" (*MT*, 308). Rather than the artist or warrior, it is the *terrorist* who represents the modern nihilist for Scholem; rather than Nietzsche, Dostoevsky should come to mind. Representing nihilists as "demons," he interprets their anti-religious intentions in a religious framework: they are demonic in that they want to rule and destroy, not out of healthy instincts but out of boredom and despair—ultimately out of God-forsakenness. Their power as well is only a pose, exercised only in terrorist groups or even more radically in total isolation, and enthusiasm for power appears as the flip side of real weakness.

In Scholem's description of figures who continue the Frankist tradition of dissimulation, demonic ambiguity plays an important role. He is interested in Hirschfeld and Dobruschka precisely due to their "tangle of reactionary and radical tendencies," an intermediate position between the Frankist Kabbalah and radical Enlightenment.[12] "In spite of the apparent contradiction, we see that mystical tendencies . . . and political orientations . . . are not incompatible. To be sure, it was necessary to be a Frankist in order to cultivate these two tendencies at the same time; in this, Schönfeld [alias Dobruschka] did nothing other than to put into practice the prophecies of . . . Jacob Frank."[13] Because of their Frankist past, these radical Jewish Enlightenment figures were disposed to work in the revolutionary underground and did not perceive any contradiction between their radical ideas and their commitment to Judaism. Scholem suggests that like the Frankists, they may have only feigned leaving Judaism while in reality remaining connected to it. Thus, a zone of transition and ambiguities emerges here, a dimension of depth that allows for a different narration of the Enlightenment.

Scholem characteristically inscribes himself into this heretical and demonic lineage when discussing Jewish historiography. In a notorious 1944 lecture, he delivers a polemical diatribe against the "science of Judaism" in order to clear the ground for himself and his own endeavor.[14] This is especially significant

---

12. Scholem, "Ein verschollener jüdischer Mystiker," 247.
13. Scholem, *Du Frankisme au Jacobinisme*, 41. Scholem also describes Dobruschka as "a man wearing several masks at the same time, disavowing all of them according to circumstance without it being possible to determine his real position: this is the position of the true Frankist according to the conception extolled by Jacob Frank" (ibid., 65–66).
14. See Weidner, "Gershom Scholem, die Wissenschaft des Judentums." Scholem describes the central image of a haunting past already in 1919: "Jewish scholarship is in an especially paradoxical and indeed extremely enviable position. It is not as if it invokes spirits

in light of his relationship to the first generation of scholars such as Leopold Zunz and Moritz Steinscheider, whom he criticizes for their merely antiquarian interest. At the same time, however, Scholem is attracted by the "zealously matter-of-fact approach," the "coolness," the "hatred" and "cynicism" of these scholars, and speaks with fascination of their "chthonian aspect" and their "demonic side": "In the case of these two, the tendency to destruction is entirely inward; their hidden nihilism contains a certain measure of nobility, which functioned within them as a kind of creative despair" (PM, 58–59). By contrast, this demonic power is absent in Heinrich Graetz, "who remained loyal to the principles of Romantic scholarship, from which he derived the natural conclusion in the constructive sense as well" (PM, 58), or David Kaufmann, for whom "this science appears in its full conservative power (not in its constructive power, Heaven forbid!), as if he had already shaken off the nods made in the direction of destruction" (PM, 64). It is also absent in the Zionist historians, although (one is tempted to say because) they have set themselves a positive goal—namely, the restoration of national identity. For them, too, "the true forces which operated in our world, the true demonics, have remained outside of the picture which we created" (PM, 70).

Surprisingly, in "natural" and "constructive" scholarship, the "demonic" element that was at work in destructive scholarship disappears, and only scholarship that flirts with radical destruction and scholarly nihilism has the chance to be truly constructive. This implies that there is no longer any natural relationship to heritage and no assured position. "History" cannot become a story of Jewish wholeness, and it cannot raise tradition into a realm beyond secularity and holiness. "And I am *really torn* between the two possibilities: to take on the yoke 'of the rebels who turned out to be followers,' or to revolt against it. And here is at once the origin of a great weakness and a great strength" (Br I, 297). Scholem remains a historian, and all ahistorical or existential updates of heritage remain suspicious to him. Yet his history is shot through with doubts regarding its own relevance and synthetic force, an attitude that could be considered typical of the late historicism of Jacob Burckhardt and Franz Overbeck or Max Weber and Ernst Troeltsch. Affected by Nietzsche's critique of history, these historians still remain true to history, and having lost the self-confidence of nineteenth-century historicism, they nonetheless hold fast

---

that refuse to come. Quite the opposite: Jewish scholarship expends its full efforts at turning away the invoked spirits, just as it denies that they're there. But the spirits come *anyway*. They are always there. Always. And they want to be redeemed through the work of insightful scholars" (LY, 312).

to historical inquiry as a way—perhaps the only way—to achieve substantial understanding.

Scholem traces the widest arc of his history in the sixth of his "Unhistorical Aphorisms."[15] Here, the entire Kabbalah is integrated into the history of nihilism: the Jews' traditional way of life stands in the "shadow of the law": "But in the Kabbalah, the stony wall of the law gradually becomes transparent; a shimmer of the reality surrounded and circumscribed by it breaks through.... But along with this ever increasing, if also ever more indistinct transparency of the law, the shadows which the law casts over Jewish life dissolve. The end of this process must, logically speaking, be Jewish 'Reform': the shadowless, backgroundless, but no longer irrational, purely abstract humanity of the law as a remnant of its mystical dissolution."[16] These lines contain the story of the Kabbalah in a nutshell. It is an ironic story, because the kabbalists wanted to make the law transparent in order to maintain while ultimately dissolving it. Ironically, it is not anarchistic will that dissipates the law but the deepening of mystical intentions. It is also ironic that the requirements of the Kabbalah itself dissipate in this development. As we saw in part 2, the Kabbalah as a historical phenomenon requires attachment to the solid word of revelation and the concreteness of legal precepts. It is this stability that counterbalances endless interpretation; through revelation, tradition is fulfilled. When the founding stability transforms into fluidity, when the solid word becomes a diffuse voice, the Kabbalah also loses the frame of reference that makes it into a collectively significant phenomenon. As soon as revelation is replaced by mystical experience, the tradition of Kabbalah transforms into subjective experience and illegible ciphers that no one can read anymore. Whereas its spirit transitions into Enlightenment, its books become completely illegible, and as a result, kabbalistic tradition cannot be perpetuated. It has to be made visible in a completely different way, through critical philology and religious-historical investigation. This breaking apart of spirit and books, of voice and writing, determines Scholem's understanding of himself as a historian as well as his understanding of Jewish modernity.

No longer a historical explanation, the above-cited aphorism revolves around a grandiose metaphor: making the law transparent. As a theory, this metaphor is weak and indeterminate, but as a metaphor, it abbreviates the plot

---

15. Scholem, "Zehn unhistorische Sätze über Kabbala," in *Judaica*, vol. 3.
16. Translation by Biale, in "Gershom Scholem's Ten Unhistorical Aphorisms on Kabbalah," 81–82.

of Scholem's research in a formula that could be called "nihilistic secularism." However, metaphors work as metaphors precisely because their meaning cannot be spelled out entirely. Indirect presentation in historical recollection is what makes it possible to express ambivalence toward one's own present and to hold one's own judgment in abeyance. Thus, in the *history* of religious nihilism, Scholem is able to articulate that which would appear empty and abstract in any theory or name we could give to it.

CONCLUSION
Authority and Silence

ROLF TIEDEMANN RECALLS THAT IN the 1960s in Frankfurt, Scholem had a curious reputation: "It was of unlimited authority, though one could not really say: authority for what."[1] Scholem appeared to his contemporaries as a distinctly strong author, with authority, charisma, and aura.[2] After finding his own specific way of writing, he no longer needed to employ forceful means of pathos or appeal, radicalism or polemics, in order to convince and pass judgment without provoking contradiction. Yet many contemporaries agreed that they often did not know much about Scholem's personal thoughts: "By no means withdrawn in other respects, he tends to speak of his true intentions with extreme reserve, in any event a little secretively."[3] Written in a way that is matter of fact, readable, and simple, what he says comes across as objective while leaving his subjective assessments obscured. The clarity of his statements is linked to a certain obscurity surrounding their author.

This obscurity also fulfills a function in Scholem's writing. Something is always at stake for him; his authority is always political, theoretical, and scholarly, not authority as such. Scholem claims authority not only for himself but for Jews, and as a Zionist, and therein lies the political dimension. He emphasizes again and again that his own work would not have been possible without

---

1. Tiedemann, "Erinnerung an Scholem," 212.
2. See Shapira: "A certain Aura enveloped Gershom Scholem, one that inspired distance and awe (though he himself seemed unaware of this)" ("The Dialectics of Continuity and Revolt," xv). Funkenstein sees Scholem's "charisma" as founded in the *kairos* of Sabbatianism and Zionism ("Gershom Scholem, Charisma, Kairos," 21ff.).
3. Adorno, "Gruß an Scholem," 483.

Zionist self-examination. Rather than a theory, Zionism is a standpoint for him, the position from which he is able to think and speak. Even when it becomes clear that this standpoint is difficult to reach, that it might be a problem instead of a fixed position, political situatedness remains essential for Scholem's writing. The result is that the word "Jewish" is always under consideration in his texts, without needing to be pronounced—and even where it could not be pronounced. When Scholem says "tradition," he means "Jewish tradition," even as the question of what is actually Jewish remains open. Tradition is the second benchmark, likewise not simply an object for Scholem but rather something that he himself refers to as a medium: a space in which his truth comes about, an area in which his writing locates itself. Here, too, the situation grows complicated when it becomes evident that this space is difficult to enter and that tradition becomes legible precisely through a break with tradition. Thus, even at the end, Scholem does not know what the Kabbalah "really is," but he can read it and comment on it. Scholem's relationship to scholarship is similarly complex, for even if at one point he only employed scholarship to bring Jewish tradition—indeed, Judaism—back to itself, it subsequently developed its own dynamics and gravity, steering the longed-for rebirth into a very particular direction—namely, that of philology. Scholem was well aware that his use of scholarship was not without its ironies: no longer unbroken in tradition, he was left with fragments of script to be set into relation by writing without losing their sites of fracture.

We have seen this play of positioning and self-concealment on various stages. In the first part of the book, I analyzed the young Scholem's political education, highlighting in his early diaries the force of his endeavor for legitimacy and its crises. He began writing as a youthful rebel, using the language typical of the day, but by the time of his confrontation with Martin Buber at the latest, he came to question this vehement position and its confessional style. Subjecting his expression to ascesis, Scholem stabilized his own position and made his writing broader and less agitated. While the wisdom of his older age remains shot through with tensions and sharp edges, also containing grounds for despair, these are concealed in later writings. The development of Scholem's intellectual ethos is also relevant because the transition from youthful radicality to a more complex position coincided with a crisis in the notion of "intellectual leadership" that was decisive for the intellectual history of the twentieth century. Indeed, this crisis might be an essential factor in the perception of Scholem's writing as "modern."

In the second part, I primarily examined Scholem's early theoretical texts, identifying a distinct trend from engagement with general philosophical problems to more specialized reflections on Judaism and individual areas of Jewish tradition. This trend can be understood in terms of Scholem's disappointment with philosophy. I have not tried to reverse this disappointment by looking for the philosophy "behind" Scholem's historiography, instead reading his theoretical writing as an experimental praxis that slowly shifted from the theological to the historical. In these texts, Scholem reflects on the Jewish tradition that he was getting to know at the time, and his reflection is simultaneously an attempt to inscribe himself into that tradition. His theses on tradition thus become legible as a poetics of his own writing. From the perspective of intellectual history, Scholem stands between liberal theology and the antiliberal countermovements of the 1920s. While he views these movements as fundamentally inadequate, he also rejects attempts to overcome them through "new thinking."

In the third part, I showed how Scholem sketches an image of the Kabbalah as a movement in the history of religion. I endeavored to shed light on the inner structure of Scholem's project, placing this project in the context of the history of scholarship to show that Scholem does not simply reconstruct the Kabbalah but reads it in a certain way, through a particular set of questions, concepts, and methods. Rather than political intentions or the underlying assumptions of the philosophy of history, these questions and methods follow from a particular logic of research—namely, the methodologically decisive paradigm of the history of religion. This contributes decisively to Scholem's scholarly authority, which in turn radiates into other areas of his activity, including political, philosophical, and theological writing.

These breaks and tensions in Scholem's writing are particularly distinct—and particularly productive—when it comes to the relationship between religion and history. This relationship crucially determines Scholem's historiography as well as his philosophical and theological speculations, and it also plays a central role in his political considerations on Zionism. The tension between history and religion has its own historical context, as the relationship between politics, religion, and history underwent a general, significant epistemological shift at the turn of the twentieth century. In the course of the nineteenth century, religious tradition had been historicized through biblical criticism, but toward the end of the century, exegetical problems and procedures emerged that undermined "history," the myth of the nineteenth century. I have only presented the relatively isolated paradigm of the history of religion as it broke with various assumptions of classical historicism, bringing into the center of attention objects such as messianism that cannot be historicized so easily. Engagement with religion was an important factor in the constitution of other new disciplines as well, including ethnology, sociology, and psychoanalysis. More generally, religion became the counterpart to what was conceived of as a fundamentally problematic modernity. The epochal break in theology around World War I released religion from a liberal framework that associated religion with morals, culture, and history. The antihistorical revolution of dialectical theology, existentialism, or "new thinking" did not simply rescind historicization—most results of historical exegesis are still presupposed—but it did tend to render it invisible through continuous polemics against historicism. This contributed decisively to the overdetermination of the concept of religion, now a collision point for various antagonistic discourses.

Scholem himself occupied both positions to a certain degree. While remaining connected to historicism through his very method, from its critics he was also aware of history's weaknesses and biases, not least because the history of religion is a deeply Protestant endeavor. Thus he incorporated tensions and resistances into his own investigations: the resistance of messianism as an effective catalyst, and the tension between tradition and history, which in general cannot be conceptually disentangled. Scholem's writings do not resolve the tensions between secular history and ahistorical religion, nor do they make them absolute. In my view, in light of the postsecular present, this is part of what makes them so interesting.

Scholem's work is thus situated in different discursive contexts. It is the tensions within these contexts as well as among these discourses that constitute the force field of his writing, which perpetuates internal inconsistencies and does not reveal a clear position on what he is writing about and against. As recounted by Hugo Bergmann, Scholem's student Isaiah Tishby asked his teacher on his sixtieth birthday to write a "synthesis" after years of historical analysis. Scholem answered that "he had made a synthesis when he began and knew nothing. He learned from Walter Benjamin what it means to think. He learned: 'When you cannot say something perfectly, it is better to be silent.'"[4]

Moments of silence are crucial for the pithiness of Scholem's writing. As we have seen in various collections of theses, moments of interruption are central to his texts, which often hint at things rather than saying everything, positing strongly but not at all unequivocally. His writing involves drawing and transgressing limits, and both moments are decisive: transgression requires limits and confirms them over and over again. Scholem's irony is not so much a paradoxical intensification: while paradox played a central role in his youthful writings, it increasingly shifted into the background of his later texts, operative

---

4. Bergmann, *Tagebücher und Briefe*, vol. 2, 264f.

but no longer explicit. Not actually comprised of aphoristic formulations, his authority is embedded in a rich, extensive research project. His is an art of the long breath, allowing him to carry out his research while letting its significance be known indirectly. The assertion that he is "really" a kabbalist is one that Scholem can confidently leave to his commentators. Let us recall the Hasidic story cited at the beginning of this book: there, too, writing engenders an excess of significance, leaving the task of executing interpretation to the reader. It is not by chance that this citation comes at the conclusion of Scholem's lectures, at the point where direct speech comes to an end and the book is passed to its readers. There is no mysterious ironist pulling the strings behind Scholem's texts or holding the reins on interpretation. In response to attempts to expose his "innermost soul," Scholem once answered: "I am well aware that I do not understand my own true depths, and I am intelligent enough to accept this" (*LL*, 371).

Writing transforms this reserve into strength. The silence that Scholem learned from Benjamin is not only a gesture of modesty but also a claim to authority. Indeed, it may even be a more or less conscious practice of the kind of self-canonization that Scholem describes with respect to Benjamin: "The gesture of the esoteric writer ... was that of the producer of authoritative sentences, and that, to be sure, also means, from the very outset and because of their essence, sentences lending themselves to quotation and interpretation" (*JJC*, 199). The sentences that lend themselves to interpretation from the outset are those that play with their own polysemy, and sentences that lend themselves to quotation from the outset are those that can be ripped out of their context without losing their significance. They lend themselves to interpretation through condensation, integrating different contexts and semantics, and through isolation, forming their own closed space of meaning. In this way, as poetic sentences, they remain transcendent in the face of all interpretations, and thus they must be repeated and passed on again and again. In the end, it is not possible to say what it is that Scholem "wanted to say," and it is not possible to abbreviate. One must say it again in his words.

BIBLIOGRAPHY

WORKS BY GERSHOM SCHOLEM

"Bekenntnis über unsere Sprache." Letter to Franz Rosenzweig, December 26, 1926. In *Der Engel der Geschichte: Franz Rosenzweig, Walter Benjamin, Gershom Scholem*, edited by Stéphane Mosès, 215–217. Frankfurt am Main: Jüdischer Verlag, 1994.

Briefe. Edited by Itta Shedletzky and Thomas Sparr. 3 vols. Munich: C. H. Beck, 1994–1999.

———, and Walter Benjamin. *Briefwechsel 1933–1940*. Edited by Gershom Scholem. Frankfurt am Main: Suhrkamp, 1980.

Das Buch Bahir: Ein Schriftdenkmal aus der Frühzeit der Kabbala auf Grund der kritischen Neuausgabe von Gerhard Scholem. Darmstadt: Wissenschaftliche Buchgesellschaft, 1980. First published 1923 (Leipzig).

———, and Walter Benjamin. *The Correspondence of Walter Benjamin and Gershom Scholem*. Edited by Gershom Scholem. Translated by Gary Smith and Andre Lefevre. Cambridge, MA: Harvard University Press, 1992.

Du frankisme au jacobinisme: La vie de Moses Dobrushka, alias Franz Thomas von Schönfeld alias Junius Frey. Paris: Gallimard, 1981.

"Franz Rosenzweig und sein Buch 'Der Stern der Erlösung': Worte des Gedenkens, gesprochen am dreißigsten Tag nach seinem Tode an der Hebräischen Universität zu Jerusalem." Introduction to *Der Stern der Erlösung*, by Franz Rosenzweig, 525–549. Translated by Michael Brocke. Frankfurt am Main: Suhrkamp, 1993.

From Berlin to Jerusalem: Memories of My Youth. Translated by Harry Zohn. New York: Schocken Books, 1980.

Die Geheimnisse der Schöpfung: Ein Kapitel aus dem kabbalistischen Buch Sohar. Frankfurt am Main: Jüdischer Verlag, 1992.
"Identifizierung und Distanz: Ein Rückblick." *Eranos-Jahrbuch* 48 (1979): 463–467.
Jewish Gnosticism, Merkabah Mysticism, and Talmudic Tradition. 2nd rev. ed. New York: Jewish Theological Seminary of America, 1965.
Judaica (vols. 1–6)
Vol. 1. Frankfurt am Main: Suhrkamp, 1963.
Vol. 2. Frankfurt am Main: Suhrkamp, 1970.
Vol. 3, *Studien zur jüdischen Mystik.* Frankfurt am Main: Suhrkamp, 1970.
Vol. 4, edited by Rolf Tiedemann. Frankfurt am Main: Suhrkamp, 1984.
Vol. 5, *Erlösung durch Sünde*, edited and translated by Michael Brocke. Frankfurt am Main: Suhrkamp, 1992.
Vol. 6, *Die Wissenschaft vom Judentum*, edited and translated by Peter Schäfer. Frankfurt am Main: Suhrkamp, 1997.
"Judaism." In *Contemporary Jewish Religious Thought: Original Essays on Critical Concepts, Movements, and Beliefs*, edited by Arthur A. Cohen and Paul Mendes-Flohr, 505–508. New York: The Free Press, 1987.
Die jüdische Mystik in ihren Hauptströmungen. Frankfurt am Main: Suhrkamp, 1967.
"Kabbala." In *Encyclopedia Judaica.* Vol. 9. Berlin: Eschkol, 1932.
"Kabbala-Forschung und jüdische Geschichtsschreibung in der Universität Jerusalem." *Der Morgen* 13 (1937/38): 26–31.
Kabbalah. Jerusalem: Keter, 1974.
Lamentations of Youth: The Diaries of Gershom Scholem, 1913–1919. Edited and translated by Anthony David Skinner. Cambridge, MA: Harvard University Press, 2007.
A Life in Letters, 1914–1982. Edited and translated by Anthony David Skinner. Cambridge, MA: Harvard University Press, 2002.
Major Trends in Jewish Mysticism. New York: Schocken Books, 1961.
The Messianic Idea in Judaism and Other Essays on Jewish Spirituality. New York: Schocken Books, 1971.
"Molitor." In *Encyclopedia Judaica.* Vol. 12. Jerusalem: Keter, 1972.
"Mysticisme et société: un paradoxe créateur." *Diogène* 58 (1967): 3–28.
"Nach der Vertreibung aus Spanien: Zur Geschichte der Kabbala." *Almanach des Schocken Verlags* 5694 (1933/34): 55–70.
"The Name of God and the Linguistic Theory of the Kabbala." Translated by Simon Pleasance. *Diogenes* 79 (1972): 59–81; 80 (1972): 164–194.
On Jews and Judaism in Crisis: Selected Essays. Edited by Werner J. Dannhauser. New York: Schocken Books, 1976.
"On Jonah and the Concept of Justice." Translated by Eric J. Schwab. *Critical Inquiry* 25, no. 2 (Winter 1999): 353–361.

"On Lament and Lamentation." In *Lament in Jewish Thought: Philosophical, Theological, and Literary Perspectives*, edited by Ilit Ferber and Paula Schwebel, 313–319. Berlin: De Gruyter, 2014.
"On Our Language: A Confession." *History and Memory* 2, no. 2 (Winter 1990): 97–99.
On the Kabbalah and Its Symbolism. Translated by Ralph Manheim. New York: Schocken Books, 1969.
On the Mystical Shape of the Godhead: Basic Concepts in the Kabbalah. Translated by Joachim Neugroschel. Edited and revised by Jonathan Chipman. New York: Schocken Books, 1991.
On the Possibility of Jewish Mysticism in Our Time and Other Essays. Translated by Jonathan Chipman. Edited and selected with an introduction by Avraham Shapira. Philadelphia: Jewish Publication Society, 1997.
"On the Social Psychology of the Jews in Germany: 1900–1930." In *Jews and Germans from 1860 to 1933: The Problematic Symbiosis*, edited by David Bronsen, 9–32. Heidelberg: Carl Winter Universitätsverlag, 1979.
Origins of the Kabbalah. Edited by R. J. Zwi Werblowsky. Translated by Allan Arkush. Philadelphia: The Jewish Publication Society and Princeton University Press, 1987.
"Philosophy and Jewish Mysticism." *The Review of Religion* 2 (1938): 385–402.
"Politik der Mystik: Zu Isaac Breuers 'Neuem Kusari.'" *Jüdische Rundschau* 57 (1934): 1–2.
"Quelques remarques sur le mythe de la peine dans le judaisme." In *Le mythe de la peine: Actes du colloque organisé par le centre international d'études humanistes et par l'institut d'études philosophiques de Rome 7–12 janvier 1967*, edited by Enrico Castelli, 135–164. Paris: Aubier-Montaigne, 1967.
Review of *Studien zum Bestschen Hasidismus*, by Torsten Ysander. *Orientalistische Literaturzeitung* 38 (1935): 441–443.
Sabbatai Sevi: The Mystical Messiah, 1626–1676. Translated by R. J. Zwi Werblowsky. Princeton, NJ: Princeton University Press, 1973.
Tagebücher nebst Aufsätzen und Entwürfen bis 1923. Edited by Herbert Kopp-Oberstebrink, Karlfried Gründer, and Friedrich Niewöhner. 2 vols. Frankfurt am Main: Suhrkamp, 1995–2000.
"Über einen Roman von S.J. Agnon." *Neue Rundschau* 76 (1965): 327–333.
Über einige Grundbegriffe des Judentums. Frankfurt am Main: Suhrkamp, 1970.
"... und alles ist Kabbala": Gershom Scholem im Gespräch mit Jörg Drews. Munich: edition text + kritik, 1980.
Ursprung und Anfänge der Kabbala. Berlin: De Gruyter, 1962.
"Ein verschollener jüdischer Mystiker in der Aufklärungszeit: E. J. Hirschfeld." *Leo Baeck Institute Yearbook* 7 (1962): 247–278.

Von Berlin nach Jerusalem: Jugenderinnerungen. Expanded ed. Translated by Michael Brocke and Andrea Schatz. Frankfurt am Main: Jüdischer Verlag, 1994.

Von der mystischen Gestalt der Gottheit: Studien zu Grundbegriffen der Kabbala. 3rd ed. Frankfurt am Main: Suhrkamp, 1991.

Walter Benjamin: Die Geschichte einer Freundschaft. Frankfurt am Main: Suhrkamp, 1975.

Walter Benjamin: The Story of a Friendship. Translated by Harry Zohn. New York: New York Review Books, 2003.

Walter Benjamin und sein Engel: Vierzehn Aufsätze und kleinere Beiträge. Edited by Rolf Tiedemann. Frankfurt am Main: Suhrkamp, 1983.

"Zionism—Dialectic of Continuity and Rebellion." In *Unease in Zion*, edited by Ehud Ben-Ezer, 263–296. New York: Quadrangle Books, 1974.

"Zum Verständnis des Sabbatianismus: Zugleich ein Beitrag zur Geschichte der 'Aufklärung.'" *Almanach des Schocken Verlags* 5697 (1936–1937): 30–42.

"Zur Frage der Entstehung der Kabbala." *Korrespondenzblatt des Vereins zur Gründung und Erhaltung einer Akademie für die Wissenschaft des Judentums* 9 (1928): 4–26.

Zur Kabbala und ihrer Symbolik. Frankfurt am Main: Suhrkamp, 1973.

UNPUBLISHED WORKS BY GERSHOM SCHOLEM FROM THE MANUSCRIPT COLLECTION OF THE NATIONAL LIBRARY OF ISRAEL, HEBREW UNIVERSITY OF JERUSALEM

"Bemerkungen über Hebräisch und Hebräischlernen." Arc 4° 1599/277-I, no. 25, 3 pp. typescript.

"Dasselbe wie stets" (1925). Arc 4° 1599/277-I, no. 54, 2 pp. typescript.

"Der Prozess von Kafka" (1926). Arc 4° 1599/277-I, no. 58, 1 p. typescript.

"Der Zionismus wird seine Katastrophe überleben" (1924). Arc 4° 1599/277-I, no. 52, 2 pp. typescript.

"Die 3 Teile des Systems der Lehre der Philosophie des Judentums oder über das Wesen des Messianismus" (1918). Arc 4° 1599/277-I, no. 22, 2 pp. manuscript.

"Die Verzweiflung der Siegenden" (1926). Arc 4° 1599/277-I, no. 57, 2 pp. typescript.

"Discussion" (1974). Arc 4° 1599/277-I, no. 118, 13 pp. typescript.

"Heute, vor 3 Jahren..." (1926). Arc 4° 1599/277-I, no. 60, 1 p. typescript.

"Konsolidierung" (1928). Arc 4° 1599/277-I, no. 69, 1 p. typescript.

"Nach fünfzehn Jahren: Selbstbetrug?" (1930–31). Arc 4° 1599/277-I, no. 72, 7 pp. typescript.

"Schwindel der Revolutionen" (1938). Arc 4° 1599/277-I, no. 88, 3 pp. typescript.

"Um was geht der Streit?" (1930). Arc 4° 1599/277-I, no. 73, 8 pp. master copy.

ALL OTHER WORKS

Adorno, Theodor W. "Gruß an Gershom G. Scholem." In *Gesammelte Schriften*, vol. 20, no. 2, edited by Rolf Tiedemann, 478–486. Frankfurt am Main: Suhrkamp, 1984.

Alter, Robert. *Hebrew and Modernity*. Bloomington: Indiana University Press, 1994.

———. *The Invention of Hebrew Prose*. Seattle: University of Washington Press, 1994.

———. *Necessary Angels: Tradition and Modernity in Kafka, Benjamin, and Scholem*. Cambridge, MA: Harvard University Press, 1991.

Althusser, Louis. *For Marx*. Translated by Allen Lane. London: Penguin Press, 1969.

———. *Philosophy and Spontaneous Philosophy of the Scientists and Other Essays*. Edited by Gregory Elliott. Translated by Ben Brewster, James H. Kavanagh, Thomas E. Lewis, Grahame Lock, and Warren Montag. London: Verso, 1990.

Altmann, Alexander. "A Discussion with Dialectical Theology." In *The Meaning of Jewish Existence: Theological Essays 1930–1939*, edited by Alfred L. Ivry, translated by Edith Ehrlich and Leonard H. Ehrlich, 77–87. Hanover, NH: Brandeis University Press, 1991.

———. "Zur Auseinandersetzung mit der dialektischen Theologie (1935)." In *Lust an der Erkenntnis: Jüdische Theologie im 20. Jahrhundert*, edited by Schalom Ben-Chorin and Verena Lenzen, 256–271. Munich: Piper, 1988.

Aschheim, Steven E. *Arendt, Klemperer: Intimate Chronicles in Turbulent Times*. Bloomington: Indiana University Press, 2001.

———. "The Metaphysical Psychologist: On the Life and Letters of Gershom Scholem." *Journal of Modern History* 76, no. 4 (2004): 903–933.

Assmann, Jan. *Herrschaft und Heil: Politische Theologie in Altägypten, Israel und Europa*. Munich: Hanser, 2000.

———. *Religio duplex: Ägyptische Mysterien und europäische Aufklärung*. Berlin: Verlag der Weltreligionen, 2010.

Assmann, Jan, and Bernd Janowski, eds. *Gerechtigkeit: Richten und Retten in der abendländischen Tradition und ihren altorientalischen Ursprüngen*. Munich: Wilhelm Fink, 1998.

Barouch, Lina. *Between German and Hebrew: The Counterlanguages of Gershom Scholem, Werner Kraft and Ludwig Strauss*. Berlin: De Gruyter Oldenbourg, 2016.

Benjamin, Walter. *Briefe*. Edited by Gershom Scholem and Theodor W. Adorno. 2 vols. Frankfurt am Main: Suhrkamp, 1966.

———. *The Correspondence of Walter Benjamin: 1910–1940*. Edited by Gershom Scholem and Theodor W. Adorno. Translated by Manfred R. Jacobson and Evelyn M. Jacobson. Chicago: University of Chicago Press, 1994.

———. *Origin of the German Trauerspiel*. Translated by Howard Eiland. Cambridge, MA: Harvard University Press, 2019.

———. *Selected Writings*. Vol. 1, *1913–1926*. Edited by Marcus Bullock and Michael W. Jennings. Cambridge, MA: The Belknap Press of Harvard University Press, 1996.

Bergmann, Schmuel Hugo. *Tagebücher und Briefe*. Edited by Miriam Sambursky. 2 vols. Königstein im Taunus: Jüdischer Verlag bei Athenäum, 1985.

Berkowitz, Michael. *Zionist Culture and West European Jewry*. New York: Cambridge University Press, 1993.

Biale, David. *Gershom Scholem: Kabbalah and Counter-History*. Rev. ed. Cambridge, MA: Harvard University Press, 1982. First published 1979 (Cambridge, MA).

———. *Gershom Scholem: Master of the Kabbalah*. New Haven, CT: Yale University Press, 2018.

———. "Gershom Scholem's Ten Unhistorical Aphorisms on Kabbalah: Text and Commentary." *Modern Judaism* 5, no. 1 (1985): 67–93.

———. "Scholem und der moderne Nationalismus." In *Gershom Scholem: Zwischen den Disziplinen*, edited by Peter Schäfer and Gary Smith, 257–274. Frankfurt am Main: Suhrkamp, 1995.

Bialik, Haim Nahman. *Revealment and Concealment: Five Essays*. Jerusalem: Ibis Editions, 2000.

Bloch, Ernst. "Bilder des Déjà vu." In *Gesamtausgabe*, vol. 9, *Literarische Aufsätze*, 232–242. Frankfurt am Main: Suhrkamp, 1965.

Bloom, Harold. *The Anxiety of Influence: A Theory of Poetry*. New York: Oxford University Press, 1997.

Blumenberg, Hans. *The Legitimacy of the Modern Age*. Translated by Robert M. Wallace. Cambridge, MA: MIT Press, 1983.

Bollack, Jean, and Pierre Bourdieu. "L'identité juive: Entretiens avec Gershom Scholem." *Actes de la recherche en sciences sociales* 35 (1980): 3–19.

Bollenbeck, Georg. *Bildung und Kultur: Glanz und Elend eines deutschen Deutungsmusters*. Frankfurt am Main: Insel, 1994.

Bornkamm, Heinrich. *Mystik, Spiritualismus und die Anfänge des Pietismus im Luthertum*. Gießen: Töpelmann, 1926.

Boschwitz, Friedemann. *Julius Wellhausen: Motive und Maßstäbe seiner Geschichtsschreibung*. Darmstadt: Wissenschaftliche Buchgesellschaft, 1968. First published 1938 (Marburg).

Bourdieu, Pierre. "Intellectual Field and Creative Project." *Social Science Information* 8, no. 2 (1969): 89–119.

———. *Language and Symbolic Power*. Edited by John B. Thompson. Translated by Gino Raymond and Matthew Adamson. Cambridge, MA: Polity Press, 1991.

Bousset, Wilhelm. "Gnosis, Gnostiker (1912)." In *Religionsgeschichtliche Studien: Aufsätze zur Religionsgeschichte des hellenistischen Zeitalters*, edited by Anthonie F. Verheule, 44–52. Leiden: Brill, 1979.
———. *Hauptprobleme der Gnosis*. Forschungen zur Religion und Literatur des Alten und Neuen Testaments 10. Göttingen: Vandenhoeck & Ruprecht, 1907.
———. *Die jüdische Apokalyptik, ihre religionsgeschichtliche Herkunft und ihre Bedeutung für das neue Testament*. Berlin: Reuther & Reichard, 1903.
———. *Kyrios Christos: A History of the Belief in Christ from the Beginnings of Christianity to Irenaeus*. Translated by John E. Steely. Nashville: Abingdon Press, 1970.
———. *Kyrios Christos: Geschichte des Christusglaubens von den Anfängen des Christentums bis Irenaeus*. Göttingen: Vandenhoeck & Ruprecht, 1913.
———. *Die Religion des Judentums im neutestamentlichen Zeitalter*. Berlin: Reuther & Reichard, 1906.
Breuer, Mordechai. *Modernity within Tradition*. Translated by Elizabeth Petuchowski. New York: Columbia University Press, 1992.
Brocke, Michael. "Franz Rosenzweig und Gerhard Gershom Scholem." In *Juden in der Weimarer Republik*, edited by Walter Grab and Julius H. Schoeps, 127–151. Stuttgart: Burg, 1986.
Buber, Martin. *On Judaism*. Edited by Nahum N. Glatzer. New York: Schocken Books, 1967.
Cassirer, Ernst. *The Problem of Knowledge: Philosophy, Science, and History since Hegel*. Translated by William H. Woglom. New Haven, CT: Yale University Press, 2012. First published 1950 (New Haven).
Cohen, Hermann. *Kants Theorie der Erfahrung*. Berlin: Dümmler, 1871.
———. *Werke*. Vol. 6, *Logik der reinen Erkenntnis*. Hildesheim: Georg Olms, 1977.
Colpe, Carsten. *Die religionsgeschichtliche Schule: Darstellung und Kritik ihres Bildes vom gnostischen Erlösermythus*. Forschungen zur Religion und Literatur des Alten und Neuen Testaments 78. Göttingen: Vandenhoeck & Ruprecht, 1961.
Dan, Joseph. "Gershom Scholem: Mystiker oder Geschichtsschreiber des Mystischen?" In *Gershom Scholem: Zwischen den Disziplinen*, edited by Peter Schäfer and Gary Smith, 33–69. Frankfurt am Main: Suhrkamp, 1995.
———. *Gershom Scholem and the Mystical Dimension of Jewish History*. New York: NYU Press, 1987.
———. "Jewish Studies after Gershom Scholem" *Encyclopedia Judaica Yearbook 1983–1985*: 138–145. Jerusalem: Keter Publishing House, 1985.
Davidowicz, Klaus S. *Gershom Scholem und Martin Buber: Die Geschichte eines Mißverständnisses*. Neukirchen-Vluyn: Neukirchener Verlag, 1995.
Davies, William D. "From Schweitzer to Scholem: Reflections on Sabbatai Svi." *Journal of Biblical Literature* 95 (1976): 529–558.

De Certeau, Michel. *The Writing of History*. Translated by Tom Conley. New York: Columbia University Press, 1992.

Deuber-Mankowsky, Astrid. *Der frühe Walter Benjamin und Hermann Cohen: Jüdische Werte, kritische Philosophie, vergängliche Erfahrung*. Berlin: Vorwerk 8, 2000.

Deutsch, Nathaniel. *The Gnostic Imagination: Gnosticism, Mandaeism and Merkabah Mysticism*. Leiden: Brill, 1995.

Eisenstadt, Shmuel N. *Tradition, Change, and Modernity*. New York: Wiley, 1973.

Engel, Amir. *Gershom Scholem: An Intellectual Biography*. Chicago: University of Chicago Press, 2017.

Feisel, Evyatar. "Criteria and Conception in the Historiography of German and American Zionism (1980)." In *Essential Papers on Zionism*, edited by Jehuda Reinharz and Anita Shapira, 298–317. New York: NYU Press, 1996.

Ferber, Ilit. "A Language of the Border: On Scholem's Theory of Lament." *Journal of Jewish Thought and Philosophy* 12, no. 2 (2013): 161–186.

Fiorato, Pierfrancesco. "Die Erfahrung, das Unbedingte und die Religion: Walter Benjamin als Leser von Kants Theorie der Erfahrung." In *Hermann Cohen's Philosophy of Religion: International Conference in Jerusalem, 1996*, edited by Stéphane Mosès and Hartwig Wiedebach, 71–84. Hildesheim: Georg Olms, 1997.

———. "Unendliche Aufgabe und System der Wahrheit: Die Auseinandersetzung des jungen Walter Benjamin mit der Philosophie Hermann Cohens." In *Philosophisches Denken--Politisches Wirken: Hermann-Cohen-Kolloquium Marburg 1992*, edited by Reinhard Brandt and Frank Orlik, 163–178. Hildesheim: Georg Olms, 1993.

Fischer, Hermann. "Die Ambivalenz der Moderne: Zu Troeltschs Verhältnisbestimmung von Reformation und Neuzeit." In *Protestantismus und Neuzeit*. Troeltsch Studien 3, edited by Horst Renz and Friedrich W. Graf, 54–77. Gütersloh: Gütersloher Verlagshaus, 1984.

Franck, Adolphe. *The Kabbalah, or, The Religious Philosophy of the Hebrews*. Revised and enlarged translation by Dr. I. Sossnitz. New York: The Kabbalah Publishing Company, Morris Reiss Press, 1926.

Frank, Manfred. *Der kommende Gott: Vorlesungen über die Neue Mythologie*. Frankfurt am Main: Suhrkamp, 1982.

Frankel, Jonathan. "The 'Yiskor' Book of 1911: A Note on National Myths in the Second Aliya (1986)." In *Essential Papers on Zionism*, edited by Jehuda Reinharz and Anita Shapira, 422–453. New York: NYU Press, 1996.

Freedman, Maurice. *Martin Buber's Life and Work*. Vol. 3, *The Middle Years, 1923–1945*. New York: E. P. Dutton, 1983.

Funkenstein, Amos. "Gershom Scholem: Charisma, Kairos und messianische Dialektik." In *Gershom Scholem: Zwischen den Disziplinen*, edited by Peter Schäfer and Gary Smith, 14–31. Frankfurt am Main: Suhrkamp 1995.

———. *Perceptions of Jewish History*. Berkeley: University of California Press, 1993.

Geller, Jay H. *The Scholems: A Story of the German-Jewish Bourgeoisie from Emancipation to Destruction*. Ithaca, NY: Cornell University Press, 2019.

Genette, Gérard. *Paratexts: Thresholds of Interpretation*. Translated by Jane E. Lewin. Cambridge, UK: Cambridge University Press, 1997.

Goetschel, Willi. "Scholem's Diaries, Letters, and New Literature on His Work." *The Germanic Review* 72, no. 1 (1997): 77–91.

Graetz, Heinrich. *Geschichte der Juden: Von den ältesten Zeiten bis auf die Gegenwart*. 11 vols. Reprint of the definitive edition 1908 (Leipzig). Berlin: Arani, 1998.

———. *Gnosticismus und Judentum*. Korotschin: B. L. Monasch & Sohn, 1846.

Gressmann, Hugo. *Albert Eichhorn und die Religionsgeschichtliche Schule*. Göttingen: Vandenhoeck & Ruprecht, 1914.

———. *Der Messias*. Göttingen: Vandenhoeck & Ruprecht, 1929.

Gruenwald, Ithamar. *From Apocalypticism to Gnosticism: Studies in Apocalypticism, Merkavah Mysticism and Gnosticism*. Beiträge zur Erforschung des Alten Testaments und des Antiken Judentums 14. Frankfurt am Main: Peter Lang, 1988.

Gunkel, Hermann. *Creation and Chaos in the Primeval Era and the Eschaton: Religio-Historical Study of Genesis 1 and Revelation 12*. Translated by K. William Whitney Jr. Grand Rapids, MI: Wm. B. Eerdmans Publishing Co., 2006.

———. "Literaturgeschichte Israels." In *Religion in Geschichte und Gegenwart*, vol. 1, cols. 1189–1194, edited by Hermann Gunkel and Leopold Zscharnack. Tübingen: J. C. B. Mohr (Paul Siebeck), 1909.

———. *Schöpfung und Chaos in Urzeit und Endzeit: Eine religionsgeschichtliche Untersuchung über Gen 1 und Ap Joh 12*. Göttingen: Vandenhoeck & Ruprecht, 1895.

Guttmann, Julius. *Philosophies of Judaism: The History of Jewish Philosophy from Biblical Times to Franz Rosenzweig*. Translated by David W. Silverman. New York: Holt, Rinehart and Winston, 1964.

Ha'am, Ahad. *Am Scheidewege: Ausgewählte Essays*. 2 vols. Translated by Israel Friedländer and Harry Torzyner. Berlin: Jüdischer Verlag, 1904–1916.

Haardt, Robert. "Bemerkungen zu den Methoden der Ursprungsbestimmung von Gnosis (1966)." In *Gnosis und Gnostizisimus*. Wege der Forschung 262, edited by Kurt Rudolph, 654–667. Darmstadt: Wissenschaftliche Buchgesellschaft, 1975.

Hamacher, Elisabeth. *Gershom Scholem und die allgemeine Religionsgeschichte*. Religionsgeschichtliche Versuche und Vorarbeiten 45. Berlin: De Gruyter, 1999.

Hamacher, Werner. "Bemerkungen zur Klage." In *Lament in Jewish Thought: Philosophical, Theological, and Literary Perspectives*, edited by Ilit Ferber and Paula Schwebel, 89–110. Berlin: De Gruyter, 2014.

Harshav. Benjamin. *Language in the Time of Revolution*. Los Angeles: University of California Press, 1993.

Hellige, Hans D. "Generationskonflikt, Selbsthaß und die Entstehung antikapitalistischer Positionen im Judentum: Der Einfluß des Antisemitismus auf das Sozialverhalten jüdischer Kaufmanns- und Unternehmersöhne im Deutschen Kaiserreich und in der K.u.K. Monarchie." *Geschichte und Gesellschaft* 5 (1974): 476–518.

Hermann, Ulrich. "Die Jugendkulturbewegung: Der Kampf um die höhere Schule." In *'Mit uns zieht die neue Zeit': Der Mythos Jugend*, edited by Thomas Koebner, Rolf-Peter Janz, and Frank Trommler, 224–244. Frankfurt am Main: Suhrkamp, 1985.

Hertzberg, Arthur. "Gershom Scholem as a Zionist and Believer." In *Gershom Scholem (Modern Critical Views)*, edited by Harold Bloom, 189–206. New York: Chelsea House, 1987.

Hirsch, Samson Raphael. *The Nineteen Letters*. Edited by Joseph Elias. Translated by Karin Paritzky. Jerusalem: Feldheim, 1995.

Hobsbawm, Eric, and Terence Ranger, eds. *The Invention of Tradition*. Cambridge, MA: Cambridge University Press, 1992.

Hoffrogge, Ralf. *Werner Scholem: Eine politische Biographie (1895–1940)*. Konstanz: UVK Verlagsgesellschaft, 2014.

Huss, Boaz. "Ask No Questions: Gershom Scholem and the Study of Contemporary Jewish Mysticism." *Modern Judaism* 25, no. 2 (2005): 141–158.

Idel, Moshe. *Kabbalah: New Perspectives*. New Haven, CT: Yale University Press, 1988.

———. "Subversive Katalysatoren: Gnosis und Messianismus in Gershom Scholems Verständnis der jüdischen Mystik." In *Gershom Scholem: Zwischen den Disziplinen*, edited by Peter Schäfer and Gary Smith, 80–121. Frankfurt am Main: Suhrkamp, 1995.

———. "Zur Funktion von Symbolen bei G. G. Scholem." In *Gershom Scholem: Literatur und Rhetorik*. Literatur—Kultur—Geschlecht, kl. Reihe 15, edited by Stéphane Mosès and Sigrid Weigel, 51–92. Cologne: Böhlau, 2000.

Jacobson, Eric. *Metaphysics of the Profane: The Political Theology of Walter Benjamin and Gershom Scholem*. New York: Columbia University Press, 2003.

Jakobson, Roman. "Closing Statement: Linguistics and Poetics." In *Style in Language*, edited by Thomas A. Sebeok, 350–377. Cambridge, MA: The Technology Press of Massachusetts Institute of Technology, 1960.

Jonas, Hans. *Gnosis und spätantiker Geist*. Vol. 1, *Die mythologische Gnosis*. Göttingen: Vandenhoeck & Ruprecht, 1964. First published 1934 (Göttingen).

Kant, Immanuel. *Werkausgabe*. Vol. 3/4, *Kritik der reinen Vernunft*. Edited by Wilhelm Weischedel. Frankfurt am Main: Suhrkamp, 1974.

Kierkegaard, Søren. *Concluding Unscientific Postscript to the Philosophical Crumbs*. Edited and translated by Alastair Hannay. Cambridge, UK: Cambridge University Press, 2009.

———. *Fear and Trembling and The Sickness unto Death*. Translated by Walter Lowrie. Princeton, NJ: Princeton University Press, 1968.

———. *Gesammelte Werke*. Vol. 16, *Abschließende unwissenschaftliche Nachschrift zu den philosophischen Brocken*. Translated by Hans Martin Junghans. Düsseldorf: Diederichs, 1959.

Kilcher, Andreas B. "Figuren des Endes: Historie und Aktualität der Kabbala bei Gershom Scholem." In *Gershom Scholem: Literatur und Rhetorik*. Literatur—Kultur—Geschlecht, kl. Reihe 15, edited by Stéphane Mosès and Sigrid Weigel, 153–199. Cologne: Böhlau, 2000.

———. "Franz Joseph Molitors Kabbala-Projekt vor dem Hintergrund seiner intellektuellen Biographie." *Zeitschrift für Religions- und Geistesgeschichte* 55, no. 2 (2003): 138–166.

———. *Die Sprachtheorie der Kabbala als ästhetisches Paradigma: Die Konstruktion einer ästhetischen Kabbala seit der frühen Neuzeit*. Stuttgart: J. B. Metzler, 1998.

Koch, Klaus. *The Growth of Biblical Tradition: The Form-Critical Method*. Translated by S. M. Cupitt. London: A. & C. Black, 1969.

———. *The Rediscovery of Apocalyptic: A Polemical Work on a Neglected Area of Biblical Studies and Its Damaging Effects on Theology and Philosophy*. Studies in Biblical Theology, Second Series 22. London: SCM Press, 1972.

———. "Sädaq und Ma'at. Konnektive Gerechtigkeit in Israel und Ägypten?" In *Gerechtigkeit: Richten und Retten in der abendländischen Tradition und ihren altorientalischen Ursprüngen*, edited by Jan Assmann, Bernd Janowski, and Michael Welker, 37–64. Munich: Wilhelm Fink, 1998.

———. *Was ist Formgeschichte? Neue Wege der Bibelexegese*. 2nd ed. Berlin: Evangelische Verlagsanstalt, 1968.

Köhnke, Klaus C. *Entstehung und Aufstieg des Neukantianismus: Die deutsche Universitätsphilosophie zwischen Idealismus und Positivismus*. Frankfurt am Main: Suhrkamp, 1986.

Krochmalnik, Daniel. "Neue Tafeln: Nietzsche und die jüdische Counter-History." In *Jüdischer Nietzscheanismus*. Monographien und Texte zur Nietzsche-Forschung 36, edited by Werner Stegmaier and Daniel Krochmalnik, 53–81. Berlin: De Gruyter, 1999.

LaCapra, Dominick. *Rethinking Intellectual History: Texts, Contexts, Language*. Ithaca, NY: Cornell University Press, 1983.

Laor, Dan. "Agnon in Deutschland." *Münchner Beiträge zur Jüdischen Geschichte und Kultur* 1 (2009): 9–32.

Lejeune, Philippe. *On Diary*. Biography Monograph Series, edited by Jeremy D. Popkin and Julie Rak. Translated by Kathy Durnin. Honolulu: University of Hawai'i Press, 2009.

Liebes, Yehuda. "Myth vs. Symbol in the Zohar and in Lurianic Kabbalah." In *Essential Papers on Kabbalah*, edited by Lawrence Fine, 212–242. New York: NYU Press, 1995.

Linse, Ulrich. "Die Jugendkulturbewegung." In *Das wilhelminische Bildungsbürgertum*, edited by Klaus Vondung, 119–137. Göttingen: Vandenhoeck & Ruprecht, 1976.

Liska, Vivian. *German-Jewish Thought and Its Afterlife: A Tenuous Legacy*. Bloomington: Indiana University Press, 2016.

Löwy, Michael. *Redemption and Utopia: A Study in Elective Affinity*. Translated by Hope Heany. Stanford, CA: Stanford University Press, 1992.

Lübbe, Hermann. *Säkularisierung: Geschichte eines ideenpolitischen Begriffs*. 2nd ed. Freiburg: Karl Alber, 1975.

Magid, Shaul. "For the Sake of a Jewish Revival: Gershom Scholem on Hasidism and Its Relationship to Martin Buber." In *Scholar and Kabbalist: The Life and Work of Gershom Scholem*, edited by Mirjam Zadoff and Noam Zadoff, 39–75. Leiden: Brill, 2018.

Mattenklott, Gert. *Jüdische Intelligenz in deutschen Briefen 1619–1988*. Frankfurt am Main: Frankfurter Bund für Volksbildung, 1988.

———. "'Nicht durch Kampfesmacht und nicht durch Körperkraft...': Alternativen Jüdischer Jugendbewegung in Deutschland vom 'Anfang' bis 1933." In *'Mit uns zieht die neue Zeit': Der Mythos Jugend*, edited by Thomas Koebner, Rolf-Peter Janz, and Frank Trommler, 338–359. Frankfurt am Main: Suhrkamp, 1985.

McCole, John. *Walter Benjamin and the Antinomies of Tradition*. Ithaca, NY: Cornell University Press, 1993.

McGinn, Bernard. *Die Mystik im Abendland*. 3 vols. Translated by Clemens Maaß, Wolfgang Scheuermann, and Bernardin Schellenberger. Freiburg: Herder, 1994–2008.

Mendes-Flohr, Paul. *Divided Passions: Jewish Intellectuals and the Experience of Modernity*. Detroit: Wayne State University Press, 1991.

———. *From Mysticism to Dialogue: Martin Buber's Transformation of German Social Thought*. Detroit, MI: Wayne State University Press, 1989.

Menke, Bettine. "Benjamin vor dem Gesetz: Die Kritik der Gewalt in der Lektüre Derridas." In *Gewalt und Gerechtigkeit: Derrida—Benjamin*, edited by Anselm Haverkamp, 217–275. Frankfurt am Main: Suhrkamp, 1994.

Menninghaus, Winfried. *Unendliche Verdoppelung: Die frühromantische Grundlegung der Kunsttheorie im Begriff absoluter Selbstreflexion*. Frankfurt am Main: Suhrkamp, 1987.

———. *Walter Benjamins Theorie der Sprachmagie*. Frankfurt am Main: Suhrkamp, 1980.
Meyer, Michael A., ed. *Deutsch-Jüdische Geschichte in der Neuzeit*. 4 vols. Munich: C. H. Beck, 1996–2000.
Mintz, Alan. *Hurban: Responses to Catastrophe in Hebrew Literature*. New York: Columbia University Press, 1984.
Mintz, Matiyahu. "Work for the Land of Israel and 'Work in the Present': A Concept of Unity, a Reality of Contradiction (1987)." In *Essential Papers on Zionism*, edited by Jehuda Reinharz and Anita Shapira, 161–170. New York: NYU Press, 1996.
Molitor, Franz Joseph. *Philosophie der Geschichte oder über die Tradition*. 4 vols. Münster: Theissing, 1827–1857.
Mosès, Stéphane. *The Angel of History: Rosenzweig, Benjamin, Scholem*. Translated by Barbara Harshav. Stanford, CA: Stanford University Press, 2009.
———. "Gershom Scholems Autobiographie." In *Gershom Scholem: Literatur und Rhetorik*. Literatur—Kultur—Geschlecht, kl. Reihe 15, edited by Stéphane Mosès and Sigrid Weigel, 3–15. Cologne: Böhlau, 2000.
Mosse, George L. "Gershom Scholem as a German Jew." *Modern Judaism* 10 (1990): 117–133.
Murrmann-Kahl, Michael. *Die entzauberte Heilsgeschichte: Der Historismus erobert die Theologie 1880–1920*. Gütersloh: Gütersloher Verlagshaus, 1992.
Myers, David N. *Re-Inventing the Jewish Past: European Jewish Intellectuals and the Zionist Return to History*. New York: Oxford University Press, 1995.
Niewöhner, Friedrich "'Ich habe keinen Garten und habe kein Haus': Ein unbekanntes Gedicht Schmuel Josef Agnons in der Übersetzung von Gershom Scholem. Auch Anmerkungen zur Geschichte einer zerbrochenen Freundschaft." In *Disjecta Membra: Studien Karlfried Gründer zum 60. Geburtstag*, 82–92. Basel: Schwabe, 1989.
Palonen, Kari. *Quentin Skinner: History, Politics, Rhetoric*. Cambridge, MA: Polity Press, 2003.
Perlitt, Lothar. *Vatke und Wellhausen: Geschichtsphilosophische Voraussetzungen und historiographische Motive für die Darstellung der Religion und Geschichte Israels durch Wilhelm Vatke und Julius Wellhausen*. Berlin: Töpelmann, 1965.
Prickett, Stephen. *Modernity and the Reinvention of Tradition: Backing into the Future*. Cambridge, UK: Cambridge University Press, 2009.
Puech, Henri C. "Das Problem des Gnostizismus (1933/34)." In *Gnosis und Gnostizisimus*, Wege der Forschung 262, edited by Kurt Rudolph, 306–351. Darmstadt: Wissenschaftliche Buchgesellschaft, 1975.
Rabin, Chaim. "The National Idea and the Revival of Hebrew (1983)." In *Essential Papers on Zionism*, edited by Jehuda Reinharz and Anita Shapira, 745–762. New York: NYU Press, 1996.

Reinharz, Jehuda, ed. *Dokumente zur Geschichte des deutschen Zionismus 1882–1933*. Tübingen: J. C. B. Mohr (Paul Siebeck), 1981.

Ricoeur, Paul. *Freud and Philosophy: An Essay on Interpretation*. Translated by Denis Savage. New Haven, CT: Yale University Press, 1970.

———. *Time and Narrative*. 3 vols. Translated by Kathleen McLaughlin and David Pellauer. Chicago: University of Chicago Press, 1983–1988.

Riffaterre, Michel. *The Semiotics of Poetry*. Bloomington: Indiana University Press, 1978.

Ringer, Fritz K. *The Decline of the German Mandarins: The German Academic Community 1890–1933*. Cambridge, MA: Harvard University Press, 1969.

———. "The Intellectual Field, Intellectual History, and the Sociology of Knowledge." *Theory and Society* 19 (1990): 269–294.

Rosenberg, Göran. *Das Verlorene Land: Israel—eine persönliche Geschichte*. Frankfurt am Main: Jüdischer Verlag, 1998.

Rosenzweig, Franz. *Der Mensch und Sein Werk. Gesammelte Schriften*. Vol. 1 (2 parts), *Briefe und Tagebücher*. Haag: Martinus Nijhoff, 1979.

Rotenstreich, Nathan. *Jewish Philosophy in Modern Times: From Mendelssohn to Rosenzweig*. New York: Holt, Rinehart and Winston, 1968.

———. "Symbolism and Transcendence: On Some Philosophical Aspects of Gershom Scholem's Opus." *Review of Metaphysics* 31 (1997): 604–614.

———. *Tradition and Reality: The Impact of History on Modern Jewish Thought*. New York: Random House, 1972.

Rubin, Abraham. "The 'German-Jewish Dialogue' and Its Literary Refractions: The Case of Margarete Susman and Gershom Scholem." *Modern Judaism—A Journal of Jewish Ideas and Experience* 35, no. 1 (2015): 1–17.

Schäfer, Peter. "'Die Philologie der Kabbalah ist nur eine Projektion auf eine Fläche': Gershom Scholem über die wahren Absichten seines Kabbalastudiums." *Jewish Studies Quarterly* 5 (1999): 1–25.

Schäfer, Peter, and Joseph Dan. "Introduction." In *Gershom Scholem's Major Trends in Jewish Mysticism 50 Years After: Proceedings of the Sixth International Conference on the History of Jewish Mysticism*, 5–12. Tübingen: J. C. B. Mohr (Paul Siebeck), 1993.

Schatzker, Chaim. *Jüdische Jugend im zweiten Kaiserreich: Sozialisations- und Erziehungsprozesse der jüdischen Jugendbewegung in Deutschland 1870–1917*. Frankfurt am Main: Peter Lang, 1998.

———. "Martin Buber's Influence on the Jewish Youth Movement in Germany." *Leo Baeck Institute Yearbook* 23 (1978): 151–171.

Schlegel, Friedrich. *Kritische Friedrich-Schlegel-Ausgabe*. Edited by Ernst Behler et al. 35 vols. Paderborn: Schöningh, 1958ff.

Schmidt, Christoph. "Der häretische Imperativ: Gershom Scholems Kabbala als politische Theologie?" *Zeitschrift für Religions- und Geistesgeschichte* 50 (1998): 61–83.

Schmidt, Hans H. *Gerechtigkeit als Weltordnung.* Beiträge zur historischen Theologie 40. Tübingen: J. C. B. Mohr (Paul Siebeck), 1968.
Schmidt, Johann Michael. *Die jüdische Apokalyptik: Die Geschichte ihrer Erforschung von den Anfängen bis zu den Textfunden vom Qumran.* Neukirchen-Vluyn: Neukirchener Verlag des Erziehungsvereins, 1969.
Schoeps, Hans Joachim. *Ja—Nein—und Trotzdem.* Mainz: Hase & Koehler, 1974.
———. *Jüdischer Glaube in dieser Zeit: Prolegomena zur Grundlegung einer systematischen Theologie des Judentums.* Berlin: Vortrupp, 1932.
Schulte, Christoph. "'Die Buchstaben haben ... ihre Wurzeln oben': Scholem und Molitor." In *Kabbala und Romantik.* Conditio Judaica 7, edited by Eveline Goodman-Thau, Gert Mattenklott, and Christoph Schulte, 143–164. Tübingen: De Gruyter, 1994.
———. "Kabbala in der deutschen Romantik." In *Kabbala und Romantik.* Conditio Judaica 7, edited by Eveline Goodman-Thau, Gert Mattenklott, and Christoph Schulte, 1–19. Tübingen: De Gruyter, 1994.
Schweid, Eliezer. *Judaism and Mysticism According to Gershom Scholem: A Critical Analysis and Programmatic Discussion.* Atlanta: Scholars Press, 1985.
———. "The Rejection of the Diaspora in Zionist Thought: Two Approaches (1984)." In *Essential Papers on Zionism,* edited by Jehuda Reinharz and Anita Shapira, 133–159. New York: NYU Press, 1996.
Schweitzer, Albert. *The Quest of the Historical Jesus.* Expanded ed. Edited by John Bowden. Translated by W. Montgomery. Minneapolis, MN: Fortress Press, 2001.
Shaked, Gershon. "Shall All Hopes Be Fulfilled? Genre and Anti-Genre in the Hebrew Literature of Palestine (1982)." In *Essential Papers on Zionism,* edited by Jehuda Reinharz and Anita Shapira, 763–789. New York: NYU Press, 1996.
Shapira, Avraham. "The Dialectics of Continuity and Revolt." In *On the Possibility of Jewish Mysticism in Our Time and Other Essays,* XI–XIX. Philadelphia: Jewish Publication Society, 1997.
Shils, Edward. *Tradition.* Chicago: University of Chicago Press, 1981.
Simon, Ernst. "Über einige theologische Sätze von Gershom Scholem." In *Entscheidung zum Judentum: Essays und Vorträge,* 160–182. Frankfurt am Main: Suhrkamp, 1979.
Skinner, Quentin. "Meaning and Understanding in the History of Ideas." *History and Theory* 8, no. 1 (1969): 3–53.
Steiner, Uwe. *Die Geburt der Kritik aus dem Geist der Kunst: Untersuchungen zum Begriff der Kritik in den frühen Schriften Walter Benjamins.* Würzburg: Königshausen und Neumann, 1989.
Steinheim, Solomon Ludwig. *The Revelation According to the Doctrine of Judaism, A Criterion.* In *Philosopher of Revelation: The Life and Thought of S. L. Steinheim,*

edited and translated by Joshua Haberman, 29–276. Philadelphia: Jewish Publication Society, 1990.

Strauss, Leo. *Spinoza's Critique of Religion*. New York: Schocken Books, 1965.

Tal, Uriel. *Christians and Jews in Germany: Religion, Politics and Ideology in the Second Reich 1870–1914*. Ithaca, NY: Cornell University Press, 1975.

Taubes, Jacob. *From Cult to Culture: Fragments toward a Critique of Historical Reason*. Edited by Charlotte Elisheva Fonrobert and Amir Engel. Stanford, CA: Stanford University Press: 2009.

———. *The Political Theology of Paul*. Translated by Dana Hollander. Stanford, CA: Stanford University Press, 2003.

Tiedemann, Rolf. "Erinnerung an Scholem." In *Walter Benjamin und sein Engel: Vierzehn Aufsätze und kleinere Beiträge* by Gershom Scholem, 211–221. Edited by Rolf Tiedemann. Frankfurt am Main: Suhrkamp, 1983.

Troeltsch, Ernst. *Gesammelte Schriften*. 4 vols. Tübingen: J. C. B. Mohr (Paul Siebeck), 1922–1925. First published 1912–1922 (Tübingen).

———. *Protestantism and Progress: A Historical Study of the Relation of Protestantism to the Modern World*. Translated by W. Montgomery. Boston: Beacon Press, 1958.

———. *The Social Teaching of the Christian Churches*. Vol. 2. Translated by Olive Wyon. Chicago: University of Chicago Press, 1981. First published 1931 (London).

Twardella, Johannes. "Gershom Scholem: Prophet und Wissenschaftler." *Aschkenas: Zeitschrift für Geschichte und Kultur der Juden* 10, no. 2 (2000): 513–523.

Veyne, Paul. *Writing History: Essays on Epistemology*. Translated by Mina Moore-Rinvolucri. Manchester, UK: Manchester University Press, 1984.

Vogelsang, Claus. "Das Tagebuch." In *Prosakunst ohne Erzählen: Die Gattungen der nicht-fiktionalen Kunstprosa*, edited by Klaus Weissenberger, 185–202. Tübingen: Niemeyer, 1985.

Voigts, Manfred. "Das Machtwort: Scholems Position zum 'deutsch-jüdischen Gespräch.'" *Aschkenas: Zeitschrift für Geschichte und Kultur der Juden* 15, no. 1 (2005): 209–224.

Volkov, Shulamit. *Jüdisches Leben und Antisemitismus im 19. und 20. Jahrhundert: 10 Essays*. Munich: C. H. Beck, 1990.

Von Harnack, Adolf. *Lehrbuch der Dogmengeschichte*. 3 vols. Tübingen: J. C. B. Mohr (Paul Siebeck), 1909.

Von Rad, Gerhard. *Old Testament Theology*. Vol. 1, *The Theology of Israel's Historical Traditions*, translated by D. M. G. Stalker. Edinburgh: Oliver and Boyd, 1962.

Weber, Samuel. *Benjamin's -abilities*. Cambridge, MA: Harvard University Press, 2010.

Weidner, Daniel. "Berlin und Jerusalem: Gershom Scholem, 'Zion' und Europa." In *Figuren des Europäischen*, 57–78. Munich: Wilhelm Fink, 2006.

———. "'Das große Problem bleibt hier die Sprache': Jüdische Autoren und deutsche Sprachkultur in der Bibelwissenschaft und Religionsgeschichte." In *Sprache, Erkenntnis und Bedeutung: Deutsch in der jüdischen Wissenskultur*, Leipziger Beitrage zur jüdischen Geschichte und Kultur 11, edited by Arndt Engelhardt and Susanne Zepp, 37–53. Leipzig: Leipziger Universitätsverlag, 2015.

———. "Gershom Scholem, die Wissenschaft des Judentums und der 'Ort' des Historikers." *Aschkenas: Zeitschrift für Geschichte und Kultur der Juden* 11, no. 2 (2001): 435–464.

———. "'Geschichte gegen den Strich bürsten': Julius Wellhausen und die jüdische 'Gegengeschichte.'" *Zeitschrift für Religion und Geistesgeschichte* 54, no. 1 (2002): 32–61.

———. "Lernen, Lesen, Schreiben: Gershom Scholem und die 'jüdische Textgelehrsamkeit.'" In *Textgelehrte: Literaturwissenschaft und literarisches Wissen im Umfeld der Kritischen Theorie*, edited by Nicolas Berg and Dieter Burdorf, 259–279. Göttingen: Vandenhoeck & Ruprecht, 2014.

———. "'Movement of Language' and Transience: Lament, Mourning, and the Tradition of Elegy in Early Scholem." In *Lament in Jewish Thought: Philosophical, Theological, and Literary Perspectives*, edited by Ilit Ferber and Paula Schwebel, 237–254. Berlin: De Gruyter, 2014.

———. "The Political Theology of Ethical Monotheism." In *The Political Theology of Ethical Monotheism*, edited by Randi Rashkover and Martin Kavka, 178–196. Bloomington: Indiana University Press, 2013.

———. "Reading Gershom Scholem." *The Jewish Quarterly Review* 96, no. 2 (2006): 203–231.

———. "Reading the Wound: Peter Szondi's Essay on the Tragic and Walter Benjamin." In *Textual Understanding and Historical Experience*, edited by Joachin Küpper and Susanne Zepp, 55–69. Paderborn: Wilhelm Fink, 2015.

———. "Self-Deception and the Dark Side of History: Gershom Scholem's Mythology of Counter-Enlightenment." *Journal of Modern Jewish Studies* (2020): 1–14.

———. "Thinking Beyond Secularization: Walter Benjamin, the 'Religious Turn,' and the Poetics of Theory." *New German Critique* 111 (2010): 131–148.

Weigel, Sigrid. "Gershom Scholem und Ingeborg Bachmann: Ein Dialog über Messianismus und Ghetto." *Zeitschrift für deutsche Philologie* 115 (1996): 608–616.

———. "Gershom Scholems Gedichte und seine Dichtungstheorie: Klage, Adressierung, Gabe und das Problem einer Sprache in unserer Zeit." In *Gershom Scholem: Literatur und Rhetorik*. Literatur—Kultur—Geschlecht, kl. Reihe 15, edited by Stéphane Mosès and Sigrid Weigel, 16–47. Cologne: Böhlau, 2000.

Weiner, Herbert. *9½ Mystics: The Kabbala Today*. New York: Collier Books, 1969.

Weissweiler, Eva. *Das Echo deiner Frage: Dora und Walter Benjamin—Biographie einer Beziehung*. Hamburg: Hoffmann und Campe, 2020.

Wellhausen, Julius. *Grundrisse zum Alten Testament*. Edited by Rudolf Smend. Munich: C. Kaiser, 1965.

———. *Prolegomena to the History of Israel: With a Reprint of the Article Israel from the "Encyclopedia Britannica."* Translated by J. Sutherland Black and Allen Menzies. Edinburgh: Adam & Charles Black, 1885.

White, Hayden. *Metahistory: Die historische Einbildungskraft im 19. Jahrhundert in Europa*. Translated by Peter Kohlhaas. Frankfurt am Main: S. Fischer, 1994.

Wiener, Max. *Jüdische Religion im Zeitalter der Emanzipation*. Berlin: Philo Verlag und Buchhandlung, 1933.

Wohlfahrt, Irving. "'Haarscharf an der Grenze zwischen Religion und Nihilismus': Zum Motiv des Zimzum bei Gershom Scholem." In *Gershom Scholem: Zwischen den Disziplinen*, edited by Peter Schäfer and Gary Smith, 176–256. Frankfurt am Main: Suhrkamp, 1995.

Wolff, Hans W. *Dodekapropheton*. Biblischer Kommentar 14. Neukirchen-Vluyn: Neukirchener Verlag, 1977.

Yerushalmi, Josef H. *Zachor: Erinnere Dich! Jüdische Geschichte und jüdisches Gedächtnis*. Translated by Wolfgang Heuss. Berlin: Wagenbach, 1988.

Zadoff, Mirjam. *Der rote Hiob: Das Leben des Werner Scholem*. Munich: Hanser, 2014.

Zadoff, Noam. *Gershom Scholem: From Berlin to Jerusalem and Back*. Translated by Jeffrey Green. Waltham, MA: Brandeis University Press, 2017.

INDEX

Agnon, Shmuel Yosef, 2, 64–66
Ahad Ha'am, 20–21
Altmann, Alexander, 132–133
Anarchism, 18–19, 137–143, 203–207
Apocalypticism, 52–54, 127, 132–133, 188–191, 196, 200
Arendt, Hannah, 3, 4, 58

Benjamin, Dora, 33, 112, 119
Benjamin, Walter, 4, 32–33, 42, 47–48, 62–64, 76–77, 81–82, 85, 87–89, 109, 115, 119, 133–137, 146, 152, 160, 193, 213
Bergmann Escha, 29n2
Bergmann, Schmuel Hugo, 100, 199, 212
Bialik, Haim Nahman, 49–52
Bloch, Ernst, 93n18, 152
Bousset, Wilhelm, 164, 180, 181
Buber, Martin, 3, 8, 15, 17, 22–31, 41, 69, 75, 77, 92, 140, 169, 172–173, 210

Cohen, Hermann, 69, 73, 76–78, 80, 87, 100–1, 103, 111, 179
Commentary, 35, 62–63, 68–71, 90–94, 102–110, 112–119, 130–131, 145

Dialectics, 48, 77–78, 98–103, 120–121, 190–193, 198–200
Dostoevsky, Fyodor, 32, 205

Esotericism, 7, 40–43, 62–64, 89–91, 199, 213.

Fanck, Adolphe, 91–92, 175, 182–183

German Jews, 16–19, 59–62
Gnosticism, 170–171, 178–184
Graetz, Heinrich, 170, 175, 181, 187–188, 206
Gunkel, Hermann, 164, 166, 171n7, 189,

Hasidism, 28–30, 187, 201
Hebrew language, 48–55, 64–66, 72–73, 117–119, 210–211
Hegel, Georg Wilhelm Friedrich, 18, 77, 170, 199n17; Hegelian, 68, 79
Hiller, Kurt, 19
Hirsch, Samson Raphael, 67, 89, 93–95, 96, 106, 128, 145
Historiography, 116–117, 150, 161–162
History of Religion, 6, 124–125, 163–168, 172–177, 179–182, 188–189, 196–197
Hölderlin, Friedrich, 85

Jonas, Hans, 166n5, 180, 181, 184

Kabbalah, notion of, 89–93, 147–157, 175–176, 185; origin of 163–165, 178–179, 181–183
Kafka, Franz, 62, 88, 133–34, 136–37, 152
Kant, Immanuel, 75–79, 100, 105, 128; Kantian Philosophy, 67, 74, 76, 78–79, 96, 102, 126, 129
Kierkegaard, Søren, 75, 98, 99–100, 128
Kraft, Werner, 17, 25, 29, 48, 72, 80, 133

Language, theory of 23–26, 30–35, 38, 44–55, 64–66, 72–74, 80–86, 102–105, 108, 117–119

Marx, Karl, 18; Marxist, 64; Marxism, 79
Mathematics, 28, 742, 2–75, 80–81,
Mauthner, Fritz, 24, 72, 74, 75–76
Messianism (see also Apocalypticism), 39–40, 58, 101–104, 111–121, 154–155, 187–191, 192–198
Misunderstanding, productive, 30, 113–117, 180n, 183–185, 190–191, 195, 199–200
Molitor, Franz Joseph, 67, 89–93, 95, 103, 145
Mysticism, 94, 105, 145, 172–177
Myth, 24–25, 169–172, 187, 194n

Nietzsche, Friedrich, 18, 75–76, 205, 206; Nietzschean, 19, 24
Nihilism, 30, 50, 82–84, 99, 132n, 203–208
Novalis, 74–75, 98

Orthodoxy, 93–95, 119. 137–139.

Paradox, Irony, 25, 72–73, 98–110, 122–124, 147, 150–154, 171, 175–176, 196–197
Philology, 144–157, 166–167, 176
Philosophy, 18–19, 75–79. 80–85, 103–105, 126–128, 159–160, 163–164, 170, 175, 198
Politics, 13–14, 20–23, 27, 34–43, 45–48, 58, 176

Revelation, 38, 63, 115–125, 128–143
Romanticism, 8, 67, 100–4, 111, 145
Rosenzweig, Franz, 41, 53, 79, 126–128, 135

Sabbatianism, 186–189, 192–198.
Schlegel, Friedrich, 98, 104–105, 145n
Schoeps, Hans Joachim, 129–33, 135–136, 138–139
Scholem, Gershom; Works: Aphorisms, Fragments, Theses 67–68, 104–110, 153–157, 207–208; Diaries 6–7, 12–14, 67–69, 104–105; 95 Theses on Judaism and Theology, 105–110; On Lament and Lamentations, 80–86, On the book of Jonah, 112–122, Redemption through Sin, 195–199; Unhistorical Aphorisms, 153–156; Walter Benjamin; Story of a Friendship, 62–64
Scholem, Werner, 8, 16, 18
Secularization, 21, 52–54, 202–204
Silence, 31–35, 81–86, 100n, 102–103
Socialism, 18–19, 26–27, 200
Steinheim, Salomon Ludwig, 128–31, 140
Symbol, 184–185

Theology, 62–63, 79, 126–143
Tradition, 35, 39, 49–53, 65–66, 69–71, 87–97, 102–103, 105–109, 120–121, 130–133, 137–138, 140–143, 144–147, 153–155, 165, 174–175,
Troeltsch, Ernst, 164, 172–73, 202–206

Wellhausen, Julius, 164–166

Youth Movement, 22–24, 34–35, 87, 99, 102, 107

Zionism, 13–15, 19–21, 26–27, 34–48, 56–59, 92–93

DANIEL WEIDNER is Professor of Comparative Literature at Martin Luther University of Halle-Wittenberg. He is author of *Bibel und Literatur um 1800* and editor of *Handbuch Literatur und Religion, Blumenberg Lesen: Ein Glossar,* and *Profanes Leben: Walter Benjamins Dialektik der Säkularisierung.*